D0760028

CHRISTIANITY AND THE TRANSFORMATION OF THE BOOK
Origen, Eusebius, and the Library of Caesarea
By Anthony Grafton
Publication Date: November 2006
Price: $29.95
ISBN: 0-674-02134-5
357 pages, 15 halftones
The Belknap Press of Harvard University Press

For more information, please contact:
Rose Ann Miller
Senior Publicist
Phone 617.495.4714
Fax 617.349.5244
roseann_miller@harvard.edu

Visit our Web sites
www.hup.harvard.edu

CHRISTIANITY *and the* TRANSFORMATION *of the* BOOK

Christianity and the Transformation of the Book

ORIGEN, EUSEBIUS, AND THE LIBRARY OF CAESAREA

Anthony Grafton

Megan Williams

HARVARD UNIVERSITY PRESS

Cambridge, Massachusetts
London, England
2006

Library of Congress Cataloging-in-Publication Data

[to come]

To Peter Brown

Contents

Preface   *ii*

Cast of Characters   *xv*

Introduction: Scholars, Books, and Libraries in the
Christian Tradition   *1*

1   Origen at Caesarea: A Christian Philosopher among
his Books   *22*

2   Origen's Hexapla: Scholarship, Culture, and Power   *86*

3   Eusebius's *Chronicle:* History Made Visible   *133*

4   Eusebius at Caesarea: A Christian Impresario
of the Codex   *178*

Coda: Caesarea in History and Tradition   *233*

Abbreviations   *246*

Bibliography   *247*

CONTENTS

Notes   291

Acknowledgments   355

Index   359

Illustrations

The ecclesiastical scholar and his patron, Johannes Trithemius, from *Polygraphia* (Oppenheim, 1518). Courtesy of the Princeton University Library.

Wall painting from the "banker's house" at Pompeii, showing at least three different kinds of writing surfaces. Photo: Erich Lessing / Art Resource, NY (ART162496).

The scribe Ezra rewriting the sacred records. Photo: Scala / Art Resource, NY (ART2510).

Map of the Mediterranean world as Origen and Eusebius knew it.

Plan of the Villa dei Papiri at Herculaneum.

Fragment of the Geniza Hexapla.

Layout of the Hexapla leaf from the Cairo Genizah, showing its actual arrangement in white and a hypothetical reconstruction of the original folio in six columns in gray.

An opening from a papyrus codex of Numbers, copied in the second or early third century CE. Courtesy of the Chester Beatty Library, Dublin.

An opening from the chronological table of Eusebius, from the *Chronicle*, as translated by Jerome, in a manuscript of the fifth century CE. Courtesy of the Bibliothèque Nationale de France.

A chronicle of the third century BCE: the Parian Chronicle. Courtesy of the Ashmolean Museum.

A subscription by Pamphilus as entered in the Codex Sinaiticus, reproduced from the facsimile, *Codex sinaiticvs petropolitanvs et Friderico-Avgvstanvs lipsiensis.*

A set of Eusebius's canon tables, showing parallel passages from the Four Gospels, from a Byzantine manuscript. Courtesy of Princeton University Library.

A section of Gospel text, showing Eusebius's canon numbers on the left margin. Courtesy of Princeton University Library.

A leaf from the chronological table of Eusebius, as translated by Jerome, in a manuscript of the fifth century CE. Courtesy of Bibliothèque Nationale de France.

An opening of the Codex Sinaiticus, fourth century, showing two pages of the Gospel of Luke. Courtesy of the British Library.

Preface

This book deals with the new ways of organizing scholarly inquiry and collaboration that took shape in the seacoast city of Caesarea during the third and fourth centuries. It seems somehow appropriate that the book itself took shape in a way that is customary nowadays in the sciences, but relatively unusual in the humanities: as a collaboration between two scholars of very different formation, generation, and approach. It is also appropriate that a study of new technologies of the book in the ancient world could be composed, debated, and revised by authors who were usually hundreds of miles apart, thanks to the new technologies of the computer. We began to discuss the problems investigated here around the year 2000, while Megan Williams was finishing her time in residence as a graduate student in Princeton University's Department of Religion. We were both struck by the fact that Origen's Hexapla and Eusebius's *Chronicle*, two massive and original works of Christian scholarship, were laid out in parallel columns, and we knew that Eusebius had certainly used Origen's work. And we began to wonder what this innovative format had meant to the two men and their readers.

Megan Williams was studying Origen's biblical philology, as part of the research for her dissertation, now a book, on Jerome. Tony Grafton had investigated ancient chronography in the 1980s and early 1990s, as part of the preparation for the second volume of his biography of Joseph Scaliger. We began to follow parallel trails, Megan working on the Hexapla and Tony on the *Chronicle*. Eventually, we set out to write an article on these two enterprises and their connections, and began to send each other short texts for discussion.

By the academic year 2001–02, we had begun to lecture, individually and together, on our findings. Inquisitive and critical audiences—at a University of Pennsylvania conference entitled "Time in the Ancient World," and at the Center for Advanced Judaic Studies, the Seminar on the History of Material Texts at the University of Pennsylvania, the Group for the Study of Late Antiquity at Princeton, Oxford University, the University of Chicago, and Syracuse University—encouraged us to press on, but also raised new questions about our core documents and their wider contexts. In 2003 and 2004, the planned article grew into a much larger synthetic work. We now tried not only to identify what Eusebius learned from Origen, but also to show, far more generally, that these two men and other residents of their city created a set of new and influential models for Christian scholarship. Each of the authors researched and drafted roughly half of the original manuscript: Megan Williams wrote what became Chapters 1 and 2, Tony Grafton Chapters 3 and 4. But in the course of revision, each of us has intervened so often in the other's sections that the whole book is really our joint work.

As we have worked together over the years, each of us has developed a new appreciation for forms of scholarship that he or she had not known, for ways of reading and arguing that he or she had not practiced, and for the sheer excitement that comes from working with a partner on complex and demanding historical problems. Writing this book has forced both of us not only to read widely in new materials, but also to think fast and argue hard. It has also given both of us much excitement and more than a little sheer fun. In the future, we very much hope to see more modern humanists engage in the sort of teamwork that was second nature, more than 1,500 years ago, to our protagonists.

Cast of Characters

Sextus Julius **Africanus,** a Christian scholar of the first half of the third century CE, wrote an elaborate chronology and corresponded with Origen.

Ammonius Saccas, a Platonic philosopher of the first half of the third century CE, was active in Alexandria. He was the teacher of Plotinus and many others.

Andronicus of Rhodes, a Peripatetic philosopher of the first century BCE, did substantial editorial work on the Aristotelian corpus.

Clement of Alexandria, a Christian scholar who wrote extensively in both philosophical and homiletic genres, was born around 150 CE and died between 211 and 216.

Lucius Annaeus **Cornutus,** a Stoic philosopher of the first century CE, taught the poets Lucan and Persius and wrote extensively on the interpretation of poetry and myth.

Epiphanius, a monk and bishop who became famous as an opponent of heretics, among whom he included Origen, lived from around 315 to 403 CE.

Eusebius of Caesarea, born around 260 CE, wrote extensively as a historian of and apologist for the Christian church. Around 313 he became bishop of Caesarea, and held that position until his death in 339.

Gregory Thaumaturgus, who lived in the first three quarters of the third century CE, was converted to Christianity by Origen at Caesarea after studying law at Berytus. He became bishop of Neocaesarea in Pontus.

Hippolytus, who lived from around 170 to 236 CE, was referred to by some as bishop of Rome. A number of works, including a *Chronicle* and a *Refutation of all Heresies*, are traditionally ascribed to him, but controversy swirls around these ascriptions and the figure of Hippolytus himself.

Jerome (Eusebius Hieronymus), who founded the tradition of biblical scholarship and translation in the Western church, lived from around 347 to 420 CE.

Cassius **Longinus**, who lived in the first three quarters of the third century CE, wrote on philosophical subjects but achieved his real prominence as a rhetorician.

Origen, who lived from around 184 to around 255 CE, was born and educated at Alexandria, where he mastered pagan philosophy and philological methods. He applied the latter systematically in his massive work on the text and interpretation of the Bible.

Pamphilus, a wealthy presbyter who died in 310 CE, assembled a rich collection of the writings of Origen and other texts in

Caesarea and trained Eusebius and other young men as Christian scholars.

Aulus **Persius** Flaccus, a satirical poet and Stoic philosopher, lived from 34 to 62 CE.

Philodemus, a Greek poet and philosopher, wrote extensively on a wide range of issues and found important patrons at Rome, though his works never became canonical. He lived from around 110 to around 40/35 BCE, and may well have been personally connected with the Villa dei Papyri at Herculaneum, among the ruins of which his writings were preserved.

L. Flavius **Philostratus,** who lived in the first half of the third century CE, wrote a life of Apollonius of Tyana, a holy man, and *Lives of the Sophists.*

Plotinus, a highly influential Platonic philosopher, settled eventually in Rome, where he exerted great personal influence and wrote widely on philosophical themes. He lived from 205 to 269/70 CE.

Porphyry, who was Plotinus's disciple, lived from 234 to around 305 CE. He edited Plotinus's *Enneads* and wrote his biography as well as an important polemical work, *Against the Christians.*

Lucius Annaeus **Seneca,** a Stoic philosopher and moralist, lived from the beginning of the Christian era until 65 CE, when Nero, whose adviser he had been, forced him to commit suicide.

Johannes **Trithemius** (1462–1518), a Benedictine abbot and bibliophile, was a pioneering literary historian as well as a forger, cryptographer, and much else.

CHRISTIANITY *and the*
TRANSFORMATION
of the BOOK

Introduction:
Scholars, Books, and Libraries
in the Christian Tradition

*T*HE Benedictine abbot, scholar, and literary forger Johannes
Trithemius (1452–1516), compiled innovative histories of the
church, of Germany, and of his own and other monastic orders.[1] He produced these works using manuscripts he had already assembled, in the vast and specialized libraries that he created in monasteries at Sponheim and Würzburg. Trithemius
was a firm believer in the value of the ancient Benedictine discipline of copying sacred and secular books. The library therefore
served, in part, as a resource for monastic discipline: when he
could not beg or buy the originals, Trithemius made his novices
transcribe the treasures that he discovered.[2] But he also used
these materials extensively in his scholarly work. When discussing the work of Freculf of Lisieux, for example, Trithemius
could describe some of his most important writings at first
hand, because, as he wrote, "I have read a large and splendid
volume, containing histories from the creation of the world to
the birth of our lord Jesus Christ."[3] Trithemius could sort out in

print the identity of a Greek writer named Sixtus, whose work Rufinus had translated into Latin, explaining that he had been a pagan philosopher, not an early pope, because he had already solved this bibliographical problem when he catalogued another manuscript.[4] And he could retell the life of Hildegard of Bingen because he had already entered a draft of what he had to say on the flyleaf of his manuscript of her letters.[5] Trithemius housed his first, immense collection—one almost half the size of that of the Vatican, and half again as big as the legendary library of Pico della Mirandola—in a splendid suite of rooms at Sponheim. This became a center for learned conversation as well as intense study. The stately humanists of central Europe, from Desiderius Erasmus to Johannes Reuchlin, came, saw, and were conquered by what they praised as Germany's "Academy." Some paid literal, as well as literary, tribute to its founder, as Conrad Celtes did when he deposited with Trithemius for a time the unique manuscript of Hroswitha's sacred comedies.

Trithemius produced scholarly works as complex and demanding in *mise-en-page* and presentation as they were rich in content. Each of his literary histories, for example, was arranged in chronological order, which made it possible to draw historical conclusions from the materials he collected. By listing the works of numerous scholars in the eighth and ninth centuries, Trithemius suggested, for the first time, the existence of a general Carolingian Renaissance, and the role that Charlemagne himself had played in it.[6] But each of his works was also equipped, as printed books readily could be, with indexes that made its content accessible for reference. Trithemius not only drew up a massive chronicle for the history of the abbey of Hirsau, but also produced a second, far longer recension of the

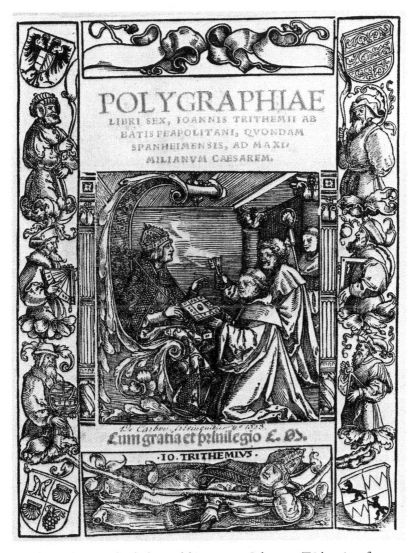

The ecclesiastical scholar and his patron, Johannes Trithemius, from *Polygraphia* (Oppenheim, 1518).

work. In the second version, which he called *Annals,* he tied all the events he recounted both to a chronology based on years of the Lord and to a list of the abbots of Hirsau—just one of eleven such tables that he drew up, even though he believed that the contents of his work were too varied for a single index to be helpful, and preferred that readers work through the whole text. After all, he admitted, using a striking term, his friends in Hirsau wanted "to *contemplate* the deeds and merits of their Fathers in a single series."[7]

Book historians remember Trithemius nowadays for a pamphlet, *In Praise of Scribes,* in which he argued that the fragile, ugly products of the printing press could never match the durable, magnificent creations of the skilled scribe's pen. The products of print—Trithemius claimed—were fragile and riddled with errors. The painstakingly accurate creations of the scribe, by contrast, would live forever, and the intense and craftsmanlike labor that went into them sanctified their makers. Trithemius described a monk who died after working for decades as a scribe. When his body was disinterred, the three writing fingers of his right hand were incorrupt, a sure sign of holiness.[8] In theory, then, Trithemius glorified the fine work of the hand as eloquently as a sixteenth-century William Morris. In practice, however, he combined the ancient skills of Benedictine scholarship, developed over centuries of copying and cataloguing manuscripts, with the new techniques of philology, forgery, and publicity that Italian humanists had revived or created in the fourteenth and fifteenth centuries, and to which the printing press gave a vast new diffusion. For all his dislike of mechanical reproduction, he proved particularly deft at exploiting the printing press for his own work. He had his book in praise of scribes, for example, published in Mainz by Peter von

Friedberg, his favorite printer, and he had Peter set the work not in the Gothic type normally used in Germany but in an innovative and attractive Roman font. Only someone who commanded as many resources—human and literary, textual and technical—as Trithemius did could possibly have brought off this tour de force.

In drawing up his pioneering bibliography of earlier ecclesiastical writers, Trithemius took a special interest in the ways in which they had produced and collected books. A humanist and reformer who believed he was helping Erasmus and others to restore the Catholic church to the pristine condition of its early centuries, Trithemius found powerful precedents for his collecting zeal in the uncorrupted church of the Great Persecution and the age of Constantine the Great. Three early Christian writers in particular claimed his attention for their services to the libraries of the Christian church. Origen, he noted, displayed "such a remarkable memory and such subtlety when he dictated the Scriptures that he exhausted seven notaries, and as many girls who wrote very quickly, as well as other youths who all took down different things as he spoke." Pamphilus the presbyter amassed a great library in Caesarea, "so that in all the world, there was no more celebrated library." He also copied in his own hand the bulk of Origen's works and deposited them in the same collection. Eusebius, for his part, shared the honor of "restoring the ecclesiastical library" with Pamphilus, from whom he took his cognomen, Pamphili. According to Trithemius, he deserved as much credit for these services to learning as for the erudite works he himself composed.[9] Trithemius's history of Christian writers was, in part, a history of Christian libraries—especially those of Caesarea Maritima in Palestine.

When Trithemius praised Origen, Pamphilus, and Eusebius,

we will argue, he noted something more than a chance resemblance between his work and that of some exemplary early figures—something vital, in fact, that many more recent scholars have missed, despite the far richer base of technical information they could draw on. Like Trithemius, the scholars of Christian Caesarea lived in a time of seismic cultural change, a time when one regime of book production and storage supplanted another, and when the nature and practices of Christian scholarship were being redefined. Like Trithemius, moreover, they were themselves impresarios of the scriptorium and the library, and developed new forms of scholarship that depended on their abilities to collect and produce new kinds of book. Like Trithemius, they struggled to devise texts that could impose order on highly varied forms of information, and took a deep interest in the visual presentation of their work. For Trithemius, furthermore, these varied enterprises—at Caesarea as at Sponheim—were tightly connected. Trithemius saw the collection of books and their interpretation, the writing of literary histories and the design of new formats for them, as organically related activities. In doing so, we will argue, he followed precedents first set at Caesarea, by the protagonists of our book. Starting from his compilations, even though they reached completion five hundred years ago, may help us shed a new kind of light on the origins of the tradition to which he belonged, and to which we do not—for all that we, too, live in a period of radical change in the realm of the book and the library.

Viewing the careers of Origen, Pamphilus, and Eusebius through this lens gives new cogency to the observations that Arnaldo Momigliano made in a classic article on Christian historiography. Momigliano suggested that, in creating the new genre of ecclesiastical history, Christian writers—specifically, Eusebius—had introduced an emphasis on documentary evidence. They thus transformed the practice of historiography as it had developed in Greece and Rome. This observation, we will argue, can be extended to characterize an important strand within the Christian intellectual tradition as a whole, at least from Origen to Trithemius. Christian scholars used written materials—both those they inherited from others, and those they created themselves—in ways that drew upon classical precedents, but they also developed these in new directions. They made their technical mastery of the production of complex books the basis of new kinds of intellectual authority, which in turn shaped new modes of scholarly inquiry. Eusebius, moreover, took the first tentative steps to provide his research and writing, and the human and physical infrastructure that supported those activities, with new forms of institutional support. Eventually, these new contexts for scholarship would allow Christian scholarship to declare its independence—as at Sponheim under Trithemius—from private patronage, which in the classical Mediterranean world had provided the resources for almost all intellectual life. We in the modern university owe a great debt to this particular strand of the Christian intellectual tradition. Through Trithemius's eyes—those of a scholar who participated himself in what was, in his day, a living reality—we can appreciate the power and coherence of that tradition anew.

A vast technical literature—one that began to flourish in later antiquity itself, and that has exploded in the last four decades—deals with the intellectual achievements of scholars in our period. Henri-Irénée Marrou and Peter Brown, Robert Kaster and

Hervé Inglebert, Arnaldo Momigliano and Timothy Barnes have taught us a great deal about how third- and fourth-century intellectuals sorted out the tangled textual and historical traditions that confronted them.[10] They have traced the development of new forms of exegesis and commentary, followed the transformations of historiography, and showed us how scholars asserted their own rights to select the texts that fell within a philosophical, theological, or literary canon and to define how these should be read. More recently, Carol Quillen, Brian Stock, and others have devoted pioneering studies to the forms of reading—as opposed to formal exegesis—practiced in late antiquity.[11] These scholars have described and analyzed the methods, passions, and obsessions of late antique readers in a detailed and profound way.

A second body of scholarship, equally informative and challenging, deals with the technical transformation of books and libraries in the same period. C. H. Roberts and T. C. Skeat have attempted to account for the revolutionary changes in the physical form of books that took place in the second through the fourth centuries, as the codex form preferred by Christians gradually became more popular than the roll.[12] Guglielmo Cavallo, Lionel Casson, and Harry Gamble have recreated the libraries used by Christian and pagan scholars.[13] Bruce Metzger and Kim Haines-Eitzen have analyzed the practices of Christian scribes and traced the networks—normally personal ones, held together by common purpose and affection, rather than commercial or professional ones—that made the transmission of Christian books possible.[14]

These rich bodies of scholarship, complementary in so many respects, have remained largely independent of one another in

Wall painting from the "banker's house" at Pompeii, showing at least three different kinds of writing surfaces: a wooden writing-tablet at the left, a papyrus notebook leaning against the *capsa* in the center, and roll books with their shelf-tags inside the *capsa*. Now in the Museo Archeologico Nazionale, Naples, Italy.

practice. Even the most elaborate studies of late antique scholarship usually devote little attention to the material forms that recensions, commentaries, and histories took, or to the connections between the techniques of scholarship and those of book production. And even the most technically adept studies of ancient books and libraries have shed little light on the extent to which these were shaped by, or shaped, the concerns of scholars. The interdisciplinary modes of inquiry that pioneers of book history in the modern world have called for, and that medievalists, Sinologists, and others have actually devised and applied to the books of other times and places, have, as yet, rarely been brought to bear on late antique topics.[15] We believe, therefore, that a fresh examination of the most famous center of Christian scholarship in antiquity, Caesarea, and of the books and libraries produced and collected there, will fill a substantial void in current understandings of the period, and of the entire history of the Western book.

Roger Chartier, Robert Darnton, and other historians of the book have made scholars newly sensitive to the need to determine afresh, for every historical setting, the meanings and connotations of key terms like "book" and "library." Nowhere is the potential for confusion greater than in late antiquity—a period relatively little studied from this point of view. For this was a crucial time of transition in the material history of texts in the West. The basic physical form of the book was in a state of flux. Greek and Roman writers normally confided their prose and verse to rolls, most of them made from papyrus. The great library collections at Alexandria and Pergamum consisted of rolls, arranged in vast sets of pigeonholes. *Capsae*—round leather cases—contained smaller book collections, and made rolls portable. Wooden writing tablets, and later, parchment and papyrus leaves, were bound up together in notebooks known as codices. Occasionally, writers adopted the codex—the form of book with which we are most familiar—for literary purposes. But for first- and second-century authors, such as Martial, this form of book remained an unusual expedient. In our period, by contrast, the codex came to dominate the making and reading of books in the Roman world. Collections of codices, lying flat on shelves in large cupboards, took shape, and gradually replaced the older collections of rolls.

But the transition from roll to codex happened only very gradually. Both forms remained simultaneously in use for at least a century and a half, probably much longer. During that period, the likelihood that a specific book would take one of the

The scribe Ezra rewriting the sacred records. Codex Amiatinus, fol. 5 r. Jarrow, early eighth century. Biblioteca Laurenziana, Florence, Italy.

two available forms rather than the other depended primarily on the genre and readership of the text(s) that it enclosed. Thus when we deal with late antique materials, the apparently clear terms "book" and "library" require analysis every time they appear. Otherwise, they call up what may prove to be highly deceptive and inappropriate images in a modern reader's mind—rather as they did in the minds of the scholars and artists who decorated the Salone Sistino of the Vatican Library, late in the sixteenth century, with splendid frescos of Greek and Roman readers handling codices long before they actually existed.

Not only was the physical form of the book in flux in late antiquity: the rise of the codex threw into question existing assumptions regarding the natural relation between the book as material object and as unit of meaning. The existence of two equally viable alternative forms of the book makes it impossible to assume that a "book" was a standard, easily recognizable, agreed-upon physical unit. Over the course of the third century, moreover, the codex developed so as to allow an individual book to contain far longer, or far more, texts than any single roll could. The book as unit therefore began to function as a small library had once done, rather than as a single or partial text or even an anthology of texts. Several of the books we will discuss exemplify this new potential. Furthermore, as the same examples will show, the codex offered possibilities different from those the roll had for the expression of extra-textual meaning. As authors and copyists learned to exploit these characteristics of the codex, the book reached new levels of complexity both as a material object and as a collection of texts. Naturally, the transformation of the book entailed a transformation of the library, though collections changed more slowly and in more subtle ways than the books they contained.

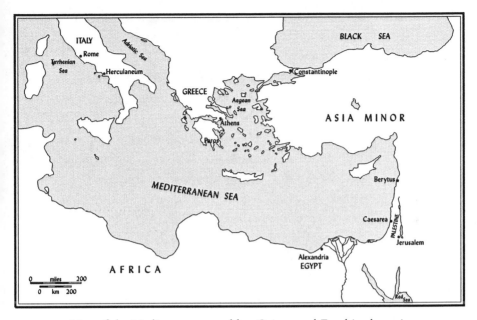

Map of the Mediterranean world as Origen and Eusebius knew it.

Before the rise of the book trade as the primary means of book dissemination, any library had to include facilities for the making of books as well as for their preservation and use. There was no publishing industry, or indeed any other formal mechanism for the copying and distribution of literary texts, in the ancient Mediterranean world. Book dealers existed, and collectors could sell their books either to these tradespeople or to other readers, but the monetary economy seems to have played little role in determining how readers gained access to books. Instead, books circulated largely through informal patterns of exchange: the author, or a reader, might prepare a copy as a gift to a friend or patron; one reader might lend another a book to copy; recipients could pass on texts to others in the same manner. In order to build his collection, the impoverished bibliophile might have to learn to write a good book hand, while a richer one could keep a staff of slave secretaries on hand.

The linkage of collection to production integrated libraries in the Roman world into an economy of gift exchange that connected literate elites across the Mediterranean. This economy involved the circulation of a variety of material objects, and also of social and political interventions. Within it, books could hold social and emotional charges that they rarely carry today, even when given as gifts. The book, in antiquity, was not a commodity, but had a status closer to that of a work of art—as Martial's positioning of the long list of books he includes in his *Apophoreta,* or *Holiday Gifts,* immediately before an even more impressive list of objets d'art, implies.[16] Books, like other costly gifts, traveled the Roman world from one member of the literate elite to another. But they bore a special implication of shared intellectual interests, and served as particularly powerful expressions of the links between like-minded members of an inward-looking social group. From the perspective of the collector, accordingly, a library was worth far more than its cash equivalent. It was, like a modern library, a means of storing cultural capital in material form.[17] But in late antiquity that capital could much more readily be transformed into social capital than it is today, through the process of copying and dissemination. To give a book to a patron, for example, was to bid for favors in return, perhaps in the form of offices and benefactions.[18] The intensity of the effort required to amass even a modest library under late Roman conditions, and even more important the nature of that effort, made the library a privileged locus for the accumulation and storage of influence. The rise of the codex, with its compact proportions, greatly intensified the physical—as well as the symbolic—concentration of cultural power that a sizable library embodied. The libraries built up at Caesarea by our protagonists, therefore, did not merely symbolize, but actually helped to create, the nascent cultural power of Christians in the Roman world of the third and early fourth centuries.

The scholarly worlds of Origen and Eusebius invite a broad-gauged investigation, embracing the material histories of books and libraries, and the social, intellectual, and cultural histories of the scholarly communities whose activities they supported. Surprisingly large amounts of evidence survive. Subscriptions in biblical manuscripts and massive literary and historical texts, manuscript fragments and complete works, complement one another, enabling us to gain a vivid sense of the different ways in which Origen, Eusebius, and the latter's mentor and patron, Pamphilus, gathered and studied earlier texts and produced new ones of their own. These pioneering Christian scholars devised new genres of learned literature, from critical editions of the Bible to world chronicles. At the same time, they created new settings for book production and consumption: scriptoria that could turn out complex and even unprecedented works of technical literature and libraries where the sources they drew upon were assembled. As the creators gave accounts of what they had done and looked for patrons who could support their work, materially and financially, they offered new definitions of what it meant to be a Christian scholar. By studying these aspects of their activities together, we can gain a sense of three different moments in the history of Christian scholarship and even of three different scholarly personae. We can offer a model for a history of scholarship that takes due account of both the cultural and the material history of scholars' work. And we can detect the first traces of a unique, and immensely productive, strand within the intellectual history of Christianity, one characterized above all by its composite and polyglot character and by its openness to non-Greek, non-Roman learning—to the scholarly traditions of "barbarians," as our subjects would have seen them.

Origen, active in Alexandria and then in Palestine in the first half of the third century, is famous as the first Christian biblical scholar and a pioneering philosophical theologian. His life unfolded as an ascetic struggle to follow and defend the central tenets of Christian orthodoxy. In his youth, Origen carried the pursuit of holiness to the point of self-castration, a literal-minded and radical step that he later regretted. As a mature scholar, he devoted a vast amount of time and effort to refuting both pagan critics of Christianity and wrong-headed Christians, like the Gnostics, whom he condemned as heretics.[19] For all Origen's zeal, however, he remained a wide-ranging and eclectic thinker, one who learned a vast amount not only from earlier orthodox writers like Clement of Alexandria and Jewish thinkers like Philo, but also from the Gnostics and the pagans. He made a life-long effort to master all of these materials and apply them to what he saw as proper Christian ends.

In particular, this effort found expression in a massive exegetical corpus, including commentaries *(tomoi)*, homilies, and collections of brief notes on virtually every book of the Christian Bible, both Old and New Testaments. This mass of materials has sunk almost without trace, yet even the debris that remains is of monumental proportions. As Origen's commentaries reveal, he was a biblical philologist as well as an exegete of the historical and allegorical senses. In order to set the study of the literal sense on solid foundations, he conceived and prepared the Hexapla, an elaborate tool for textual criticism of the Hebrew Scriptures. The Hexapla was an Old Testament written in six parallel columns laid out across each opening of a series of massive codices. Origen carried out this immense project sometime after his relocation from Alexandria to Palestine in 234, probably soon after his arrival there.[20] The epochal importance of the work lies above all in its arrangement. The Hexapla was perhaps the first book—as opposed to official documents—ever to display information in tabular form: in columns intended to be read across rather than down the page. Modern scholarship on Origen tends to emphasize his spirituality, his philosophical—or rather, theological—insight, and the originality of his thought. But he was no impractical religious genius, receiving inspiration from on high. Rather, he was a meticulous, energetic scholar who drew heavily on long-standing traditions for the study of authoritative texts. He followed patterns first laid out in the Greek philosophical schools and both imitated and developed by a range of Jewish and Christian groups under the Roman Empire. Seen in this context, Origen's bibliographic activities come to seem at once more central to his career as a Christian intellectual and more comprehensible.

Eusebius rose to prominence about seventy years after Origen died in 254. He idolized his predecessor, propagating his methods and building on his technical innovations. Like Origen, Eusebius defended Christian truths against all comers. And like Origen, he found the weapons he wielded in his life-long combat on behalf of orthodoxy not only in the Bible and in earlier Christian thinkers, but also in a wide range of pagan and Jewish texts. As priest and eventual bishop of Caesarea, however, Eusebius operated under conditions rather different from Origen's. While we have comparatively little direct information about Eusebius's scriptorium and library, rich evidence proves that he received a formal training in Christian scholarship from his first patron, Pamphilus. His own works and other manuscripts that descend from the products of his workshop show that he eventually commanded a sizable staff, capable of impressive technical feats. The scriptorium that Eusebius built up at Caesarea produced a variety of elaborate biblical manuscripts, possibly including copies of the Hexapla. Eusebius's own *Chronicle,* or history of the world, and the editions of Scripture produced to his specifications used the tabular form pioneered by Origen for several novel purposes. Of necessity, Eusebius relied on a rich library of previous works, including Origen's, as the basis for his literary production. His library exemplifies, on a particularly impressive scale, the linking of collection, production, and dissemination so typical of the book culture of the ancient Mediterranean—and of much later Christian scholars like Trithemius. Indeed, the close parallels between the activities of Eusebius and Trithemius support particularly well our claim that links like these became a deep structure of Christian scholarship, forged in late antiquity, then reproduced again and again in the Middle Ages and the early modern period.

The background to much of our story is the city of Caesarea, the Palestinian port where Origen, Pamphilus, and Eusebius all found homes. Its qualities made it an especially favorable habitat for Christian scholars, both comfortable and challenging. Founded as Strato's Tower, a small Hellenistic outpost of the

Phoenician city of Sidon, Caesarea was rebuilt and dedicated to Augustus by Herod. Deeply committed to Rome and Roman culture, Herod laid out his city on a splendid scale, with a magnificent palace for himself, a hippodrome and theater near it for games and performances, and all the practical equipment and amenities anyone could want. Aqueducts brought fresh water from the springs of Mount Carmel, sewers kept the streets clean, extensive port facilities favored trade, and further adornments, including new temples, sidewalks, statues, and colonnades, enhanced the city's beauty during the early centuries of the Roman Empire. It soon became the seat of the Roman procurators of Judaea, and after the terrible siege of Jerusalem in 70, Caesarea replaced it as the capital of Palestine. A fictional epistle ascribed to Apollonius of Tyana described Caesarea as "the biggest [city] in Palestine, and at the forefront in size and laws and customs and the military virtues of ancestors, and still more in the mores that are appropriate to peace."[21] Later geographers noted its beauty.

Caesarea housed a substantial population—perhaps 35,000 to 45,000 in the third and fourth centuries—made up of varied elements in a highly unstable suspension. Pagans and Christians, Jews and Samaritans, Gnostics and sectaries jostled and argued in the markets, the squares, and the theater—a theater where Jews could watch performances satirizing them, and where at least one Jewish mime performed. Caesarea boasted erudite rabbis. Some of them had to make difficult accommodations with the Jewish population, many of whom prayed not in Hebrew but in Greek; yet a number of rabbis were able to attract circles of students. At the same time, Caesarea was a center of Christian learning and scribal culture. Jews and Christians regularly met, and both regularly encountered pagans, some of them learned. Members of different communities tried to convert one another, and sometimes succeeded. And even as they debated and struggled, they also traded precise information about their own traditions of biblical exegesis and theology. A microcosm of multiple traditions, a little vortex into which several distinct, but related, Mediterranean traditions drained, Caesarea made an ideal stage on which Christian scholars could enact the demonstration that their faith had superseded Judaism and incorporated the high truths at the heart of the best pagan philosophies.[22]

Behind Origen and Eusebius loom a number of mistier, but equally vital figures. Two play particularly important roles in our story: Julius Africanus and Pamphilus. Africanus, Christian chronologer and student of magic and technology, was a friend, correspondent, and critic of Origen. A collector of exotic texts, Africanus laid at least some of the foundations on which Eusebius reared the structures of his *Chronicle*. He was the first Christian scholar to confront the historical works on ancient Chaldea and Egypt compiled, in the third century BCE, by the priests Berossos and Manetho—texts that played a crucial role in Eusebius's work.[23] In fact, however, his library researches extended far beyond the dry realm of chronicles. In Africanus's *Kestoi (Embroideries)*, he cited magical verses that he claimed to have found in manuscripts of the *Odyssey* preserved in the great Carian library at Nysa, in "the archives of the ancient fatherland of Colonia Aelia Capitolina of Palestine [Jerusalem]," and even, though in this case only partially preserved, "in Rome near the baths of Alexander in the beautiful library in the Pantheon, which I myself designed for the emperor."[24] Whatever the truth of this account, its wording shows that Africanus knew about some of the most refined techniques of ancient literary scholarship, like the systematic collation of manuscripts practiced in the Alexandrian Museum and described in detail by Galen.

The presbyter and martyr Pamphilus created the collection at Caesarea that Eusebius himself used and continued to expand. Pamphilus dedicated himself to gathering, hunting, and producing Christian books, from the works of Origen to the volumes of the Gospels that he distributed to any Christian he thought worthy. It is likely that he also provided the primary support for the early stages of Eusebius's career, when the younger man produced some of his most complex and most characteristic works.[25] Throughout this study, we will refer to these less famous Christian scholars whenever their activities help to set those of our central figures into context. In particular, we are concerned to show that Origen and Eusebius, whatever their achievements, did not emerge from a vacuum. Rather, they are merely the best documented—probably the most influential, perhaps the most brilliant—of several generations of learned Christians who together forged a new scholarly culture in late antiquity. Their works, too, allow us to trace with new clarity the contours of a specific tradition of learning that outlasted that culture, going on to shape the lives and the work of many others, through Trithemius and his contemporaries, and beyond.

1

Origen at Caesarea: A Christian Philosopher among His Books

SINCE antiquity, Origen's reputation has been immense. Eusebius applied to him the sobriquet Adamantius, or "man of steel," and portrayed Origen as a kind of superhero of Christian piety and scholarship.[1] The tendency ever since has been for Origen's biographers to represent him as sui generis.[2] His own accomplishments, and his posthumous reputation, have set him apart from his contemporary cultural and social context. Despite his fame and his vast literary output, however, we have little information about the contents of Origen's library or the concrete uses to which he put his books. Eusebius's biography provides tantalizing, yet sparse, anecdotal evidence; Origen's own works contain a variety of hints; other texts add precious tidbits to the picture. But in the end, the sources cannot take us very far, which makes context crucial for any reconstruction. The Christian communities of the third century, and their shared culture and institutions, cannot provide it. Christians were simply too few, too scattered, too disorganized, and mostly too poor to support a phalanx of academicians capable of developing their own independent scholarly culture. Rather, despite Origen's eccentric Christian views, his best parallels in the intellectual world of the Roman Empire are the philosophers. For our purposes, it is as a philosopher that he is best approached.

We are not unaware that in some quarters, this claim may seem controversial. For the last century, scholars have quarreled over Origen's relation to contemporary Greek philosophy, particularly Middle and Neo-Platonism.[3] Indeed, the confusion can be traced to antiquity. Origen's contemporaries, and his biographer, Eusebius, understood his career in terms of philosophical norms and traditions. His own student, Gregory Thaumaturgus, in a formal farewell oration presented when he left Caesarea to return to his native Pontus, describes his initial response to Origen's influence as follows: "One thing alone was for me dear and worthy of love, philosophy and her guide, this divine man." As Gregory goes on to recount, not only did Origen present Christianity as the best form of philosophy, but Greek philosophical works played an important role in his teaching.[4] Origen's younger contemporary, the pagan philosopher Porphyry, identified Origen as "a hearer of Ammonius, who had achieved the greatest progress in philosophy in our times." This was Ammonius Saccas, an Alexandrian Platonist and the teacher of Porphyry's own revered master, Plotinus.[5] Eusebius described Origen's Christian asceticism and his biblical studies as a form of philosophical exercise: "For many years he continued to live in this philosophical way, putting aside all the fleshly things of youthful enthusiasm; all day long his discipline was to perform labors of no light character, and for most of the night he devoted himself to studying the divine Scriptures: and he persevered, as much as possible, in the most philosophic way of life."[6]

At the same time, Origen attempted to distance himself from Greek thought. In a letter to his student, Gregory, which may reply directly to Gregory's *Farewell Oration,* Origen warned him to treat philosophy as the fleeing Israelites had the wealth of Egypt:

> Take with you from the philosophy of the Greeks both those parts that are able, as it were, to serve as encyclical or propaedeutic studies for Christianity, and also those elements of geometry and astronomy that may be useful for the interpretation of the Holy Scriptures . . . Perhaps something of this sort is hinted at, in the passage of Exodus where God in person directs the sons of Israel to ask from their neighbors and those dwelling in their tents vessels of silver and of gold and clothing [Ex. 12.35–36]; thus they are to spoil the Egyptians, and so find material for the preparation of what will be required for the worship of God. For out of the things of which the sons of Israel spoiled the Egyptians the furniture of the Holy of Holies was made, the ark with its cover, and the cherubim and the mercy-seat.[7]

Philosophical learning, Origen implies, is precious, but foreign and therefore dangerous. It must be purified of the taint of its pagan context, and refashioned after a Christian model, in order to serve Christian purposes. Porphyry agreed that Christianity could not be reconciled with philosophy. He described Origen, accordingly, as a betrayer of his own philosophical formation, one who "drove headlong toward barbarian recklessness," adopted a "Christian way of life, contrary to the law," and in his allegorical interpretation of the Bible, fruitlessly "introduced Greek ideas into foreign myths."[8] Both Origen and his critic portray the distinction between Christianity and philosophy in ethnic terms. Gregory, too, seems to distinguish between philosophy, which is Greek, and "foreign" Christianity.[9] The emphasis, intriguingly, is not on content, but on origins. As we shall see in the next chapter, one of the most important differences between Origen's practice as a scholar and that of contemporary philosophers was precisely his commitment to the study of a "barbarian" literature—the Hebrew Bible—in its original language.

But for the moment, we will focus on what Origen shared with the philosophers. Several generations of scholars have debated, without apparent resolution, the actual importance of Greek philosophical ideas in Origen's thought. We see no need to resolve this debate, since our concern here is not so much with Origen's ideas as with his way of life, and the social and cultural categories through which others would have perceived it in his own day. Most observers agree that Origen's social identity, the material conditions of his intellectual work, and the physical form of his writings, have much in common with those of his philosophical peers. Yet the parallels between their textual habits and Origen's have not been fully explored.

The philosopher of the high empire was himself a composite creature, a complex and idiosyncratic blend of the itinerant sophist and the enlightened guru, a character whose peculiarities modern scholars have only begun to appreciate over the last few decades. The culture of the second century—the era of the so-called Second Sophistic, which received its name from a

third-century writer and contemporary of Origen's, Philostratus[10]—endowed all learning with an aspect of performance, while
it brought technical rigor and an enthusiasm for system to the
most arcane fringes of intellectual activity.[11] Philosophers, like
the sophists and grammarians, were erudite men, scholarly, even
bookish in their habits. Philosophy was esoteric, set apart from
the broader culture of Roman elites, the preserve of adults seeking enlightenment rather than the boys in need of basic education who filled the schools of grammarians and rhetoricians.
Philosophers from all the schools had strong tendencies toward
dogmatism, reverence for authority, and sectarian squabbling.
One important conception of philosophical legitimacy, therefore, depended upon a teacher's place in a school or a literary
tradition, which could underwrite the propositional validity of
his teachings. By Origen's day, however, the rivalry between the
schools had begun to soften. Philosophical sectarianism was replaced by a more eclectic pursuit of ancient wisdom, to be
sought in the works of a diverse array of earlier writers—poets,
philosophers of whatever school, even barbarians, so long as
they wrote or were translated into Greek. Furthermore, the true
philosopher had always exuded considerable personal charisma,
inasmuch as he might be seen as himself an embodiment of
wisdom. Charismatic authority, therefore, was repeatedly proclaimed as the final, central source of philosophical legitimacy.[12]
Throughout the Roman era, the tension between two notions
of how a student, or a critic, might distinguish the true philosopher—one based on school affiliation and book-learning, the
other on charismatic wisdom—were resolved only in the person
of the individual teacher, whose moral excellence, experienced

directly by his students, authenticated his teachings, which often made heavy use of books.[13]

Origen was not the only Christian who played the role of a philosopher in the Roman world of the late second and early third centuries. Like Justin and Clement before them, some of Origen's contemporaries clearly occupied similar niches. Africanus, for example, seems to have combined his interest in Christian chronology with equally strong passions for magical lore and ethnography. His *Kestoi* contained not a word about Christianity, but offered rich information about the weapons and tactics of the Parthians (which he had seen in the course of his travels), the religious rituals practiced in Edessa, and the magical properties of amulets.[14] It may well have been this sort of knowledge that won him the friendship of the emperor Severus Alexander, from whom he obtained the new name of Nikopolis for Emmaus.[15] As William Adler has shown, Africanus, in his intellectual and literary facility, his love for the ancient past, and his ability to sell himself to patrons, closely resembled the sophists of the Second Sophistic. He created a mode of learning that combined their skills and interests with those of Christian millenarian speculation.[16] For all his idiosyncratic preoccupations, Africanus exemplifies just as much as Origen—with whom, as we will see, he corresponded—the integration of the Christian scholar of the third and fourth centuries into existing social roles.

By Origen's own day, notoriously, the Severan dynasty had imbued the imperial court with an oriental flavor. However little we may credit the hysterical accusations of Roman traditionalists against the Syrian cults of Elagabalus, we can still appreciate that the first half of the third century was an age of religious eclecticism, even at the highest levels of imperial society.[17] The account of the personal religiosity of the emperor Severus Alexander that appears in the *Historia Augusta*—for all that its details may be fictional—seems emblematic of Origen's age. The emperor, we are told, worshipped each morning before a personal shrine that contained images of his ancestors, of deified emperors, and of "Apollonius of Tyana, Christ, Abraham, Orpheus, and others of the same character."[18] Philostratus himself, in addition to his *Lives of the Sophists,* wrote a lengthy biography of this same Apollonius, in which he portrayed him as both philosopher and holy man—a worthy object of Severus's devotions.[19] This multifaceted scholar was a protégé of the empress Julia Domna, Severus's great-aunt.[20] In such a climate, it is less difficult to imagine how a Christian biblical scholar could occupy the social status and function of a Greek philosopher—or how one trained in all the subtleties of Greek literary and philosophical learning might find, even in the peripheral world of the persecuted and barbarous Christians, adequate scope for the exercise of his prodigious intellectual gifts.

Gregory Snyder has investigated the teaching methods, and the bibliographic habits, of these pagan sages and their Jewish and Christian contemporaries, from the first century BCE through the third century CE. He draws our attention to the centrality of books and reading in the lives of philosophers throughout the period, while documenting the variations in the ways that followers of various schools read, wrote, and used books. His work on reading and writing among philosophers has provided much of the inspiration for what follows.[21] Although Snyder presents suggestive evidence for the schools' distinct styles of using and producing books, the material he surveys also makes clear that the philosophers of the Roman world shared a common culture of the book. Our focus will be on these points of intersection between disparate bodies of evidence, from literary texts of the third century CE to the paleographical details of papyri from the first century BCE. As in Origen's own case, the evidence is thin and scattered, and conclusions can only be tentative. But a coherent larger picture does emerge.

Closest to Origen's time and culture, and linked to him through a common teacher, is the Platonic philosopher Plotinus, active at Rome in the third quarter of the third century. For our purposes, the richest source for Plotinus and his circle is the *Life* of Plotinus written by his student, Porphyry, as part of the apparatus that he created for his collection of Plotinus's philosophic treatises, the *Enneads*. As we have already had reason to note, Plotinus began as a student of the Alexandrian Platonist, Ammonius Saccas.[22] His career as a teacher and writer, however, took place entirely at Rome.

Porphyry's biography is among other things a life in books, a trove of information on reading, writing, and libraries in the second half of the third century. It provides much information not only on Plotinus's habits as a writer, reader, and user of books, but on those of a whole array of his contemporaries. Many of these philosophers were prolific authors. It seems paradoxical, therefore, that Porphyry describes the philosophers of his time as hesitant to commit their teachings to writing. Yet this paradox is typical of an ambivalence toward writing, books, and literature that runs throughout the *Life of Plotinus*. As we shall see, this ambivalence had deep roots in philosophical tradition, not only in the famous warnings of Plato's dialogues against writing and against poetry,[23] but under the Roman Empire as well, in a world where the centrality of literature to culture was taken for granted as perhaps it had not yet been in Plato's Athens.

Porphyry quotes at length the preface to a philosophical treatise by his own first teacher, Longinus, a famous critic, which he wrote in response to the doctrines of Plotinus and his foremost student, Amelius. In the preface, Longinus reviews the philosophers of his time. He groups them according to their writing practices, implicitly categorizing them, and their texts, in terms of those texts' differing relations to the authoritative works of earlier writers. He begins by mentioning a number of philosophers who did not write anything at all. As Porphyry had implied earlier in the *Life,* Plotinus's teacher, Ammonius, was among those who wrote nothing. So reluctant was he to see his teachings disseminated that he even swore his students to secrecy.[24] Longinus also catalogues philosophers who did write, in a number of genres. He first describes several authors who produced only copied or compiled parts of earlier writers' texts: "some produced nothing except compilations and transcriptions of what their elders had composed, like Euclides, Democritus, and Proclinus," all Platonists. Longinus then describes others, all Stoics, who "diligently brought to mind quite small points from the investigations of the ancients, and made it their task to put together books on the same subjects." Perhaps these philosophers composed commentaries, or possibly *zetemata*—works organized around particular problems presented by an authoritative text, but not following the order of that text as a commentary would. Porphyry himself was the author of a work of this kind, *Homeric Problems.*[25] Among the commentators, Longinus lists, intriguingly, the Stoic Phoibion, who "deemed it better to be known for the elegance of his speech rather than the coherence of his thought." The question of rhetorical or literary eloquence, and its incompatibility with systematic thinking, will recur below. Of the several further philosophers whom Longinus catalogues, he concludes, "those who display true zeal for writing by the multitude of problems they have treated, and have an original way of thinking, are Plotinus and Gentilianus Amelius"—Plotinus's most prominent student. These two alone, for Longinus, are philosophical authors in the true sense.[26]

Despite the prominence eventually accorded him by Longinus, Plotinus's career as a writer began only very slowly. He had long imitated the refusal of his teacher Ammonius to write. Then, he began to work with a group of students, basing his teaching "on what he had learned during his time with Ammonius. So he continued for ten complete years, associating with a certain group of people, but writing nothing."[27] Finally overcoming his reluctance, Plotinus became a prolific author, composing the fifty-four treatises that Porphyry collected in the *Enneads.*

The avoidance of writing, as Ammonius's example suggests, was associated with esotericism. Porphyry portrays Plotinus as desiring to keep his teaching secret: as he writes, "From the first year of Gallienus, Plotinus was persuaded to write about the subjects that came up [in discussion]; in the tenth year of Gallienus, when I first knew him, I found that he had written twenty-one books, which I also discovered had been given out to few people. For the issuing of copies [*ekdosis*] was in no way straightforward, nor did it happen simply and openly and with ease, but those who received them had passed the strictest scrutiny."[28] To write down one's teachings was to risk their dissemination beyond the inner circle. Ammonius's policy was the safest one, though as his case makes clear, even a philosopher who wrote nothing could not guarantee the secrecy of his ideas.

Philosophers, especially Plotinus, also favored an obscure literary style, which prevented casual inquirers—and even some serious readers—from penetrating their works. In addition to the preface of Longinus's discussed above, Porphyry quotes a personal letter he received from his former teacher, in which he complains that the copies of Plotinus's treatises he has received from Porphyry are corrupt and incomprehensible. But as Porphyry goes on to explain, "He was mistaken in judging that the manuscripts he received from Amelius were faulty, because he did not understand the way that Plotinus usually expressed himself. For if any copies were ever carefully corrected, they were those of Amelius, which were transcribed from the autographs."[29] As Plotinus's editor, Porphyry was well aware of the oddities of his teacher's style. These resulted from his idiosyncratic mode of composition, which Porphyry describes in detail: "Plotinus could never bear to take up again a second time what he had written, nor even to read it through once and go over it . . . his handwriting was poorly formed, he did not divide his syllables correctly, he cared nothing about spelling; his one concern was for the thought."[30] Plotinus's works reflected his manner of composition in both style and content: "In his writings Plotinus is concise, dense with thought, terse, abounding in ideas rather than words, usually expressing himself as if direclty inspired [*enthusiōn*]."[31]

In his teacher's defense, Porphyry asserts that in speaking, "he was completely free of the vaporousness of the sophist or the theater; in his lectures he spoke as if he were having a conversation."[32] Philosophers who wrote well, or who seemed preoccupied with literary elegance, came in for criticism. Longinus was one such: "When Longinus's works, *On First Principles* and his *Lover of Antiquity,* were read out to him, Plotinus said, 'Longinus is a philologist, but in no way a philosopher.'"[33] Plotinus's evaluation implies an opposition between the two categories of the philosopher and the philologist, which like the ambivalent attitude of the philosophers toward writing itself, had deep roots in the philosophical tradition. Concern for style, prolixity, and an abundance of examples are all condemned as "unphilosophical." Porphyry's descriptions of philosophical writing distinguish form from content in classically Platonic terms, privileging the latter while rejecting the former as mere adornment, even as symptomatic of a lack of real content. For Porphyry, the form of philosophical discourse might usefully serve to obscure its content from undeserving readers—and should certainly never advertise it.[34]

But books nevertheless played a central role in the philosophical life as lead by Plotinus and his students. Among the philosophical genres adumbrated in Longinus's letter, Porphyry's *Life* accords a special rank to the treatise, the form chosen by Plotinus. Yet it also provides copious evidence for the importance of commentaries and doxographies. As the passage from Longinus's letter shows, third-century philosophers studied both the works of "the ancients" and those of more recent writers. Another passage of the *Life*, discussed in detail by Snyder, gives us a glimpse of commentaries in use in Plotinus's lecture room: "In our gatherings he would have the commentaries read out to him, whether they were those of Severus, or Cronius, Numenius, Gaius, or Atticus, or else among the Peripatetics those of Aspasius, Alexander, Adrastus, and others that were to hand."[35] A sizable library must have been at Plotinus's disposal.

Furthermore, the members of Plotinus's circle wrote constantly, as an integral part of the philosophic life. When Porphyry joined the group, he misunderstood Plotinus's views on a question of epistemology. He recounts,

> I produced a refutation [*antigrapsas prosēgagon*], attempting to show that the object of thought existed outside the intellect. He had Amelius read this out [*anagnōnai*] to him, and when it had been read, he smiled and said, "Let it be your task, Amelius, to resolve the confusion he has fallen into because he does not know what our view is." Amelius wrote a sizable book [*biblion ou mikron*] "On Porphyry's Confusion." Yet again I wrote a refutation against what he had written, Amelius replied to what I wrote, and on the third round I, Porphyry, understanding the argument with difficulty, changed my mind and wrote a recantation [*palinōdian*] which I read out in the lecture session. And from that time on I was entrusted with Plotinus's books, and I aroused in the teacher himself the ambition of organizing his views and writing them down at greater length. Not only that, but I encouraged Amelius too to write books [*eis to suggraphein*].[36]

Despite their ambivalence about writing, these philosophers produced a blizzard of treatises, papers, tracts, and replies in the course of their debates.. Porphyry's conversion to the teachings of Plotinus came about through reading, and especially writing. He expressed his change of heart by composing a written recantation, which he then read aloud before the entire group. Furthermore, his inclusion in the inner circle was signalized, or perhaps rewarded, by his appointment as Plotinus's editor, which put him in a position to spur his teacher on to write still more.[37]

Controversy with other philosophers, perhaps even with some outside the philosophic milieu, also involved the study and production of texts. Porphyry tells the story of Plotinus's conflict with Christians at Rome, carried out almost exclusively through the reading and writing of books rather than through face-to-face confrontation:

> There were in Plotinus's day many Christians and others, sectarians who had abandoned the old philosophy, the followers of Adelphius and Aquilinus, who possessed a great many treatises of Alexander the Libyan and Philocomus and Demostratus and Lydus, and produced revelations of Zoroaster and Zostrianus and Nicotheus and Allogenes and Messus and others like them, and so deceived many and were themselves deceived, claiming that Plato had not even approached the depths of intellectual being. Plotinus therefore often attacked them in our meetings, and he wrote the book which we have titled "Against the Gnostics," then left it to us to assess what remained. Amelius advanced as far as forty books in his refutation of the book of Zostrianus. I myself wrote long attacks on Zoroaster. I demonstrated that the book was entirely spurious and modern, a forgery made up by the adherents of the heresy,

in order to give the idea that the doctrines they had chosen to honor were those of the ancient Zoroaster.[38]

Porphyry identifies the offending Christians not by describing their religious activities, or even, except in passing, their philosophical opinions, but by cataloguing their discreditable bibliography. Plotinus himself writes a treatise against them, then delegates the task of refuting the Christians' writings to his star pupils, Amelius and Porphyry. Porphyry's own efforts take the tellingly philological form of exposing the pseudepigraphy of a volume attributed to Zoroaster.[39] Of course, the implication is that Christians, too, were busily forging the texts they circulated under the names of ancient sages.

All this reading and writing took place under challenging conditions. Writing books was hard work. Copies of new works were difficult and expensive to obtain, if they could be found at all. As we have already seen, Plotinus wrote all his books with his own hand, but his handwriting was so bad, and his spelling so inaccurate, that they required careful recopying and extensive editing to be intelligible even to initiates. His eyesight was so poor that he could not reread his own works to correct them. How many readers—to say nothing of the authors—of this very book would be similarly handicapped without their eyeglasses?

Other conveniences, too, were lacking. Porphyry inserts into his *Life* of Plotinus an extensive excerpt from a personal letter he received at Rome from Longinus, who wrote to him from Tyre, on the coast of Roman Syria. In the letter, Longinus complains about the quality of the copies of Plotinus's works that he had received. Not only did Longinus deem the manuscripts faulty, but he had had great difficulty in making a complete copy of the corpus: as he writes, "there is such a dearth of copyists here that, I assure you, all this time I have been struggling to complete my copies of the remaining works of Plotinus, and I could do so only by calling my secretary off his accustomed tasks, and setting him to this one only."[40] Porphyry can therefore expect no new works from his former teacher, since Longinus's staff has been otherwise occupied.[41] The passage thus reveals some of the physical constraints that ancient techniques of book production placed upon the circulation and production of philosophical works.

But Longinus goes even further: in his quest for more accurate texts of Plotinus's works, he urges Porphyry to travel to Tyre to bring him the books in person, "for I can never refrain from asking you repeatedly to prefer the road to us over any other, and even if for no other reason—for surely there is no wisdom for you to seek among us, if you were to come—then for the sake of our old acquaintance and the weather, which is best suited for the poor health of which you speak."[42] It seems extreme to ask a friend in poor health to travel from Rome to the neighborhood of Beirut, because one has no other way of getting copies of the books one wants to read. And not only does Longinus have trouble getting his hands on others' books: he cannot find the staff to make copies of his own works—which are otherwise unobtainable—even for a beloved, and well-situated, former student like Porphyry. Clearly, the writings of living philosophers did not quickly find their way to the bookshops.

Yet Plotinus's writings did somehow survive, which implies that they were copied and disseminated. Porphyry seems to have played an important role in this process, by assigning titles to the treatises, organizing them in thematic groups, including a catalogue in the prefatory *Life of Plotinus,* and providing other supplementary material. As he writes in the closing paragraphs of the *Life,*

> I imitated Apollodorus, the Athenian, who edited in ten volumes the collected works of Epicharmus, the comedy writer, and Andronicus, the Peripatetic, who classified the works of Aristotle and of Theophrastus according to subject, bringing together the discussions of related topics. So I, too, as I had fifty-four treatises of Plotinus, divided them into six sets of nine [*enneadas*]—it gave me pleasure to find the perfection of the number six along with the nines—then to each Ennead I assigned related treatises, giving the first place to the easier questions.[43]

The role of the editor or literary executor was traditional in the philosopher's world. Sometimes it was played by an intimate friend of the author's like Theophrastus or Nicomachus, both of whom may have taken part in the editing of Aristotle's *Nicomachean Ethics,* or by a distant disciple like Andronicus, who came centuries after Aristotle. This Andronicus, by the way, is a significant figure in the history of the literary editing of philosophical corpora under the Roman Empire, to whom we shall return.[44] Porphyry's thematic arrangement of Plotinus's treatises into numerologically significant units also bears comparison with the various canons of Plato's dialogues developed by philosophers in the Roman period. Snyder, in his chapter on the use of books in Platonic instruction, discusses these in detail, and makes good sense of the lengthy tradition of scholarship that has attempted to reconstruct and interpret them.[45]

But Porphyry's labors did not stop there. The *Life* ends with a complete list of the fifty-four treatises, grouped into six Enneads by subject matter, and with the following comments:

> Thus we have arranged the books, which were fifty-four in number, so as to form six enneads; we have written, too, commentaries on some of them, irregularly, because our friends asked us to write on whatever they wanted cleared up for them. We have also composed headings for all of them, except "On Beauty," because we did not have a copy of it, according to the chronological order of the books; but we have produced not only the headings for each book but also summaries, which are numbered in the same way as the headings. Now we shall try to go through each of the books and put in the punctuation and correct whatever errors there may be in wording; and whatever else may occur to us, the work itself will indicate.[46]

We learn several things from this valedictory statement. Even Porphyry himself did not have a complete set of Plotinus's writings always to hand. Nor did his devotion to his teacher impede him from adding material of his own to the texts, when it seemed helpful to clarify their meaning. Finally, the apparatus of which the *Life of Plotinus* forms a part is revealed as a fully articulated skeleton, supporting the interpretation, and also the preservation, of Plotinus's work as a whole. Porphyry—at least in his own telling—neglected neither the details of spelling and punctuation nor the overall structure of the corpus, in his service to his master's writings.

Here we see one important implication of a final passage from the *Life,* which presents Plotinus the writer as divinely inspired. Porphyry comments on a passage from a lengthy hexameter oracle on Plotinus, given by Apollo to Amelius, which has just been cited in full. He writes, "Also it is said that the gods often set him straight when he was going on a crooked path, 'sending down a solid shaft of light,' which means that he wrote what he wrote under their inspection and supervision."[47] Only an author so gifted with holy wisdom could deserve the efforts Porphyry poured into assuring the preservation of his corpus. Conversely, by treating his master's works as he did, Porphyry bid to place them in the same company as those of the great men of old, those authors who, like Aristotle at the hands of Andronicus, had merited such careful handling.

The habits of Plotinus and his circle were by no means unique to their place and time, but represent the fruition of a long-standing tradition, dating back at least to the beginning of the Roman Empire, and probably well into the Hellenistic period. Philosophers of a much earlier era, and a quite different school tradition, display many of the same habits and preoccupations in relation to books. These were the Stoics of Nero's Rome, whose literary remains allow us to tease out some of the roots of the philosophical culture of the book so fully developed in the world of Plotinus. The early Stoics—Zeno, Chysippus, and Cleanthes, the founders of the school—are unfortunately too poorly documented to play much part in the discussion. Unlike Plato, however, they seem to have taken an interest in literary studies: Zeno, for example, produced five books on

Homer, probably of a philological character.[48] This interest in literature, alongside a countervailing rejection of mere bookishness as unphilosophical, sets up a founding tension that seems to characterize the later, better-known figures in the tradition as well.

We are particularly well informed regarding several Stoic philosophers at Rome in the sixties CE, under the reign of Nero: Seneca, Cornutus, and their respective disciples.[49] Seneca stands at one pole of the spectrum, obsessed with the role of books in the philosophic life, while deeply suspicious of mere philology. His *Letters to Lucilius,* written in 64 CE, are particularly informative in this respect. The overarching purpose of the letters is to set forth for Lucilius an ideal portrait of the quest for virtue. As he does so, Seneca traces a fine line between bookishness and bibliophobia. On the one hand, he treats the authoritative texts of his school quite cavalierly, rejecting the authority even of the founder, Zeno of Cition.[50] Furthermore, he makes a sharp distinction between philologists and philosophers, assigning to the latter the knowledge of the proper sense even of Virgil. Though he is well acquainted with the methods of the *philologi* and the *grammatici,* his portrayal of their modes of reading places them on a lower level of seriousness. Clearly, he took it for granted that his addressee, Lucilius, and all other potential readers had received a literary education and would read Virgil and the other poets. Then too, Seneca was a poet himself, the author of numerous tragedies based on mythological themes. But in his description of the modes of reading of the philosopher, on the one hand, and the *philologus* and *grammaticus* on the other, he distinguishes sharply between them. The philosopher, confronted with a Virgilian tag, only finds in it confirmation for the truth he already knows, while the others embark on a seemingly endless voyage into trivia. Seneca's depiction of these competing ways of reading makes it hard to imagine that he could have envisioned writing commentaries on Virgil—or on Homer, as the early Stoics did—as an appropriate philosophical pursuit.[51]

Seneca's equivocal attitude toward books comes across clearly in a famous passage in which he describes large libraries as merely pretentious, evidence of their owners' illiteracy, while advocating immersion in a small, carefully selected corpus of the classics:

> Even for studies, where expenditure is most honorable, it is justifiable only so long as it is kept within bounds. What is the use of having countless books, and libraries whose mere titles their owners can scarcely read through in a whole lifetime? The mass of them does not instruct but rather burdens the student; and it is much better to surrender yourself to a few authors than to wander through many. Forty thousand books were burned at Alexandria; let someone else praise this library as the most noble monument to the wealth of kings, as did Titus Livius, who says that it was the most distinguished achievement of the good taste and solicitude of kings. There was no "good taste" or "solicitude" about it, but only learned luxury—no, not even learned, since they had collected the books, not for the sake of learning, but to make a show, just as many who lack even a child's knowledge of letters use books, not as the tools of learning, but as decorations for the dining room.[52]

Throughout his letters to Lucilius, as Snyder shows, Seneca portrays appropriate modes of reading and writing as forms of *askesis,* exercises in philosophic virtue. Books—the proper, carefully chosen books—are not merely sources of information, but serve an almost medicinal function in healing the troubled soul.[53] Yet in the passage just quoted, mere bookishness is portrayed not only as wasteful, but as a tell-tale sign of the insecurity of the arriviste—or perhaps of the immoral laxity of the decadent Greek. In sum, Seneca's attitude toward books, reading, and writing was profoundly ambivalent, a trait we have already met among other philosophers.[54]

By contrast with Seneca, a close contemporary and fellow Stoic, Cornutus, seems to have combined his philosophical interests not only with literary but even with grammatical and rhetorical studies. Unlike Seneca, Cornutus—who was probably a freedman[55]—may have been a professional teacher, and certainly did take on young students as his personal disciples. Two of these became famous poets: Persius, author of six surviving satires, and Lucan, whose epic *Pharsalia* has been interpreted as a sort of anti-*Aeneid.* Interestingly, through Lucan, who was Seneca's nephew, Cornutus may have been connected with Seneca himself, although the two make no reference to each other in their surviving works. The titles, or at least the subjects, of several of Cornutus's works survive, exemplifying his varied interests: a work on Aristotle's *Categories;* the treatises *On Figures of Speech, On the Art of Rhetoric, On Pronunciation* (or perhaps, *On Spelling*); a satire of his own; and commentaries in at least ten books on Virgil's *Aeneid.* Only one work has been transmitted intact: the *Introduction to Greek Theology,* which consists largely of etymological interpretations of myth—as transmitted in poetry, painting, ritual, and other forms—in terms of Stoic physics.[56] The *Introduction,* in its combination of serious, even abstruse philosophical learning with a close engagement with verses of Hesiod, among a variety of other texts and sources, demonstrates an attitude toward the relation between philosophy and literary study that is almost the inverse of Seneca's. For Cornutus, philology was a necessary support to philosophical investigation, one of whose richest sources was the archaic poetry that transmitted, albeit distorted by poetic license, the profound insights of the earliest men.

Persius, one of the poets among Cornutus's coterie, has left a moving portrait of his teacher's influence and of their relations in the beginning of his fifth satire, which as a whole is an exhortation to philosophic conversion. According to the *Life of Persius,* he began to work with Cornutus when he was only sixteen, having already completed his grammatical and rhetorical studies. Persius describes Cornutus's influence in terms that would have fit well with Seneca's ethical ideals. As Persius recounts the experience, Cornutus's "skilful rule was applied unawares and it straightened out my twisted ways, and my mind was overcome by reason and strove to surrender and took on its features, molded by your thumb." The two spent long days in study together, then dined "at a serious table," where work and rest became one. It is hard to extract much detail from this description. On the one hand, Cornutus's ethical influence, as Persius portrays it, would have fit well with Seneca's ideals. But it may not be too imaginative to suggest, as well, that the shared studies that filled the days of master and disciple included philological research of the kind represented by the *Introduction to Greek Theology.* Indeed, philosophy and philology, in the way that Cornutus practiced it, could have been experienced as a single ascetic discipline aimed at knowledge of the divine.

One interesting passage of the *Life of Persius* shows that books did play an important role in his philosophical studies: on his premature death, Persius bequeathed to his teacher his library, which contained seven hundred rolls of the works of the Stoic founder Chrysippus. In return, Cornutus acted as Persius's literary executor, taking responsibility for the editing of his surviving poetic corpus—though he did not edit the *Satires* himself, but delegated the task to a friend, Caesius Bassus. Persius's other writings, produced in his youth—"a comedy, and a few verses upon Arria, the mother-in-law of Thrasea"—Cornutus ordered destroyed.[57] Clearly, the interplay of philosophical and literary pursuits in the two men's relations was close.

Our scanty evidence does not support a confident interpretation of how Seneca, Cornutus, and Persius used and regarded books. But certain patterns do emerge. Reading, writing, and collecting books were integral to the philosophic life as these men lived it. Philosophy, though it was not merely an extension of the literary culture common to the elites of the Greco-Roman world, was by no means incompatible with literature. Persius's remarkable collection of Chrysippus shares key features with other philosophical libraries, too. Persius's library was large, but very specialized, and contained a rich hoard of books now entirely lost. Not one of Chrysippus's works was transmitted intact in the literary tradition.[58] Finally, the philosophers' bookish pursuits were but one element within a life of learning grounded in intimate friendship. Friendship, in turn, shaped the fate of their books—those they owned, and those they wrote—as well as their habits as readers and writers. The Stoics of Nero's Rome, in other words, lived a life much like that of Plotinus and his students two centuries later, in which books played very similar roles. One might even go so far as to say that Plotinus's circle and its literary activities, as we know them through the writings of Porphyry, somehow managed to fuse Seneca's snobbish spasms of bibliophobia with the literary, exegetical, and even grammatical concerns of Cornutus, in the service of a new elitism of the Mind.

It seems, then, that a certain characteristic philosophical mode of using books persisted, even among members of different schools and across two centuries. This finding gives us license to turn to an even earlier example, which despite its distance in time from Origen, nevertheless has the advantage of bringing us much closer to our goal of watching a philosopher at work: reading, interpreting, and, particularly, composing books. The destruction of Herculaneum, a city on the Bay of Naples buried under volcanic ash in the eruption of Mount Vesuvius in 79 CE, entombed among many other things a sizable library. Since the eighteenth century, archaeological excavation at the site of a magnificent seaside villa—termed the Villa dei Papiri after its precious contents—has unearthed this library, in the form of several hundred carbonized papyrus rolls. The books are mostly Epicurean writings, and have come to be identified with Philodemus, a figure well known from other sources.[59] This material is tantalizing in its richness, yet frustrating in its fragmentary character, and needs to be treated with caution. In particular, we must bear in mind that the identification of the library as Philodemus's working collection, and even more so of the villa as that of Calpurnius Piso, who is then proposed as Philodemus's patron, remain—for all their brilliance—conjectures unsupported by direct evidence.[60]

Nevertheless, the library from Herculaneum provides unparalleled evidence for philosophers' use of books, material of an

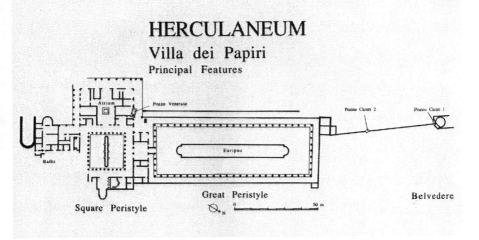

Plan of the Villa dei Papiri at Herculaneum, from Parslow 1995, 78.

entirely different order from the literary references that we have considered thus far. It cannot therefore be left out of account, despite its distance in time from Origen's world and the continuing uncertainty over its precise historical context. The library as reconstructed included a variety of works. Some are perhaps unrelated to the philosophical core collection, such as the fragment of a Latin epic poem on the Battle of Actium.[61] Other works were added after Philodemus's death.[62] But most of the books recovered from the villa probably belonged to Philodemus's personal library. This core collection includes the works of Epicurus himself, sometimes in multiple copies; of another of the Epicurean founders, Metrodorus; of recent Epicureans, like the late second-century author Demetrius of Laconia; of philosophers of other schools, such as the Stoic Chrysippus; and above all, Philodemus's own, copious writings. The total number of works forming this collection is on the order of sixty or so, of which more than half are those of Philodemus.[63] These texts are preserved in about 230 decipherable scrolls. Many of the works were long enough to fill several scrolls, and a number are preserved in more than one copy. Perhaps as many as 1,100 rolls made up the original collection, before the eruption of 79 CE. Many of these have been destroyed, while hundreds more survive but are undecipherable or have yet to be unrolled for examination.[64]

The scope and the contents of this collection are evidence for the intense bookishness of first-century BCE Epicureans, among whom Philodemus was probably quite unexceptional. Many philosophers from the late Hellenistic period through the end of antiquity treated the works of their founding thinkers almost as Scripture. The Epicureans were particularly reverential toward their eponymous founder's voluminous corpus.[65] The centrality of canonical writings in the philosophical tradition did not, however, inhibit the emergence of new ideas and the production of new works, but rather served to spur on later writers—whether their productivity, like that of the third-century philosophers catalogued by Longinus, took the form of independent treatises or of derivative or parasitic works, like doxographies and commentaries and other aids to the study of the central texts.[66]

Philodemus himself wrote in all of these genres, except perhaps commentary. His writings seem to fall into two main phases. Earlier in his career, he wrote lengthy histories of the various philosophical schools, while in later years he began to take on new issues in works on rhetoric, poetry, and music—topics that had not normally preoccupied earlier generations of

Epicureans, but ones that were of great interest to the wealthy and aristocratic Romans among whom Philodemus now found himself. Throughout his career, he also produced study aids of various kinds for those approaching Epicurus's thought, and polemical works, whether against the ideas of other philosophical schools or against other Epicureans' interpretations of the Master.[67]

Both the genre and the methods of Philodemus's works show that books and scholarship were central to philosophy as he practiced it. One of Philodemus's major contributions was to the history of philosophy—a field that modern philosophers sometimes regard as outside their purview. Philodemus's histories of the philosophical schools make up an important part of the collection found at Herculaneum, and survived in antiquity to be consulted by Diogenes Laertius in the third century CE.[68] These works would have required Philodemus to amass and study a wide range of earlier philosophical writings, as well as personal data on the major figures in the various schools. For example, in composing his work *On the Stoics,* his collection of Chrysippus—now represented by four surviving rolls—probably played an important role.[69] Perhaps Philodemus also relied upon earlier historical and biographical works now unknown, which may be represented by anonymous lives of Epicurus and Philonides found at Herculaneum.[70]

Technical philology, applied to the canonical writings of the founders, was an important weapon in the Epicurean polemical arsenal, wielded chiefly against those who put forward rival interpretations of the Master's works. The library from Herculaneum includes twenty-five or more separate rolls containing parts of Epicurus's *On Nature,* several books of which appear in multiple copies.[71] A number of those rolls have been paleo-graphically dated to the third century BCE, more than a hundred years before Philodemus used them.[72] Philodemus must have gone to considerable lengths to lay hands on these precious ex-emplars of the Master's great work. Such a collection would have provided a rich resource for textual studies, especially the collation of different versions of authoritative texts—a corner-stone of the philological method developed at Alexandria in the third and second centuries BCE. A number of Epicurean works found at Herculaneum reflect studies of this kind, though none of Philodemus's preserved writings present original text-critical arguments.[73] The identification of pseudepigrapha was a stan-dard tool of ancient philology, all the more important when a canon of authors or texts had gained authoritative status. Three centuries later, as we have already seen, Plotinus and his stu-dents used the same approach in combating the views of Chris-tian teachers at Rome.

The library from Herculaneum provides rich evidence for an-other side of Philodemus's bookish activities. Among the multi-ple copies of some of Philodemus's writings found in the library, considerable variation occurs. Guglielmo Cavallo—one of the leading students of ancient writing and libraries—has made a careful paleographic study of the rolls from Philodemus's li-brary. Some copies carry extensive marginal annotations. These may be working drafts dictated by the author. Other rolls seem to contain corrected exemplars from which copies were pre-pared for dissemination.[74] These books, therefore, may repre-sent the material remains of a scriptorium devoted to the dis-semination of Philodemus' writings, whether the work was done at the site where the rolls were discovered or at some other, unknown location.[75] Observing that some of the rolls were copied by several scribes working together, all writing an almost identical hand, Cavallo has proposed an attractive conjecture. He suggests that the teams of scribes who produced these manuscripts had been trained in Philodemus's library—as their counterparts would be centuries later in medieval scriptoria—to write bookhands, and to lay out text, so consistently that sections of these books written by different scribes nevertheless present an almost identical appearance.[76] The philosophical collection discovered at Herculaneum thus provides striking evidence for the inseparable linkage of the two central functions of the ancient library: the collection of books and their production and reproduction. It also gives precious insight into the complexity, and high professional standards, of the scriptorium available to even such a relatively obscure figure as Philodemus, whose own philosophical contributions modern readers have sometimes judged little more than mediocre.

Both Philodemus's close engagement with a sizable repertoire of earlier texts, and his use of a staff of scribes, would have made his brand of philosophy a costly pursuit, at home in the context of the luxurious villa where his library was entombed. To accumulate the number of books that he needed to support his researches on the history of philosophy alone would have been expensive as well as difficult.[77] To be sure, the books Philodemus needed could not have been found in the West in the first century BCE, and therefore cannot represent the fruits of Piso's patronage. Instead, Philodemus probably obtained them before he went to Italy, during the years he spent in eastern centers of

philosophical teaching, like Athens, where he studied under
Zeno, then successor to Epicurus as leader of the school. In the
West, such a collection of rare and precious books would have
played an important part in Philodemus's self-presentation as a
philosopher, before a Roman audience in whose image of philosophers books and study formed a central part. But the production of Philodemus's own substantial corpus, and especially
his access to a stable of scribes trained in specialized skills,
do suggest an atmosphere of liberal resources, provided by a
wealthy private patron.

We cannot be certain that Philodemus lived and wrote where
his books were discovered, or that the grand seaside villa belonged to his patron Calpurnius Piso. But Philodemus would
have thrived with the support of such a wealthy and well-con-
nected Roman, in an era when Roman governors and generals
were going to great lengths to amass libraries in the East and to
transport them home to Italy.[78] A Piso would have been well
able to provide Philodemus with the staff that supported his research and writing. The size and luxury of the Villa dei Papiri—
whoever actually enjoyed its gardens, arranged its sculptures,
and gazed from its belvedere over the Bay of Naples—help us to
appreciate the sheer scale of the resources that Philodemus's
work demanded.

The library from Herculaneum has much in common with
the later collections, known only from literary sources, that we
discussed above. Clearly, the philosophers of the Roman world
developed and perpetuated a rich and long-lived culture of the
book, whose roots lay in the Hellenistic world, and which en-
dured well after Origen's day. Though our results are founded

only on scattered evidence, and must therefore remain tentative, several features emerge as typical of the ways that philosophers collected, used, and produced books. First of all, the philosophical culture of the book was part and parcel of a larger culture of reading, writing, and scholarship, shaped primarily by the grammatical schools. The devotion of the philosophers to the works of their founders was, on some level, merely an extension of the intense focus on canonical authors—Homer, Menander, Virgil, or Horace—that was the most characteristic feature of the common education shared by all literate men in the Roman Empire.[79] The scholarly methods used by philosophers, from Philodemus to Porphyry, were the same ones that the grammarians applied to the poets. The importance of exegetical genres, the commentary only one among them, also reflected the habits of mind instilled in the schools.

But philosophers also used and wrote books in ways that differentiated them from other learned men of their day. Philosophical libraries were often large, and remarkably specialized. Philosophers could be extraordinarily prolific writers. Yet many philosophical books seem to have had an extremely limited circulation. David Sedley, for example, has suggested that Philodemus never intended some of his later treatises for an audience beyond his immediate students.[80] If this were true, it would be very much in keeping with what we learn from Porphyry of the circulation of contemporary philosophical writings among the Platonists of the third century.

Perhaps it was easier to obtain copies of the works of the great philosophers of the past. But the story of the loss and reconstitution of the Aristotelian corpus, first recounted by Strabo, then repeated and amplified by Plutarch, cautions us against making a blanket assumption that the works of such founding figures were readily available. As Strabo tells the story,

> Neleus succeeded to the possession of the library of Theophrastus, which included that of Aristotle . . . Aristotle was the first person with whom we are acquainted who made a collection of books, and suggested to the kings of Egypt the formation of a library. Theophratus bequeathed it to Neleus, who carried it to Scepsis, and bequeathed it to some ignorant persons who kept the books locked up, lying in disorder. When the Scepsians understood that the Attalic kings, on whom the city was dependent, were in eager search for books, with which they intended to furnish the library at Pergamum, they hid theirs in an excavation underground; at length, but not before they had been injured by damp and worms,

the books passed into the hands of the grammarian Apellicon. From him, Plutarch informs us, they went to Andronicus of Rhodes, who catalogued the books and published them at Rome in the time of the dictator Sulla. Until this time, Aristotle's works were not widely available, even to the heads of the Peripatetic school.[81] Even a founder's books, it transpires, could go missing for several centuries. Clearly, philosophical publication could be a primitive affair.

Philosophical circles, furthermore, were bound together by intense personal ties, which shaped the ways that philosophers and their students obtained, used and produced their books. The Roman world as a whole was criss-crossed by ties of friendship among members of the ruling elite. Charisma and personal affection played many roles that more institutionalized societies reserve for formal credentials and offices. As Fergus Millar showed thirty years ago, in the absence of a large bureaucracy, or even an empire-wide law code, the Roman Empire in its first centuries—down to Origen's time, and even beyond—relied on personal relationships to mediate imperial rule to the provinces.[82] The traditional Greco-Roman conception of friendship—expressed, for example, in Aristotle's *Nicomachean Ethics*—emphasized sentiment and rejected any calculation of interest between friends. True friendship could subsist only between equals—which implies that to treat someone as a friend was to recognize him as an equal, or near-equal.[83] This understanding of friendship masked inequalities and softened the harsh edges of Roman domination.[84] Similarly, it bound philosophical teachers and their students in intensely emotional relationships, while allowing differences in personal status to give way before intellectual prowess and progress toward shared goals of wisdom and the good life.

The philosophic life was austere. Renunciation of worldly goods exempted the philosopher from the need for great wealth to support his learned leisure. But to the extent that philosophy was a bookish undertaking, it was also costly, and limited to the educated elite. Even the most ascetic philosophers could expend substantial resources on obtaining and producing books. Personal patronage was the only source of support for these activities. To be sure, a few cities had chairs of philosophy, funded at municipal expense.[85] But these were the exception that proved the rule: in general, philosophers worked within a web of per-

sonal relations, bound together by the charisma of the philosopher and the devotion of his followers, not by any institutional
structure.

Origen's bibliographic habits fit well within the philosophical
culture of the book as it emerged under the Roman Empire.
The contents and scope of Origen's collection, the uses to which
he put his books, the ways he read and the genres in which he
chose to write, and the social matrix that supported his work, all
find strong parallels among the philosophers. Origen's library
was large and varied, yet its contents were also highly specialized, omitting many works, even entire literary genres, that were
central to contemporary learned culture. Origen's literary output was diverse, but much of it was shaped by the twin philosophical imperatives of interpretation—in Origen's case, of the
Christian Scriptures—and polemic, whether against members
of one's own school or against representatives of rival traditions.
Finally, we have precious documentation both for Origen's relations with patrons and for the concrete ways that their support
enabled him to obtain and, especially, to produce books. What
we find both reflects, and helps to fill out, the picture pieced together from the evidence for more typical philosophers.

Origen's library has left no physical traces for archaeology to
uncover, nor do we have much direct evidence for its contents.
Yet we can say a good deal about the books that Origen collected and how he used them. Studies of his use of earlier texts,
in particular, can suggest what books he had on hand as he
wrote. He gathered books, it seems, from many sources over
the course of a long career, which not only saw him teaching
and writing at Alexandria and then at Caesarea for several decades, but sent him on a number of long journeys. Everywhere,

he encountered influences—in the form of both persons and books—that shaped his scholarship and presumably his library as well. His travels took him to Rome for some time, between 215 and 217, to Antioch in 231–32, to Caesarea in Cappadocia in 232, to Athens in 233 and 245, and even, around 240, to Bostra, in Roman Arabia, where he was summoned to debate the local bishop, suspected of Trinitarian heresy.[86]

Everywhere he lived and traveled, Origen accumulated Jewish and Christian books, which would have interested few contemporary philosophers. This part of his library set Origen apart from others who filled similar social roles. But close examination makes clear that these were differences of content, not of form or function. The kinds of Jewish and Christian literature that Origen had on hand, the ways that he collected books, and the uses to which he put them, closely parallel the habits of the philosophers within their own traditions. Furthermore, Origen had a rich collection of philosophical works, the same texts that contemporary philosophers read. He also seems to have owned and used other technical works, particularly historical compilations. Philosophers from Philodemus to Porphyry liked and collected books of this kind.

Origen's Christian library had at its heart, like the libraries of other kinds of philosophers, the foundational texts of his school: in his case, the Christian Bible. In antiquity, pandect Bibles—copies of the entire Christian Scriptures in a single volume—were rare, verging on nonexistent. A few examples of such huge books survive from the fourth and fifth centuries. But it is unlikely that third-century book technology would have allowed for their production, because codices at that time were too small and too poorly bound to hold so much material between a single pair of covers.[87] Origen's Bible, then, would have been a library in its own right, not merely a single book. Furthermore, Origen collected multiple copies of biblical texts, seeking out rarities wherever they could be found. Eusebius lists some of these exotica, in a passage to which we will return in our final chapter.[88] Already during his years at Alexandria, Origen had cited several different translations of the Hebrew in an early commentary on the Psalms.[89] His interest in textual problems may have been stimulated by a visit he made to Rome around the year 215.[90] There, in the course of heated controversies over Gnosticism, various Christian teachers emended the Scriptures, denounced pseudepigrapha, and generally used philology as a weapon against their adversaries.[91] Some of these men were probably among the Christians combated by Plotinus and his students thirty years later, while others may have been their teachers.

Pseudepigraphy, and its exposure, played important roles in the debates among Roman Christians in the second and early third centuries, as they did later in the attacks of Plotinus and his circle on similar-sounding Christians toward the end of the third century. From the beginning of his career, as Eusebius informs us, Origen had taken it upon himself to argue against Gnostic forms of Christianity. The use to which his Roman Christian peers—heretical and orthodox—put biblical philology would have been of great interest to him. Origen's engagement with the biblical text only intensified after his relocation to Caesarea, where he came into more frequent contact with Jews. Like many philosophers, then, Origen accumulated rare copies of authoritative works, collated them, and attempted to produce corrected texts. Like their philology, too, Origen's was far from a neutral quest for truth, but had polemical purposes, aimed against both Jews and fellow Christians. Philodemus, with his multiple copies of Epicurus's *On Nature,* and his teachers, with their polemical use of philology, provide particularly strong parallels to this aspect of Origen's activities.

Hippolytus of Rome, the so-called first anti-pope, was a generation older than Origen. In many ways, the range of his scholarly activities prefigured those of the younger man. He too collected books actively. It was the discovery of what Miroslav Marcovich calls "a *golden hoard* . . . substantial treatises belonging to no less than *eight* different Gnostic schools . . . this 'Nag Hammadi library' of his days" that enabled him to write his *Refutation of All Heresies*.[92] Like Origen, Hippolytus used the materials he assembled for polemical ends, and like Origen's, his scholarship extended more widely than modern philologists have sometimes realized. The textual resources he deployed to show that the Gnostics had plagiarized from the Greeks included not only the works of the skeptical philosopher Sextus Empiricus, but other sources as well, which he excerpted in notebooks and then pieced together to form his own mosaic-like accounts of, for example, the life and thought of Simon Magus.[93] We can only imagine the impact he might have had on Origen in 215, when the younger man was about thirty, if—as many have speculated—the two met when Origen travelled to Rome.[94]

In addition to biblical manuscripts, Origen's library contained a range of technical works for use in Bible study. In particular, he seems to have had a diverse collection of commentaries on the Scriptures, by a variety of interpreters. Origen relied heavily on the massive commentaries and other writings of the first century CE Jewish exegete Philo of Alexandria.[95] He knew something, too, of the now poorly preserved writings of Aristobulus, a Jew who had already allegorized the Scriptures in the second century BCE.[96] Origen also collected Christian exegetical works. The mid-second-century Christian teacher Basilides, later labeled a Gnostic heretic, had composed at Alexandria a commentary on the Gospels in twenty-five books, which was known to Clement at the end of the century.[97] Did Origen know, or even own, this work? On more certain ground, his commentary on John, begun at Alexandria at the end of the 220s, but only completed at Caesarea twenty years later, begins by arguing against the interpretations of a Gnostic exegete, Herakleon, author of the earliest known Christian commentary on a New Testament book. Perhaps Origen had encountered Herakleon's work at Rome, where its author had taught at the end of the second century.[98] There, Origen probably also obtained copies of the extensive commentaries on the Hebrew Scriptures attributed to Hippolytus of Rome. In his commentary on Matthew, written at Caesarea during the last decade of his life, Origen refers to the *libelli* (pamphlets) of an anonymous Christian commentator.[99] Nor should these scattered examples be taken as exhausting the Christian exegetical works that Origen would have known and used. Instead, we must take seriously the lessons to be learned from the fate of the philosophers' vast output, not to mention that of the Hellenistic grammarians and critics. So much of the literature of ancient learning has perished that we can hardly go far enough in attempting to imagine the range and variety of what once existed—Christian as well as non-Christian.[100]

Alongside the Bible and commentaries on it, Origen accumulated a range of other Jewish and Christian works, some written in genres common among the philosophers, others standing outside that spectrum. Andrew Carriker, in his remarkable study of the library that Eusebius formed several decades later, gives a convenient list of Christian and non-Christian writers whose presence in Origen's library can be securely documented. Several second-century Christian authors—Ignatius of Antioch, Irenaeus of Lyons, Melito of Sardis—reflect concerns and approaches broadly similar to those of the philosophers. All of these writers were preoccupied with precise questions of doctrine, and expended much energy on polemics against the views of rival Christians. Origen also knew the writings of his Alexandrian predecessor Clement, although it is unclear how much of Clement's sizable corpus he had on hand. Clement's works—the *Protrepticus,* an exhortation to conversion; the *Hypotyposeis,* a lost commentary on passages from the Bible; the *Paidagogus,* a guide to the Christian life; an ethical treatise, *Quis dives salvetur (Who Is the Rich Man Who Will be Saved?);* and even the peculiar *Stromateis,* or *Carpets,* a miscellany of Christian learning, interspersed with quotations from both the Bible and the Greek philosophers—all fit, more or less, into the conventions of the philosophical literature in which Clement himself was steeped. All of these Christian works would probably have filled roles in Origen's library similar to those played in the philosophical collections we examined by the numerous writings of philosophers who lived after the founders. The anonymous *Altercation of Jason and Popiscus,* a second-century Christian work that Origen seems to have known, was even written in the form of a dialogue—a genre popular among philosophers since Plato.[101]

Origen also read a range of historians, particularly those who transmitted the history of non-Greek peoples. Some of his interest in historiography can be compared to Philodemus's: just as Philodemus collected lives of philosophers, so Origen, when he read—for example—the first-century Jewish historian Josephus, was tracing the origins of his own "school," in order to defend it against its critics. Origen's repeated citations of Josephus in the polemical *Contra Celsum,* which he wrote just before his death, fit well into such a context.[102] Origen may have made similar use of the monumental, now-lost historical compilation of Alexander Polyhistor—not a Jew himself, but one of the few non-Jews, before the rise of Christianity, to take an interest in Jewish history.[103] Karl Mras, editor of Eusebius's *Preparation for the Gospel,* believed that Origen also knew the *Phoenician History* of Philo of Byblos.[104] The fragments transmitted in Eusebius show that Philo's history began with a Euhemeristic interpretation of Phoenician myth, which portrayed the gods as human inventors and kings.[105] Evidence to be discussed shortly suggests that Origen may also have read the *Egyptian History* of the first-century CE Stoic philosopher and Egyptian priest Chaeremon. It begins to seem that Origen—like his critic Porphyry—took an interest in barbarian history outside of the history of the Jews. Philosophers, by Origen's day, were eagerly mining barbarian writings for the ancient wisdom they might contain.

But Origen's use of barbarian historiography more likely served another, less typically philosophical purpose: the interpretation of the Christian Scriptures, which unlike the writings of the philosophers were themselves largely composed of detailed accounts of past events. Phoenicians and Egyptians could both be relevant to the exegesis of the Hebrew Scriptures, as Josephus's works surely were. As modern biblical scholars now use Egyptian and Assyrian royal annals, among other texts recovered by archaeologists since the eighteenth century, to interpret the Hebrew Bible in particular, so Origen likely ransacked not only the *Antiquities* of Josephus, but the writings of Philo of Byblos, Chaeremon, and others, whether directly or as compiled by authors like Alexander Polyhistor, for data that could support his biblical exegesis. Origen's immersion in a non-Greek literary tradition probably drove his interest in the histories of barbarian nations.

Origen's library was not restricted to works of his own and related "schools," whose genres might resemble those found in philosophers' libraries, but which would in themselves have been of little interest to non-Christians. Origen also had a sizable, and catholic, collection of Greek works in philosophy and other genres. The *Farewell Oration* that Gregory Thaumaturgus delivered when he left Caesarea to return to Pontus describes the philosophical instruction that Origen's students received, and by implication the texts that Origen used in his teaching. According to Gregory, Origen "saw fit for us to study philosophy by reading with our entire energies all the writings of the ancients, both philosophers and poets, rejecting nothing and refusing nothing (for we were not yet capable of critical judgment). He excepted only the works of the atheists."[106] If, as Gregory's praise implies, Origen instructed his pupils in all the philosophical schools except Epicureanism—for it was the Epicureans whom other philosophers usually charged with atheism—he surely had on hand, and used, a range of texts by all the major philosophical authors. Perhaps he and his students also used doxographic compendia, histories of philosophy like those compiled by Philodemus, and other study aids. Earlier phases of the program introduced students to astronomy, geometry, and natural philosophy.[107] Indeed, Greek literature as well as philosophy, and non-Greek authors to boot, seem to have been on the curriculum at Caesarea.[108]

Porphyry, in an excerpt from his *Against the Christians* that Eusebius inserted in his account of Origen's philosophical studies at Alexandria, describes the breadth and depth of Origen's philosophical reading. Origen "was always consorting with Plato, and was conversant with the writings of Numenius and Cronius, Apollophanes and Longinus and Moderatus, Nicomachus and the distinguished men among the Pythagoreans; and he used also the books of Chaeremon the Stoic and Cornutus."[109] The passage poses some tricky historical problems. Eusebius incorporates it within an early section of his quasi-biographical discussion of Origen, but Porphyry wrote *Against the Christians* around the year 303. Thus there is no reason to assume that in this statement, Porphyry was referring exclusively to Origen's studies as a young man. Furthermore, Porphyry's first teacher, who is probably the Longinus mentioned, was born too late to have begun his career as a writer before Origen had settled in Caesarea.[110]

Pier Franco Beatrice has made the important observation that earlier in the excerpt from his *Against the Christians,* Porphyry describes Origen as "a man whom I met [*entetuchēka,* which Beatrice translates elsewhere as "frequented"] when I was still quite young."[111] Since Porphyry was born about 233, he probably knew Origen in the last years of the 240s, before he studied with Longinus at Athens.[112] At that time, Longinus would have been about thirty-five, certainly old enough to have produced works of his own that Origen might use in his school. Furthermore, Longinus was a Syrian himself, who spent the last decades of his life at Tyre,[113] just up the coast from Caesarea, and he had begun his philosophical studies at Alexandria, where he claims to have studied for a long time with "the two Platonists, Ammonius and Origen."[114] It is unlikely that, as Beatrice contends, this Origen is the same as our subject, since even if Longinus began his philosophical studies in 228 at the tender age of fifteen (a year younger than Persius, when he began to study with Cornutus), our man would have left Alexandria shortly thereafter. Nevertheless, Longinus had a teacher in common with Origen the Christian, which makes it even more likely that the latter would have taken an interest in his works.

For all these reasons, as Beatrice argues, the list of philosophical works that Porphyry includes here should be taken as evidence not only for our Origen's philosophical interests, but for the books he had on hand at Caesarea, and perhaps even for the sources on which he based parts of his teaching.[115] What do we learn from the names that Porphyry catalogues? That Origen read Plato comes as no surprise. Numenius of Apamea was one of the most renowned philosophers of the second century, whose work creatively fused Platonism, neo-Pythagoreanism, and a range of other materials, probably including texts from the Hebrew Scriptures, on which he seems to comment allegorically in one of the few surviving fragments of his work.[116] Here again, Porphyry's evidence corroborates and extends the significance of what we know from Origen's own writings. Moderatus of Gades was an earlier Pythagorean philosopher, who flourished in the late first century CE, and wrote eleven books, now lost, of lectures on Pythagoreanism.[117] Cronius, also a Pythagorean, was the contemporary and close friend of Numenius; none of his works survive, but he is said to have written against the doctrine of metempsychosis into animals and on the allegorical interpretation of Homer.[118] Apollophanes was a figure of quite a different cast: a Stoic of the third century BCE, and a student of Ariston of Chios.[119] With Nicomachus of Gerasa, as Porphyry indicates, we are back among the Pythagoreans, around the turn of the second century CE; his extant works include *Introduction to Arithmetic* and *Manual of Harmonics,* plus substantial fragments of his *Theology of Arithmetic* and *Life of Pythagoras.*[120] Longinus is already familiar to us: of him, John Dillon writes, "He may fairly rank as the last 'regular' Middle Platonist—a most civilized and learned man, but not an original philosopher of any significance."[121]

Origen's extensive Pythagorean reading is interesting, in that it broadens the range of his philosophical interests beyond Platonism. Chaeremon the Stoic is also intriguing: we have already mentioned his *Egyptian History;* he was also responsible for a work on hieroglyphics, which argued that they carried symbolic meanings.[122] Chaeremon's Roman contemporary and fellow Stoic Cornutus, as we have already seen, composed an extant treatise on the etymological interpretation of Greek mythology. As previous scholars have suggested, these writers, independent of Philo of Alexandria and his Jewish predecessors, whose works survive only in fragments, may have influenced Origen's allegorical interpretation of the Bible.[123] The Pythagoreans' interests in the nature of God and the soul, their mathematics, and all of these writers' work on the interpretation of ancient texts fit well with various elements of the life of philosophical (or equally, theological) reflection, biblical study, writing, and teaching implied by Origen's own works, and documented in the testimony of his student, Gregory.

Gregory's indication that Origen's students at Caesarea read Greek literature under his supervision recalls an episode recounted by Eusebius, which seems to imply a rejection of that corpus. Origen had begun his career as a *grammatikos,* a teacher of Greek language and literature, in Alexandria. Eusebius tells us that when Origen decided to devote himself entirely to Christian study and teaching, he divested himself of his library of Greek literature and related works:

> Deeming the teaching of grammar discordant with training in divine learning, without hesitation [Origen] ceased to engage in grammatical studies, which he now held to be unprofitable and opposed to holy erudition. Then, having come to the conclusion that he ought not to depend upon the support of others, he gave away all the books of ancient literature that he possessed, though formerly he had fondly cherished them, and was content to receive four obols a day from the man who purchased them.[124]

This passage has sometimes been seen as a wholesale rejection of Greek learning.[125] Read together with Gregory's account of Origen's teaching, and in the context of contemporary philosophical culture, it takes on quite a different set of implications. Philosophers, as we have seen, were often deeply ambivalent toward literary culture. Yet they did not reject the approaches to texts taught in the grammatical schools, but simply transposed them to the study of new corpora. Origen, too, applied the traditional techniques of Alexandrian grammatical scholarship to the central texts of his tradition.[126] Even the allegorical method for which he has become famous was rooted in Greek *grammatikē*. It was only the preoccupation with literature for its own sake that Origen rejected. In this respect, as in so many others, he was typical of the philosophers of his day.

In any case, if Origen began his career by selling a library, he soon produced one to replace it. Origen was an immensely prolific author, whose own works would have made up a substantial part of his library. Jerome, following Pamphilus and Eusebius, attributes more than 800 works to Origen. Despite its length, this immense catalogue is incomplete.[127] Origen wrote in a number of genres, many of them paralleled among philosophical writers. He left a massive exegetical oeuvre, including *tomoi*, scholarly commentaries intended for other learned Christians; homilies, which he preached before the congregation at Caesarea in the last years of his life; and *excerpta*, or disconnected notes on specific problems in the interpretation of the scriptures.[128] He also wrote a variety of polemical works, against Christian and non-Christian opponents. As we have seen, authors' copies served as the ultimate basis for the dissemination of all literature in antiquity, so that we should imagine that Origen kept copies of all of these works on hand.[129] The concrete example of Philodemus's library can help here to reconstruct what Origen's own copies of his writings may have looked like. Philodemus kept annotated drafts alongside the exemplars from which copies for presentation would be made; perhaps Origen did too.

The comparison with Philodemus's books leads one to wonder how Origen's writings were copied. As it happens, Eusebius provides information that neatly answers this question, while raising several others. The hands in which Philodemus's works were copied show that he commanded a staff of carefully trained scribes. Similarly, Eusebius tells us that a wealthy disciple of Origen's, Ambrose, provided his teacher with an enviable support staff, including seven shorthand secretaries to take Origen's dictation as he composed, scribes to work up the secretaries' notes, and even "girls trained in beautiful writing," whose task was presumably to prepare copies to be presented to Origen's dedicatees and other privileged readers.[130]

This information raises a crucial issue: how important were Ambrose, and private patrons like him, in supporting Origen's teaching and scholarship? The philosophers we considered above were relatively isolated figures, whose careers took place in the absence of any institutional context. Personal relationships, with patrons as with students, were their lifeblood. Since Eusebius, scholars have tended to present Origen in rather different terms. They have placed him, and his work, in the context of Christian institutions and authorities, especially bishops.[131] But this picture is anachronistic. Private patronage, we will argue, likely provided the only source of support for Origen's costly brand of scholarship.[132]

Eusebius, our sole informant on this point, had already misinterpreted his sources for Origen's life by reading them against the background of the Christian institutions of his own day. The decades that separated him from Origen had seen a structural transformation of the Christian church, and particularly that of Alexandria, where Origen was born and spent the first half of his career. Eusebius was dimly aware of some of these changes, but both theological preconceptions and lack of information prevented him from portraying the early second-century church in its true colors. For example, Eusebius was committed to the theory of apostolic succession, which linked the bishops of the major sees in unbroken chains leading back to Christ. So he traced the bishops of Alexandria back to Mark, disciple of the apostle Peter, in the mid-first century.[133] But the first bishop of Alexandria was probably Demetrius (bishop 189–232), who came to power when Origen was a boy.[134] As we will see, Demetrius played an important role in Origen's life, but it was almost entirely negative.

Similarly, Eusebius's account of Origen's career as a teacher at Alexandria is refracted through the prism of Eusebius's own life at Caesarea, first as student and then as bishop. As Eusebius recounts it, Origen's career as a Christian teacher at Alexandria took place largely in the context of Christian schools, controlled by the bishop, Demetrius. Indeed, the *Church History* tells us that Origen spent the first several decades of his career— roughly from 204 to at least 230—as an official functionary of the church of Alexandria. According to Eusebius, in about 204, Demetrius appointed the young Origen—aged only eighteen years—head of the "catechetical school" at Alexandria.[135] Later, Eusebius recounts, Origen divided the school into two sections, assigning the duties of catechesis to his own student Heraclas— a future bishop of Alexandria—and creating an advanced class that he taught himself. Though Eusebius's description of this development is rather vague, he clearly places Origen's teaching throughout the period in the context of Demetrius's episcopal supervision.[136] Further on, Eusebius goes so far as to claim that Origen succeeded Clement as director of the "school" of Alexandria; Clement himself had succeeded Pantaenus.[137] This chain of succession implies that by the beginning of the third century, the catechetical school at Alexandria was a long-standing institution, presumably controled by the city's bishops, as it was in Demetrius's time. But Eusebius's story is almost certainly distorted, if not simply wrong, as its own internal inconsistencies have suggested to many readers.[138] It cannot be used as a reliable historical source. In order to reconstruct Origen's career as a teacher at Alexandria on a firmer basis, therefore, we will need to take a considerable detour, and to shift our frame of reference from the individual scholar to the larger setting within which he operated. We will need to review, at least briefly, the history, and the social structure, of the Christian church of Origen's day, as reconstructed independently of Eusebius's narrative.

In 1934, Walter Bauer claimed that before Demetrius, Alexandria had had no bishops, as we now understand that term. Instead, the Christians there had been led by a college of presbyters.[139] Recent studies have done a great deal to flesh out the broader social-historical context of Bauer's fundamental insight into the history of the Alexandrian hicrarchy. The sociologist Rodney Stark and the Roman historian Keith Hopkins have proposed that statistical models can take the place of purely inductive approaches to the reconstruction of the social position and structure of the early church.[140] Hopkins's work, in particular, makes clear how profoundly the church was transformed during the third century. From a very different point of view, Peter Lampe's massive study of another urban Christian community, that of Rome, can help to add detail to the picture. The evidence for Rome's Christians—not only textual but also inscriptional and archaeological—is uniquely rich. Lampe concluded that there, too, the first monarchical bishop emerged only at the end of the second century, in the person of Victor (bishop 189–199). Before that, Roman Christian congregations had been too fragmented either to require, or to support, a single leader. A loose association of presbyters made what collective decisions were necessary—just as Bauer had claimed for Alexandria.[141] Lampe's study of the Roman evidence can therefore be used, with caution, to set the limits of the probable for the history of the Christian community of another great city of the Roman Mediterranean. Finally, the recent work of Attila Jakab has reconstructed the social profile of the church of Alexandria from its origins through the mid-third century, when it produced its first great bishop, Dionysius. Unlike Lampe, Jakab had only exiguous primary sources—almost entirely literary, rather than epigraphic or archaeological—to work with. Nevertheless, his thorough review of this material, and of the massive secondary literature it has generated, make his study a necessary starting point for further work on the church of Alexandria during this period. Because Jakab focuses much of his attention on the issue of the "school" of Alexandria, and its evolution from the latter part of the second century through Origen's time and beyond, his work is especially relevant for the specific problem we face.[142]

Hopkins's foundational article began with the basic question of number: from the beginning through Constantine, how many Christians were there in the empire at any given time? Demographic statistics for ancient populations will never be much more than educated guesses. Nevertheless, as Hopkins argued, even conjectures can help to set boundaries within which to interpret individual items of evidence. Furthermore, the basic parameters are fairly clear. Christianity began, in the fourth decade of our era, as a very small movement—so unimportant demographically as to go almost unnoticed by outsiders—and remained obscure through at least the mid-third century. At the same time, it must have grown steadily from its limited base, since by the beginning of the fourth century Christians numbered perhaps 10 percent of the empire's population, and had become a major force in Roman culture.[143]

This apparent paradox is readily accounted for by a simple exponential growth model, which has the additional advantage of consistency with what we know of how new religious movements grow in the modern world. Surprisingly, even when mass media and easy communications allow new ideas to spread rapidly, religious conversion occurs largely on a one-to-one basis, and along the lines of preexisting social ties. Public preaching and door-to-door missionizing play little role. Under ancient conditions—when news traveled slowly, and tradition restrained the pace of cultural change far more than it does today—such patterns were likely even more dominant. A successful religious movement spreading in this manner grows exponentially at a fairly low rate. Such a model predicts that if there were 1,000 Christians in the year 40, and 6 million in 300 (roughly 10 percent, in a total population of 50 or 60 million), then in 100 there would have been 7,000, in 200 just over 200,000, but in 250 already 1 million.[144]

Lampe's research on Christians at Rome in the second century helps to flesh out Hopkins's next point. Both scholars see Christians in the first three centuries as divided into many very small groups, even within an individual city.[145] In part, this claim rests on an argument from silence: just as Christians left little trace in non-Christian literature before about 250, so there is very little archaeological evidence for their existence. Only after 200 can Christians be identified in the material record, and only after the midcentury do we begin to find significant traces of Christian buildings and Christian art.[146] The first signs of Christian presence, furthermore, are quite unassuming. The oldest identifiable Christian church is a renovated house used by Christians in the Mesopotamian border outpost of Dura Europus for a short period before the town's destruction by the Persians in 256. It was still a small, simple building, which could accommodate at most a few dozen worshippers. The town's well-preserved synagogue, with its rich wall paintings that depicted biblical stories, was considerably larger and more imposing.[147] Only in the reign of Constantine were monumental structures set aside for Christian worship.[148] Eusebius and Lactantius describe sizeable churches in the late third century, but as Eusebius acknowledges, these were a new and still relatively rare phenomenon.[149]

What, then, was the internal structure of these small Christian groups? How were they organized, who were their leaders, and perhaps most important for our purposes, what resources did they control? Early sources, through at least the mid-second century, take it as a matter of course that Christian congregations met as "house-churches," informal assemblies that came together in the home of a better-off member.[150] These groups were probably not very large, since they lacked suitable meeting places. Before the fourth century, vanishingly few Christians came from the wealthiest stratum of Roman society, who could afford grand villas equipped with ample reception rooms.[151] Although Christians began to pool their resources to provide charity as early as the 50s,[152] there is no evidence before the mid-third century for corporate ownership of church property. In the beginning, then, the typical Christian meeting place—a dining room, a shop, or perhaps a rented lecture hall—would have accommodated a congregation numbering at most a few dozen.[153] Lampe finds no evidence that this situation changed at Rome before the end of the second century.[154] The first archaeological evidence for extensive renovations on buildings in use by Roman Christians comes from the late third century, in the lowest levels of the present churches of San Clemente and SS. Giovanni e Paolo, formerly the *titulis Byzantis*.[155] Major cities, such as Origen's Alexandria, must therefore have harbored many small Christian cells, worshipping separately in their own premises.[156] The "church" as such could have had only a very blurry profile.

Jakab's study of the church of Alexandria bears out this point even more strongly. Because of the nature of the site (important districts of the ancient city now lie under water), the city's repeated reconstruction by successive Christian and Muslim rulers, and its continued occupation to the present day, archaeological evidence for Alexandria itself is almost nonexistent, especially in relation to its original scale, as what must once have been the second-largest city of the Mediterranean world. Christian literary evidence that can be firmly situated in an Alexandrian milieu is similarly—and more surprisingly—almost nonexistent before the late second century. But what texts do survive suggest a small, very loosely organized Christian community. The Christians of Alexandria perhaps shared some sense of communal identity, but most of them, Jakab argues, were relatively well-to-do spiritual seekers, who pursued their various brands of Christian salvation quite individualistically.

They did not draw sharp boundaries either between Christianity and philosophy or between "orthodox" and "heretical" forms of Christianity itself. These Christians inherited much, intellectually, from the great Jewish community that had existed at Alexandria before it was destroyed in the Jewish rebellion that erupted in Egypt in about 117. Among these inheritances were the exegetical tradition of Philo, whose works the Christians of Alexandria preserved, and the ascetic practices of groups like the Therapeutae, whom Philo described. But given the likely extirpation of Jews from Egypt after the rebellion, the Jewish community as an institutional framework would have had little ongoing relevance for Alexandrian Christians.[157]

The notion that Christians, even in large cities where they were quite numerous, at the beginning of the third century still met—if they met at all, in any formal sense—in many small, dispersed congregations bears directly on the question of communal leadership. Some quite early sources suggest that, even before 150, some cities' Christian populations were under the supervision of a single, monarchical bishop, who had the power to excommunicate dissidents and to rule on the validity of sacraments like baptism.[158] But in the largest cities, especially Rome and Alexandria, it seems improbable that a single bishop held sway over hundreds of small congregations. Indeed, the term "bishop," which derives from the Greek *episkopos,* for "supervisor" or "overseer," did not acquire a consistent Christian technical meaning, at least at Rome, until late in the second century.[159] It is at that time, too, that we encounter the first serious claimants to the title, in both Rome and Alexandria.

In the light of this larger context, it seems unlikely that Origen from his youth held an official appointment as a teacher in the institutional church of Alexandria. Eusebius's text is our only evidence for that notion, and close examination has revealed its unreliability as a historical document. Drawing on Pierre Nautin's source-critical analysis of book six of Eusebius's *Ecclesiastical History,* which contains his biography of Origen, Joseph Trigg argues that in fact Origen was never a catechist. Demetrius, far from appointing Origen to an official post, merely gave his approval after the fact to what had been entirely Origen's own initiative. Origen had begun to teach during a persecution that took place under the rule of the governor Aquila (206–210). Demetrius and his clergy had gone into hiding outside the city, leaving potential converts to Christianity with nowhere to turn. As Origen became well known as a grammarian, he began to attract students interested in the Bible rather than Greek literature.[160] The idea that Origen was head of an official catechetical school arises from an uncritical reading of Eusebius, who extrapolated from a letter of Origen's, filling in the blanks on the basis of the church institutions of his own day. Origen's teaching was never an official activity of the Alexandrian church as an institution, and his decision to change the format of his classes was purely personal.[161]

In fact, there is no evidence—outside of Eusebius's conjectures—for a catechetical school at Alexandria whose teachers were appointed by the bishop. Furthermore, no firm connection can be made between Clement and Origen. Origen knew the older man's work, and seems to show its influence, but in his extant works he never refers to him explicitly. Nor does Eusebius seem to have had concrete evidence that the two were directly in contact. Finally, both Clement and Origen ended their careers at Alexandria by fleeing for Palestine, seeking refuge from the harassment of Bishop Demetrius—Clement in the first decade of the second century, Origen in the mid-230s. Thus Demetrius can be seen not as Origen's episcopal sponsor, but rather, if anything, as a rival candidate for leadership among Alexandria's Christians, one who espoused a quite different model of authority.[162] How, then, to account for Origen's ability to pursue scholarship, on a stipend of four obols a day? As the details that Eusebius transmits make clear, private patrons were involved. Most important, during the second phase of his teaching at Alexandria, Origen met Ambrose, the wealthy layman who would be his patron for the rest of his life. It was then that Origen began to write. Far from being a result of his place in the church hierarchy, Origen's literary production was directly supported and encouraged by a private patron, a man about whom we have a fair amount of information.[163]

Origen's relationship with Ambrose, which turned on scholarship, involved much more than financial support. Both apparently saw themselves as engaged in a joint pursuit of deeply Christian ends, passionate and ascetic. In a letter to Bishop Fabian of Rome, fragmentarily preserved by later sources, Origen wrote:

> The holy Ambrose, who is genuinely dedicated to God, sends his greetings. Since he thought of me as a lover of labor and one thirsty for the divine word, he confounded me with his own love of labor and passion for divine studies. He has passed me by such a margin, that there is some danger that I will not answer his propositions. For we are not permitted to dine without discussion, or, having dined, to take a walk so that the flesh may recover. Even at

those times we are required to engage in textual studies and to correct texts. Nor are we allowed to sleep through the night for the health of the body, since our textual studies continue until late in the evening. Not to mention that we work until the ninth hour, and sometimes the tenth: for all those who really desire to love work devote those times to the study of Scripture and to readings.[164]

Naturally, we cannot verify in detail this vivid account of Ambrose's Taylorite habits as a supervisor of intellectual work. But other evidence does confirm that the two men studied the Bible together. At the end of his letter to Africanus, Origen notes that "my master and brother, the holy Ambrose, greets you. He aided me with his advice for this letter, and was with me the whole time, correcting it wherever he wanted" (24). The Christian philosopher's lifestyle, in other words, was as social and as demanding of intensive commitment, in its own way, as the pagan's.[165]

Eusebius also tells us that Origen, like Philostratus a few decades before, was summoned to the Syrian court of the philosophically inclined Julia Mamaea, grand-niece of Philostratus's patron Julia Domna, and the influential mother of the emperor Alexander Severus, who came to the throne at a very early age. There, Origen made a very favorable impression.[166] At the court of Alexander, as Eusebius portrays it—with a retrospective idealization oddly similar to that of the pagan author of the *Historia Augusta*—the combination of Christianity with philosophy could lead to intellectual prominence in the highest circles. Such advancement, we can hardly avoid inferring, might come with financial rewards. Here, as in the case of his relationship with his patron Ambrose, we see Origen operating not in the framework of the organized Christian church, much less its orthodox clergy, but outside it. He derives a cultural imprimatur, and perhaps financial resources, from the same types of private patronage by members of the elite that supported other, more typical philosophers, as well as sophists like Philostratus.

Nor did Origen's devotion to a body of authoritative texts set him apart from the Greek philosophers of his day. Origen applied the techniques of the classical grammarians, which had been the stock in trade of his first profession, to the Christian Scriptures. The analysis to which he subjected these archaic, often elusive texts was searching, but no more so than that which Alexander of Aphrodisias applied to Aristotle. His commentaries were obsessed with digging out ultimate truths hidden in recondite material, but no more so than was the exegesis of Plato and Homer developed by Platonists from Plutarch to Porphyry. The learned of the Roman world shared the assumption that truth lay hidden in ancient, cryptic writings, and that only careful interpretation could uncover it. Christians, some Stoics, and the Middle and Neo-Platonists, may have been more given than others to a particular kind of philosophical allegory. But the assumptions that made such allegoresis plausible were widespread in the culture.

Yet the library, and the learned activities, of the Christian philosopher did differ in vital ways from those of his pagan counterparts. What made Origen's case special was the nature of the texts on which he brought his interpretative tools to bear, in particular the Hebrew Scriptures. To put it bluntly: the Greek grammatical tradition, which provided the basic implements of the interpreter's art, whether literary or philosophical, was self-consciously, self-affirmingly Greek, taking precious little interest in non-Greek writings and traditions. Origen's Christianity, on the other hand, had a barbarian literature, composed in a non-Greek tongue, at its very core.[167]

True, men who read, wrote, and thought in other languages could appropriate the structure and techniques of Greek learning. The Latin literary tradition proves this beyond any question. But Latin literature, for all the learning and skill with which its authors manipulated their Greek models, and for all its readers' political power, did not exert a significant influence on the parent culture. To take an example of a different kind of relation between Greek culture and a non-Greek literature, the Mishnah was probably published around the beginning of Origen's career. The rabbis it cites, and their successors, Origen's contemporaries the early Palestinian Amoraim, all drew heavily on the methods of Greek *grammatikē* in devising their own methods of interpretation. Rabbinic culture was, in important ways, open to Greek ideas and Greek methodologies—most revealingly perhaps to Greek technical terminology transliterated into Hebrew or Aramaic.[168] But it was also self-consciously non-Greek, in language, structure, content, and orientation. The rabbis created in Hebrew and Aramaic, both of them provincial, "barbarian" tongues, a free-standing learned culture that drew upon what Greek models had to offer but transposed them into another world. In doing so, they founded a millennial tradition.[169]

Origen's task was a very different one, and one for which we find few analogues in antiquity. He had to make accessible to a Greek reading public the fullest possible range of information concerning a text whose complex history began in, and had continually to return to, an original that was not itself written in Greek. His project—whether on the level of textual criticism or of interpretation—had always to mediate between two languages, Hebrew and Greek, while presenting its results in the second of the two. Despite Origen's faith in the inspired authority of the Septuagint, and his reverence for it as the Bible of the church, the effort that he put into studying the Hebrew original of the Christian Old Testament makes clear that he appreciated its fundamental importance. This recognition of the importance of the Hebrew text drove him not only to accumulate various Greek translations as well as variant manuscripts of the Septuagint, but, as Eusebius reports, to study "the original writings in the actual Hebrew characters, which were extant among the Jews."[170] There could be no clearer testimony to Origen's uniqueness as a Greek scholar of a Near Eastern tradition. Though many ancient philosophers took a serious interest in what they regarded as the Near Eastern sources of Greek philosophy, we have no evidence that they investigated those sources in their original languages.[171]

Origen knew and took seriously the exegesis of his Jewish contemporaries, and in achieving many of his greatest works he must have relied on the assistance of Jewish collaborators. In the commentaries he wrote in Alexandria, Origen repeatedly cites information gleaned from a Jewish teacher, who may have been a convert to Christianity.[172] During the second half of his career, in Caesarea, Origen developed a special openness to Jewish learning and an unusual knowledge of it in its rabbinic expression. He clearly interacted regularly with members of Caesarea's diverse Jewish community, including those associated with the city's rabbinic academy. His exegesis, and that of rabbinic figures who were his contemporaries, reflect interaction and debate that influenced both sides.[173] Furthermore, in his attempts to cite and study the Hebrew original of the Old Testament, Origen must have relied on Jewish informants, on materials for textual study originally prepared by Jews, or both. He seems never to have learned much Hebrew, but, as we shall see, he devoted massive resources to overcoming this problem so as to access the text as transmitted by the Jews, through the medium of the Hexapla.

In his efforts to negotiate between Jewish learning, including that expressed in Hebrew and Aramaic, and his Greek Christian audience, Origen resembles not so much the rabbis of the Caesarean academy as the intellectual leaders of the other important strand of Judaism in the Roman world, which scholars today often term "Hellenistic" Judaism.[174] This form of Judaism, which eschewed the linguistic and cultural separatism of the rabbis, together with their commitment to the concept of Oral Torah and a concomitant preoccupation with adherence to a particular, highly elaborated form of Jewish ritual law, is relatively little represented in extant texts. Philo's corpus, produced in the mid-first century CE, is the most important survival.

Archaeological excavation, however, both in the various cities of the Roman Mediterranean that were centers of the vast Hellenistic Diaspora and in Palestine itself, has revealed that this variety of Judaism was far more widespread, and probably far more influential—both among Jews themselves and among their non-Jewish neighbors—than was rabbinic Judaism in Origen's day.[175] Numerous synagogue buildings have been excavated, whose construction reveals the influence of classical norms, whose decorations are Greco-Roman in both style and content, and whose inscriptions combine the routine use of Greek to convey information with a ritualized, almost talismanic deployment of Hebrew phrases. Their evidence makes clear that the primary form of Judaism in late antique Palestine, as in other parts of the Mediterranean, was not rabbinic, but Hellenistic.[176] Even rabbinic literature testifies at numerous points to the vitality, even the dominance, of Hellenistic Judaism in Origen's day.[177]

For Hellenistic Judaism, Hebrew remained a sacred tongue, and the Bible in its most essential form was the Hebrew original, rather than any Greek translation. Yet many Jews in the Roman world—perhaps the vast majority of the numerous Jewish Diaspora—knew no Hebrew, or very little. They relied on Greek translations for their access to the Scriptures. The language of their liturgy, like that of the inscriptions that adorn their synagogues, commemorate their dedications, and mark their graves, was presumably Greek. Since the second century BCE, they had had a Greek version of their Bible, in the form of the Septuagint. If Hebrew had lost all significance for these Jewish communities, as it eventually did for the mainstream of Christianity, they would presumably have felt no need to return to it. In fact, the contrary was true: translation remained a crucial and ongoing project for the Jews of the Roman world well down to Origen's time. Although some of the later Jewish Greek translations have been placed in the context of rabbinic Judaism, the very existence of these versions attests to the need of Jews to continue to expound their sacred texts in Greek, the lingua franca of the entire eastern Roman Empire.[178] It attests, therefore, to the continuing vitality of Hellenistic Judaism in the Roman world.

The impressive, yet often uneasy, synthesis of Greek approaches to learning with non-Greek material that is so characteristic of Origen's learning, and that drove him to his most innovative undertakings, is therefore best understood as part of the cultural milieu of a fully Hellenized Jewish Palestine. At Caesarea, a welter of different varieties of Judaism, Christianity, and related cults competed for influence in a largely Greek-speaking milieu, where the Greek culture of the eastern Roman Empire was the common heritage of all. Other ancient Near Eastern cultural traditions had attempted their own versions of the *translatio Graeca* carried out by Origen's Hellenistic Jewish predecessors. The expression of Egyptian religious wisdom in the philosophical and technical *Hermetica,* and in the Mediterranean-wide diffusion of magical texts and techniques of essentially Egyptian origins, is a strong parallel.[179] But the Jewish case has its unique features. Perhaps the most curious, and certainly the most important for our purposes, is the seriousness of the intellectual investment that the Hellenized Jews of the Roman world made in the ongoing congress between the two languages of their faith, Hebrew and Greek. It is ironic, but perhaps unsurprising, that this culture should find its ultimate expression in the work of a Christian, Origen.

Origen's Hexapla: Scholarship, Culture, and Power

*O*RIGEN, like his contemporaries the philosophers, applied the full range of grammatical and philological tools—developed since the Hellenistic period for the study of Greek literature—to interpret the central texts of his school. In his case, however, those texts presented unique problems. The Old Testament formed a vital part of the Christian canon. It had, however, originally been composed in Hebrew.[1] Christians and Hellenized Jews read it in any of a number of Greek versions that often differed both from the original and from one another. No classical text existed in so wide a variety of forms. The Hexapla brought many of these together in a single, radically innovative work. Complex, difficult to produce, and extremely expensive, its production would have required tremendous resources, both in terms of patronage and in terms of learning and labor. Furthermore, in order to incorporate in a foreign, barbarian tongue, written in a non-Greek alphabet, into his great compilation, Origen would have had to turn outside the Greek Christian community for key components of the work—whether these were available in the form of preexisting texts or Jewish scholars willing to cooperate in this Christian undertaking. No exaggeration is needed to make clear how impressive an accomplishment the Hexapla was. Yet its form, its contents, and above all its purpose remain unclear. We cannot hope to resolve these questions permanently, but in exploring possible answers, we will learn a great deal about the milieux and the mentality that shaped Origen's biblical philology, and made possible this milestone in the history of the book.

Modern scholarly controversy over the nature and contents of the Hexapla dates at least to the seventeenth century.[2] In recent decades, the disagreements have become sharper, even as scholarship has assimilated considerable new evidence. As several studies have suggested, however, a reasonably secure and detailed reconstruction of the original work is possible.[3] The details, as we will see, remain uncertain. But enough information existsto allow us to appreciate in concrete terms the vast expenditure of time, resources, and innovation that Origen's great scholarly tool required. Our evidence is scattered, its usefulness and reliability variable. In his few surviving works, Origen himself never refers to the Hexapla. Two passages describe the text-critical researches that it was presumably designed to support.[4] These texts will be discussed below, as evidence for the purpose for which Origen created the Hexapla. But they give little if any information as to its physical form. A few fourth-century Christian writers had the opportunity to examine the Hexapla. Their remarks—usually comments made in passing—provide evidence for its contents and appearance. Finally, two fragmentary copies of the work preserve material from the original, although in altered forms. These fragments, which very likely rest on textual traditions going back to the library of Caesarea, provide our most important data, but they are by no means easy to interpret. Because the evidence is so thin, and the debates so complex, we will open our discussion of the work and its implications with a brief description of the Hexapla as we would reconstruct it, in full awareness that every detail is controversial.

Imagine, then, an armarium loaded down with forty matching codices. Across each opening of each volume, six or more parallel columns appear. They present a Hebrew text in Hebrew letters at the far left, followed by a Greek transliteration of the Hebrew, then by the Greek versions of Aquila, Symmachus, the Septuagint, and Theodotion, in that order. The translation of Aquila was a hyper-literal version of the Hebrew, allowing a reader with little knowledge of the original to assess its content. Symmachus's Greek version was more fluent. Like Aquila, it rested on a text similar to the Hebrew that appeared in the first two columns rather than on the widely different Hebrew original of the Septuagint, which is now extant in part only among the Dead Sea Scrolls. The fifth column contained a Septuagint text that adopted the Jewish scribal convention of writing the name of God in square Hebrew letters. Many scholars hold that Origen furnished this column with the Alexandrian critical signs, the obelus and the asterisk, and that its text was supplemented from that of Theodotion, given in the next column to the right.[5] There is no reason to believe them. Rather, where one column lacked material to parallel that presented in others, it was simply left blank. The translation of Theodotion, in the sixth column, was also a Jewish product of the Roman period, drawing on a Hebrew tradition similar to that which underlay

the work of Aquila, though its Greek was less heavily Sem-
iticizing.[6]

For some books of the Bible, particularly those written in
verse, as many as three additional columns containing anonymous Greek translations appeared to the right of the sixth column. Origen had assembled these versions—known only by the
numbers Quinta, Sexta, and Septima—from a range of sources.
Among them was a Greek text of the Psalms found hidden in an
earthenware jar in the Judean desert. Although the presence of
these versions is well attested, we have no concrete evidence as
to how their inclusion affected the *mise-en-page* of the books for
which they appeared, nor do we know much about the nature
of their text. For the Pentateuch, the Hexapla may also have included a column containing the Samaritan text.

Eusebius's *Church History* is the earliest surviving text to refer
explicitly to the Hexapla. What he says can probably be trusted.
Much evidence, to be considered in Chapters 3 and 4, shows
that he saw and used the original Hexapla in the library created
by his mentor Pamphilus at Caesarea, which included many
of Origen's other books as well. But Eusebius's description is
vague, allowing considerable room for interpretation:

> So accurate was the examination that Origen brought to
> bear upon the sacred Scriptures, that he learned the He-
> brew language thoroughly, and obtained his own copies of
> the Hebrew originals in circulation among the Jews, and
> tracked down the other versions of the Holy Scriptures be-
> sides that of the Seventy [translators]. Besides the beaten
> track of translations, those of Aquila and Symmachus and
> Theodotion, he found some others . . . [so that] in the

Hexapla on the Psalms after the four famous versions he added not only a fifth, but a sixth and a seventh translation . . . Bringing all of these together into the same [copy], he separated them by cola [phrases] and juxtaposed them to each other, [placing them] after the very Hebrew letters themselves, and so he left us the copies of the Hexapla, as they are called; and separately he arranged Aquila, Symmachus, and Theodotion, together with the version of the Seventy, in the Tetrassa.[7]

Eusebius lists the three main translations that Origen placed alongside the Septuagint, though not in the order in which they appear in the two surviving fragments. He then digresses to recount Origen's efforts to obtain exotic biblical translations. Eusebius also informs us that the texts presented in the Hexapla were divided "by cola." Finally, he specifies that Origen presented a column of Hebrew *autēs tēs Hebraiōn sēmeiōseōs*, which probably means "in the very Hebrew letters themselves." Despite Pierre Nautin's argument that this phrase refers to the Hebrew in Greek transliteration, the natural sense of the passage, as several commentators have remarked, is that Origen included a column in Hebrew letters.[8]

For all the information Eusebius provides on the content of the Hexapla, though, he leaves important questions unanswered. For example, his description seems to allow no place for the Greek transliteration of the Hebrew, whose presence cannot convincingly be questioned. Furthermore, if this passage were our only evidence, we would be hard put to decide how Origen arranged the materials that he assembled. Clearly, Eusebius's primary goal was not to describe with precision the format of the Hexapla, but rather to emphasize the impressive range of texts Origen had on hand and the zeal with which he pursued his philological inquiries. This passage of the *Church History,* accordingly, has resisted the efforts of some of its modern interpreters to see its every detail as referring to some concrete feature of the Hexapla.[9]

Our best ancient evidence for the form and content of the Hexapla comes from Jerome, writing in Palestine at the end of the fourth century. Jerome knew the work well. Not only did he possess Hexaplaric volumes of his own, which he used extensively in his translations and commentaries, but he also consulted the original at Caesarea. In a brief aside in his commentary on the pseudo-Pauline letter to Titus, he gives a detailed account of the work. Jerome says that in the original Hexapla preserved at Caesarea,

> the very Hebrew words, too, are copied in their own letters, and expressed in Greek letters in the neighboring column. Aquila also, and Symmachus, the Septuagint and Theodotion hold their places. But for not a few books, and especially those which among the Hebrews are composed in verse, three other editions have been added, which are called the fifth, sixth, and seventh translations: they are considered authoritative though the names of the translators are lost.[10]

Jerome thus confirms the presence of a Hebrew column in Hebrew letters as well as a column in Greek transliteration, while giving an unambiguous description of the order of the columns. The original Hebrew in the first column was followed by the transliteration and then by the translations of Aquila, Symmachus, the Septuagint, and Theodotion, in that order. For some books of the Bible, three further, numbered translations appeared at the far right. Jerome's voluminous and highly technical commentaries on the Prophets cite the additional translations repeatedly, providing further evidence that they were present in the original synopsis.[11]

Two other fourth-century writers, Epiphanius of Salamis and Rufinus, also refer to the Hexapla, describing it in terms that corroborate the testimony of Eusebius and Jerome. Both writers spent substantial amounts of time in Palestine, both were scholars with an interest in Christian literary history and the Bible, and both could have visited the library in Caesarea where the original was kept. Epiphanius, for all that modern scholars have questioned his intellectual seriousness, was an avid compiler of curious texts, and a native of Palestine who maintained strong ties to his home territory after he became bishop of Salamis on Cyprus. In his *Panarion*, he gives a brief and somewhat incoherent description of the Hexapla:

Ambrose provided him with what was necessary for his nourishment and that of the stenographers who were assisting him, and papyrus and the other costs, and Origen, working day and night and with the greatest expense of time, carried out this laborious task of writing. First of all, he was eager carefully to bring together the six translations: Aquila, Symmachus, the Seventy-two, and Theodotion, the fifth and the sixth versions. Then he set alongside each word, together with it, the Hebrew [equivalents], in their very own letters. Opposite them, in parallel, in the second column, in the form of a sort of mixture, which was in Hebrew words, but in Greek letters—he made this mixture yet another [column]. So these [books] were in fact, and were called, Six-fold, since in addition to the Greek translations there were two additional juxtaposed [columns], Hebrew in the natural manner with Hebrew letters, and Hebrew with Greek letters, so that he put the entire Old Testament in this so-called Six-fold form, named because of the two [columns] in Hebrew words.[12]

The passage is somewhat confused, in particular in its explanation of the term "Hexapla," for what Epiphanius describes is, surely, an "Octapla." But it clearly attests the presence of two Hebrew columns, written in Hebrew and Greek letters, and the insertion of additional translations beyond the four named versions.

In his *On Weights and Measures,* which despite its name mostly deals with translations and texts of the Bible, Epiphanius gives another, much longer description, which is rather more coherent in substance, despite its often tortured syntax and wandering train of thought. Here, Epiphanius observes that Origen made the Hexapla so that it could be read both down and across the columns; admires Origen's use of the Greek letters as numbers to label the nameless fifth and sixth translations; then finally, after again cataloguing the variant synopses he refers to as the Tetrapla, Hexapla, and Octapla according to the number of their columns, dispels the misapprehension—so he puts it—that might arise in a viewer of the work, who assumed that Origen had placed the columns in the order in which they were translated. Rather, Epiphanius claims, Origen put the Septuagint version, which he observed to be most accurate, in the center, "so that he might utterly refute those on either side."[13]

It seems unlikely that Epiphanius had any independent sources of accurate information to draw upon here. Rather, he probably conflates data from Eusebius, from traditions that were more than a century old by the time he wrote, and from his own guesswork, to provide an intepretation of the Hexapla's arrangement and purpose, which stands at the head of more than fifteen hundred years of speculation to follow. It is interesting as being the reaction of an ancient reader accustomed to books similar to those in use in Origen's day. Epiphanius fears that a reader would interpret the order of the columns as historical, rather as a modern reader might do. He, like modern scholars, saw the order of the columns as a problem. His solution, which explains the arrangement in sharply polemical terms, has the advantage of clarity, and as we shall see, was probably very close to Origen's own views about the value of the various translations.

As for Rufinus, Jerome tells us that he possessed copies of the Jewish translations compiled in the Hexapla, obtained at considerable expense.[14] Rufinus's interest in such matters would likely have extended to the great philological tool prepared by his hero, Origen. In his *Ecclesiastical History*, which was in part a translation of Eusebius's work but here clearly diverges from its model, Rufinus writes,

> So [Origen] also first composed those most renowned codices, in which he wrote down the work of each one of the translators separately, in small individual columns, placing the very Hebrew words in Hebrew letters first of all, and

transcribing the Hebrew words with Greek letters, in the same order, right next to them in the second place; third he added the edition of Aquila, fourth that of Symmachus, fifth that of the Seventy translators, which is our own, sixth he placed alongside Theodotion's version. And because it was composed in this manner he called the exemplar itself Hexapla, which means "written in sixfold order."[15]

Again, Rufinus clearly attests the presence of both the Hebrew column in Hebrew letters and the transliteration, as well as the order of the Greek versions. It seems likely, therefore, despite the skepticism of some modern critics, that both writers saw the original Hexapla. Their statements, however, add little to what we already know. All of these early descriptions are strikingly similar, which adds to their credibility.

Finally, it is possible that the Hexapla of the Pentateuch included a column containing some version of the Samaritan text. The evidence of the Syro-Hexapla indicates that such a column existed. Eusebius also attests to its presence. A passage of Jerome's commentary on Galatians, which was a virtual paraphrase of Origen's work on the same letter, refers (in the first person) to research on Samaritan Hebrew manuscripts of the Pentateuch. Does Jerome here echo Origen's description of his own investigations, appropriating it for himself? We cannot be sure, but among the other mysteries of the Hexapla—why, for example, does the Septuagint column give the name of God in square Hebrew letters?—the possibility of a further column, containing either a Greek translation of the Samaritan Hebrew or perhaps even an additional Hebrew column, for the first five books of the Bible must be entertained. For the Syriac translators, familiar with a dialect of Aramaic, even a column in Hebrew might have been accessible; if on the other hand Origen obtained a Greek version of the Samaritan Pentateuch, it would only add to the range of biblical exotica he had already collected. Caesarea, a primarily Greek-speaking city with a sizable Samaritan population, would surely have been the place to find it.

But the patristic testimonia support only a skeletal reconstruction of the Hexapla. A detailed description of its arrangement, form, and extent must depend primarily on the surviving fragments of the work. The two extant fragments are much later than both the original and the descriptions discussed so far. Their evidence, therefore, must be interpreted with due allowance for the distance in time and in the culture of the book that separates them from Origen's Hexapla itself.[16] Furthermore, both fragments come from the Hexapla on Psalms. This may or may not be accidental. In either case, they show us only how Origen handled a text where the variation between the Septuagint and the other versions was relatively restricted. We have no direct evidence for how he treated texts where a comparison of the contemporary Hebrew text, and the versions based on it, with the Greek Bible of the church revealed substantial additions, subtractions, or transpositions. The two fragments also share another curious feature: although the testimonia claim that it was for the Psalms in particular that Origen had assembled the three anonymous translations, both fragments contain only five columns, all written in Greek letters. They cannot help us, therefore, to reconstruct the fullest version of the syn-

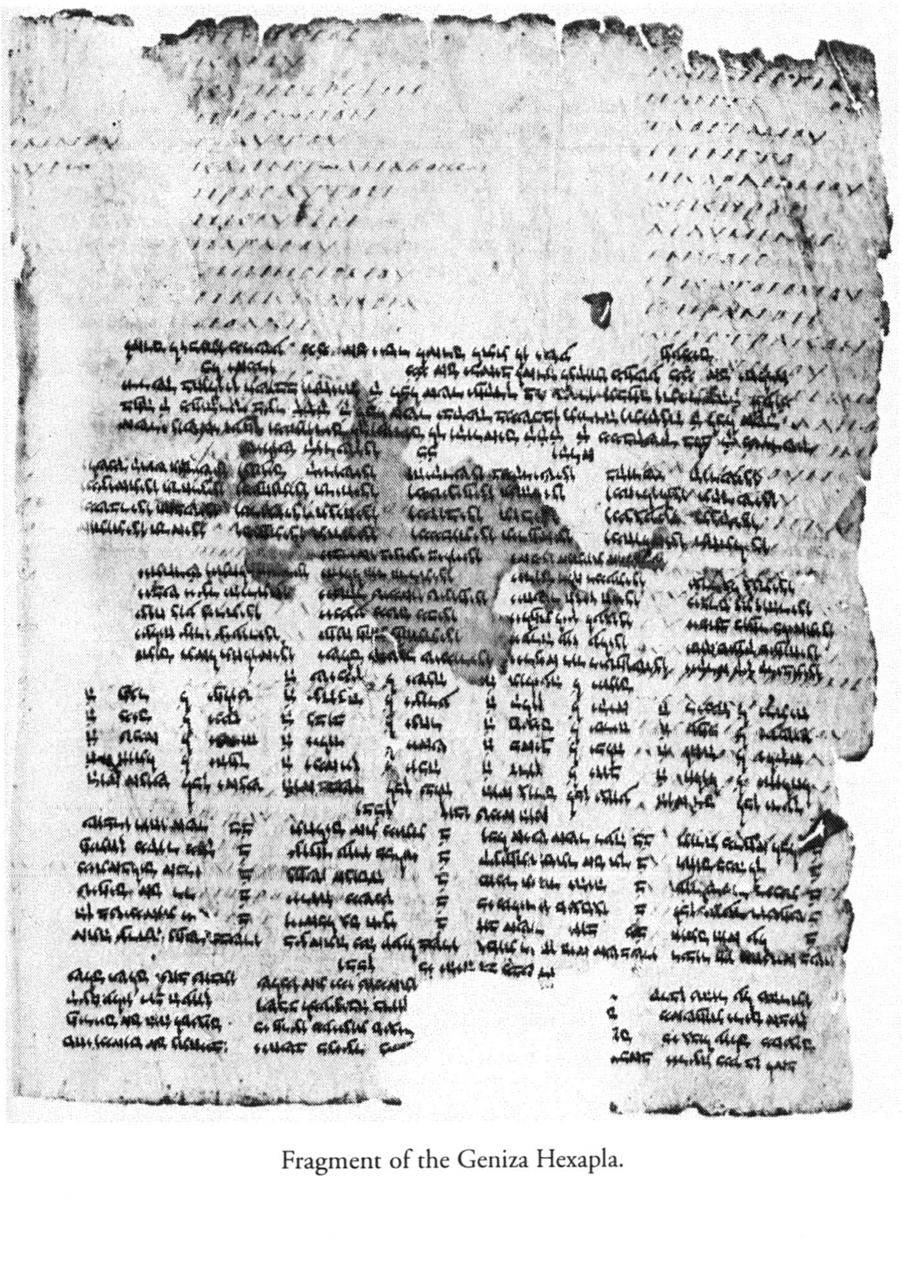

Fragment of the Geniza Hexapla.

opsis, and must represent a substantial modification of Origen's original.

The earlier fragment, published by Charles Taylor in 1900, consists of a single palimpsest leaf found in the Cairo Genizah. The overwriting, in a medieval Hebrew hand, contains fragments of a late antique Jewish liturgical poem. The underwriting, described by Taylor as a sloping uncial hand of the eighth century, contains passages from the Hexapla on Psalm 32, including the Greek transliteration of the Hebrew and the texts of Aquila, Symmachus, the Septuagint, and Theodotion in that order.[17] An entire folio of the Hexapla manuscript was reused to prepare the extant leaf. The folio was cut down on two sides, so that we now have a portion of both original leaves; the original gutter is still visible. The six Hexaplaric columns are spread out over the two halves of the original folio. Each page of the fragment contains 33 lines, and each line gives one Hebrew word with its Greek equivalents. On the basis of the number of words of the psalm missing between the two original leaves, Taylor estimated that the original had forty lines per page.[18] In 1994 R. J. Jenkins presented a new reconstruction based on a reexamination of the Genizah fragment, held at Cambridge. He agreed with Taylor's conclusion that the original leaf had forty lines per page, and argued further that an entire column had been trimmed away at each side of the fragment when it was prepared for reuse. He hypothesized, naturally, that this column had contained the Hebrew text in Hebrew characters, which the scribe of the Hebrew overwriting had hesitated to use.[19]

Giovanni Mercati, in an article of 1896, announced the discovery of another fragment of the Hexapla on Psalms, in the underwriting of a thirteenth- or fourteenth-century Greek pa-

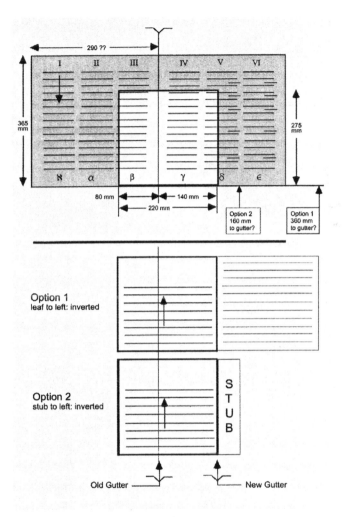

Layout of the Hexapla leaf from the Cairo Genizah, showing its actual arrangement in white and a hypothetical reconstruction of the original folio in six columns in gray. Adapted from Jenkins 1998, 94.

limpsest manuscript of the Octateuch in the Biblioteca Ambrosiana in Milan. This fragment was published only in 1958, after the death of its discoverer, in an elaborately produced facsimile edition.[20] The hand of the underwriting is a Greek minuscule of around the year 900.[21] The use of the smaller minuscule, rather than an uncial hand like the one used to write the fragment from the Genizah, allowed the scribe of the Mercati fragment to lay out the Hexaplaric columns five per page, rather than six per opening as in the Genizah fragment. Like the Genizah fragment in its current condition, the Mercati manuscript contains the transliteration of the Hebrew in Greek letters, followed by the translations of Aquila, Symmachus, the LXX, and Theodotion. It, too, entirely omits the Quinta, Sexta, and Septa, which were certainly present in the original Hexapla on the Psalms. Unlike the Genizah fragment, the Ambrosiana manuscript never contained a column in Hebrew letters. Each line of the five-column synopsis normally contains a single Hebrew word in Greek transliteration, followed by its four Greek equivalents. Occasionally, a single line represents two or even three brief Hebrew words, but these exceptions are quite rare.[22]

This later manuscript was of a different order entirely from the one represented by the Genizah fragment. Almost forty-four pages of the original survive. These show that the Hexaplaric material formed only one part of a larger scholarly compilation designed to assist the textual study and interpretation of the Psalms.[23] The compiler began with the Hexaplaric text of each psalm, followed by a Septuagint text, then by a lengthy *catena* of patristic commentary on each verse of the psalm. The work probably contained the entire corpus of the Psalms. This was a very large and costly manuscript, produced for a scholar of some means. In Mercati's judgment, it was a copy of an already existing work, rather than a new composition. The hand and layout betray no signs of experimentation or hesitation.[24]

Though the gap between the dates of the two fragments may be less than two centuries, they stand on opposite sides of a great divide in the culture of the Greek book. During this period, the new minuscule bookhand gradually replaced older majuscule hands for literary and liturgical purposes. Scribes and scholars collaborated on what amounted to a vast transliteration project—one so massive that few classical texts that were not recopied at this time now survive, except in the form of epitomes. The change from majuscule to minuscule had a tremendous impact on the form and *mise-en-page* of Greek books.[25] The Hexaplaric material from the Ambrosian palimpsest, therefore, is separated by a much greater distance from the books of Origen's day than the single leaf from the Genizah. It can add few new data to our understanding of the contents and arrangement of the original.

Nevertheless, it is valuable to have two separate fragments of the Hexapla. The two fragments are clearly unrelated to each other. This allows us to infer that features they share—which might otherwise seem arbitrary—probably derive from their common source. We may conjecture that this was Origen's Hexapla itself.[26] Both present one Hebrew word, with its Greek equivalents, per line. Furthermore, both have forty lines per page. The more extensive later fragment presents occasional exceptions to this rule, but they are very infrequent. It seems likely that this was also the arrangement of the original. The evidence of the fragments thus permits a more detailed, if ultimately speculative, reconstruction of the form and extent of the

Hexapla, and perhaps more significant, a clearer idea of its original purpose.

The Hexapla, as reconstructed, would have stood out as very different from other contemporary books. In order to appreciate what Origen accomplished in making it, we will need to be familiar with the book technology current in his day. In the third century, the roll was still the dominant form of book. Most books or book fragments preserved from the third century are rolls.[27] The roll book of the later Roman world was a refined example of the bookmaker's art, its form, layout, and use well established and deeply familiar to readers throughout the Mediterranean and beyond. Roll books were normally laid out in narrow columns written down the short dimension of the roll. The reader unrolled the book a column at a time along the roll's long dimension, rolling up the text he had already read on the other side. This arrangement had evolved to reflect both the natural limitations of the papyrus roll and the quirks of the human eye.[28] In theory, book-rolls could be of any length, but it seems that standardized, blank rolls were widely available and influenced the form of roll books in general. Very long rolls were cumbersome and therefore rare.[29] Presumably, ancient readers found these handsome and convenient books satisfactory for most of their needs.

Codices, by contrast, remained relatively crude even in the third century. Perhaps because their ideal form had not yet evolved, makers of codex books were willing to experiment, even in matters as basic as the material on which the books were written. Most roll books were written on papyrus, the traditional material of ancient Mediterranean books. But a relatively high proportion of third-century codices seem to have been written on parchment, a new-fangled and expensive material.[30] Furthermore, no firm conventions governed the number of columns of text written on each page of an early codex. The majority of codices, whatever their material, were written in a single column per page.[31] But a small but important percentage of third-century codices were written in multiple columns—as many as three per page for literary texts, and more for documentary codices.[32] The evidence is far from conclusive, but it allows us to estimate that roughly five or six manuscripts were written in one column per page for every one written in several. In other words, it was possible, but rather unusual, for a third-century codex (whatever its material) to be written in more than one column per page.

As its name implies, the Hexapla was written in at least six columns, probably laid out across each opening of a series of large codices, as in the Genizah fragment. That the extant fragments come from codices is unsurprising. By the date when they were written, the roll had gone out of use in the Greek world for all but certain specialist purposes. But in the first half of the third century, a collection of elaborate codices like the Hexapla would have been very unusual. True, Christians were early adopters of the codex, especially for biblical manuscripts.[33] Among Christian manuscripts of the third century, the ratio of rolls to codices is roughly the opposite of that among Greek literary texts.[34] The Hexapla, therefore, extended and amplified a trend already under way among Christian copyists: the development of codex technology to accommodate ever longer texts. Origen's elaboration of the codex form must have pushed the limits of what was possible in his day.

Given its contents, the Hexapla could never have been a

An opening from a papyrus codex of Numbers, copied in the second or early third century CE. The Chester Beatty Library, Dublin, P. Chester Beatty VI, ff. IIv-12.

"book" in the modern sense, that is a single codex, enclosed between two covers. Rather, it must have occupied a series of codices (rather as almost all "Bibles," until the High Middle Ages, were collections of rolls or smaller codices). If we follow the evidence of the surviving fragments, we can assume that in the original as well each line was devoted to one Hebrew word, in the original and in its Greek equivalents. Perhaps Origen's

Hexapla, like the fragments, also had forty lines per page. These data yield a picture of the original Hexapla as a veritable library in itself, a collection that would fill almost forty codices of 400 leaves (800 pages) each.[35]

To realize how vast, and how complex, the Hexapla actually was, is to confront the enigma of its production: how was it made, how was it paid for, and where did Origen obtain its specialized contents and the expertise that made their assembly possible? No direct evidence provides answers to these questions, but context can provide a sense of the parameters of the possible. Laying out the columns and copying the texts would have been an immense task. How was it carried out? The books themselves would also have been extremely costly, far beyond the reach of any but the wealthiest—and those who benefited from their patronage. Here, we are back on familiar territory: it was surely Origen's patron, Ambrose, who funded the undertaking, as he supported Origen's biblical scholarship in general. In his description of the Hexapla in the *Panarion,* Epiphanius opens by recounting the support that Origen received from Ambrose. Jerome, too, noted the expense involved in obtaining a copy. Ancient readers could immediately appreciate the resources that went into making such a book, or rather library of books.

The complex *mise-en-page* of the Hexaplaric columns must have presented a major logistical challenge to the scribes who created and reproduced them. Contrary to the impression one might gain from late antique depictions of writers at work—from early evangelist portraits, for example—ancient scribes wrote not in bound books but on separate sheets, which were later assembled and bound. Whether the Hexapla was first writ-

ten on papyrus or parchment, the pages were probably ruled be-
forehand, to lay out the columns into which the various texts
were then written. We can only begin to imagine how Origen
and his scribes worked together to create the complex guidelines
necessary to govern the arrangement of the many columns, especially when we consider that their number differed from one
biblical book to another.

Our reconstruction, furthermore, implies that to produce or
even to copy the Hexapla was extraordinarily expensive. Our
only real data for the cost of books in the late antique Mediterranean come from a single source, the Price Edict posted by
Diocletian throughout the empire in 303. But the interpretation
of the Price Edict poses so many problems that it cannot support a firm estimate of the original cost of the Hexapla.[36] What
it does allow for is a rough comparison of the cost of a copy of
the Hexapla with the cost of other books, and with the wages of
various workers. For example, Robert Marichal estimated on
the basis of the Latin text of the edict that a high-quality manuscript of Virgil's *Aeneid* would have cost 3,400 denarii. A sec-
ond-quality manuscript, written in uncial letters rather than in
capitalis, would have cost 2,600.[37] For the Hexapla as we have
reconstructed it, the cost of the writing alone would have been
approximately 75,000 denarii.[38] Unfortunately, the passage of
the Price Edict regulating the cost of papyrus has not survived.
The parchment required for a copy written on that relatively
luxurious material would have cost another 75,000 denarii, for a
total of approximately 150,000 denarii.[39] This estimate leaves
out any supplement for the copying of the Hebrew column in
Hebrew letters, surely a specialized and therefore potentially a
costly task in a Christian scriptorium.

A copy of the Hexapla clearly cost more than any but the wealthiest could afford. Origen's own case provides a helpful basis for comparison. Before he became a Christian teacher, Origen had briefly worked as a grammarian at Alexandria. The Price Edict sets the grammarian's pay at 200 denarii per student per month.[40] A successful teacher's class included perhaps thirty students.[41] Origen's annual income, in the terms set by the Price Edict, might therefore have amounted to something on the order of seventy thousand denarii—less than the cost of the writing alone in a single copy of the Hexapla. The resources of grammarians and their ilk, members of the educated sub-elite, were not adequate to support such expensive projects.[42] But a copy of the Hexapla would have been well within the reach of a bishop like Cornelius of Rome in the 250s, since he annually disbursed the equivalent of 6 million denarii (in the inflated terms of the Price Edict) in food for the poor.[43] And someone from the very highest stratum of Roman society, with the vast wealth that group commanded—someone like Origen's patron Ambrose—could easily have paid for even an undertaking as immense as the Hexapla.[44]

The content of the Hexapla raises different kinds of questions: what cultural resources did Origen draw upon in assembling the Jewish materials he used, and how did the work itself fit into his larger program of philological research? The first two columns gave a text in Hebrew, written first in Hebrew letters and then in Greek transliteration. Where did Origen obtain these materials, and how did he have access to the skills necessary to copy them into his six-column Old Testament? Again, we have very little evidence, but the range of possibilities must be explored, and their implications drawn out. Then there is the problem of the fifth column, which contained the Greek text of the Septuagint. Many scholars have concluded that the critical signs, the obelus that Origen used to distinguish material in the Septuagint that was absent from the Hebrew tradition, and the asterisk with which he marked material lacking in the Septuagint but present in the Hebrew, were inserted in this column. Others maintain that the addition of the critical signs was part of a separate project, a recension of the Septuagint that reflected its divergences from the Hebrew tradition. We cannot decide for certain between these alternatives, although we incline toward the latter. But simply to pose the question is to raise the larger problem of the place of the Hexapla in Origen's philological research on the Old Testament. Surely, his work did not begin and end with the production of this massive set of codices. How did the Hexapla fit into his other activities, especially his exegesis? Why did Origen create it, and how did he use it? What, finally, motivated this immense undertaking? Here again, the evidence is very thin. However, close attention to historical context can help to explain some of the questions that have puzzled scholars for a century or more. Ruth Clements has recently reexamined many of these problems, with particular attention to the Caesarean context of Origen's later writings, and has thereby placed the topic on a much sounder footing. Her work will inform much of what follows.[45]

Correlating the various texts contained in the Hexapla posed two distinct challenges. First, only someone who could read both Hebrew and Greek with confidence could correlate the Hebrew columns with the Greek. One Hebrew word often corresponds to two or more Greek words. To produce a synopsis presenting one Hebrew word and its Greek equivalents per line required knowledge of both languages.[46] Second, for some books, correlating the different Greek texts would have presented problems. The Hebrew used in the first two columns was, on any plausible theory of its origins, a text found among the Jews in the second or third century. The base texts from which the *recentiores* were translated would have been very similar, since by the time they were made the Hebrew text had been largely standardized. But the base text used by the early Greek translators in the Hellenistic period—the translators of the Greek version Origen knew as the Septuagint—was quite different from the Hebrew text used by his Jewish contemporaries. How did he go about arranging the two different text forms—one represented in a single column, the others in four or more—in parallel?[47] These two different problems must be considered separately, since each raises a different set of questions related to the context in which the Hexapla was produced, and its purpose and setting within Origen's larger philological project. No smoothly articulated historical narrative can do justice to the confused and fragmentary evidence, or to the mutually contradictory hypotheses that generations of scholars have advanced to account for it. But close attention to the range of possibilities can help to draw out what the technical problems involved in the creation of the Hexapla imply for the variety of cultural resources that Origen drew upon, and thus for the larger context of his enterprise.

In theory, there are three possible ways to account for the correlation of the Hebrew with the Greek columns. First, Origen could have obtained a preexisting synopsis containing at least the Hebrew material and one or more Greek translations, which he used as the basis for his Hexapla. Since the beginning of the twentieth century, numerous scholars have explored the possibility that Origen used preexisting Jewish materials in creating the Hexapla. Their starting point was the notion that Jews who did not know Hebrew might nevertheless have felt a religious obligation to read the Scriptures in their original language in a liturgical context, and so had a transliteration made.[48] But this view is problematic on two counts. First, as Clements has observed, it assumes a degree of uniformity—and tacitly at least, of rabbinic influence—that is out of keeping with what we now know of the Hellenistic synagogues of the second and third centuries. There is no real reason to believe that in that era, Jews in the Diaspora, or even Greek-speaking Jews in Palestine, saw any problem with worshipping in their native language.[49] Second, it does nothing to explain how the transliteration was correlated with the Greek versions, since in order to understand—rather than merely read aloud—even the transliteration, a reader would need knowledge of Hebrew. Pierre Nautin suggested that Jews who had use for such a transliteration might also have produced a synopsis placing the transliteration alongside the versions of Aquila and Symmachus. This view has met with some skepticism, but it deserves consideration.[50] If Origen had had access to such a text—a hypothesis that we cannot hope to prove or to disprove, but whose implications are worth considering—he would only have had to add the Septuagint, Theodotion, and the anonymous versions to produce the full Hexapla. As Nautin argued, this reconstruction helps to account for the order of the columns, which is otherwise perplexing.[51]

The idea of a preexisting Jewish synopsis has generally been associated with the idea that Origen began work on the Hexapla while still in Alexandria.[52] We know that he used the *recentiores* in works he wrote there.[53] But there is little evidence to suggest that a sizable Jewish population had reemerged in Egypt by the early 200s, only a century or so after the disastrous rebellion of 117. Only in the fourth century and later do the papyri begin to document again a significant Jewish presence in Egypt.[54] The hypothesis that Origen used a preexisting Jewish synopsis or transliteration better fits a project carried out in Caesarea than in Alexandria. There, such a text might have been in use among the significant population of Greek-speaking Jews. Perhaps they felt the influence of other Jews whose liturgy was celebrated in Hebrew, and therefore felt the need for liturgical readings pronounced in the original. No evidence supports any of these speculations. Taken together, however, they suggest that in compiling the Hexapla, Origen may have drawn on textual resources originally produced by Jews who wanted access both to the Hebrew original of their Scriptures and its translation into Greek.

Alternatively, Origen could have employed an assistant who knew enough Hebrew to correlate the Hebrew with one or more Greek translations. Nicholas De Lange has argued that it is quite plausible that Origen had assistants literate in Hebrew as well as Greek, and Ruth Clements concurs with him, though she casts Origen's relations with the Jewish community in a rather less irenic light than de Lange did.[55] Origen's numerous references to Jewish informants certainly support this view. They grow much more frequent in the more abundantly preserved works from his Caesarean period.[56] In theory, Origen could have found Jewish help either in Alexandria or in Caesarea. Indeed, in works he wrote at Alexandria he cites exegetical material he learned from a Jewish interlocutor. But the trinitarian content of an interpretation that Origen attributes to this informant implies that he was a convert to Christianity. Some have speculated that he was a Palestinian Jew who moved to Alexandria after becoming a Christian. He remains a shadowy figure, and it is hard to say if he had much real expertise in Hebrew. It is more likely that Origen found an assistant proficient in Hebrew at Caesarea, where it is certain that some Jews used the language as a primary medium of their scholarship. Wherever these transactions took place, producing a new synopsis of the Hebrew and Greek columns would have required Origen to recruit and work closely with learned Jews or converts.

Or perhaps Origen himself knew Hebrew well enough to correlate the Hebrew with the Greek. When Origen puts forward arguments based on the Hebrew, he makes so many mistakes that this seems unlikely.[57] However, the entire undertaking makes more sense if we assume that Origen did know some Hebrew. The Hexapla would have been most useful for someone who could read some Hebrew, but only with a good deal of help. For one fluent in Hebrew, the four columns containing the additional translations would have been redundant; for one with no knowledge whatsoever of the language, the Hebrew columns would have been useless. Its very existence, therefore, suggests that Origen was interested in accessing the Hebrew, but needed considerable assistance in doing so—not only in the form of the tool whose creation he supervised, but also in the massive philological task of compiling it. There is no contradiction between the ideas that Origen had extensive access to Jewish assistants and that he knew some Hebrew himself. Rather, the two possibilities complement each other.[58]

This discussion of the problems presented by correlating the

Hebrew and Greek columns in the Hexapla raises a related question: did Origen produce another, truncated synopsis, a "Tetrapla" containing only the Greek translations? Early sources, from Eusebius on, claim that he did.[59] Numerous subscriptions and marginal annotations in Septuagint manuscripts claim that their authors consulted the Tetrapla. Indeed, the tradition, from Epiphanius of Salamis onward, refers to synopses with various numbers of columns, from four to eight. Ruth Clements makes the sensible suggestion that, with respect to the Tetrapla itself, the order in which the story is conventionally told should be reversed. Eusebius makes it sound like the Tetrapla was a secondary effort, coming after the original, six-column synopsis, and his readers have tended to interpret his text as proof that this was so.[60]

But perhaps he was misinformed. Clements argues that Origen probably began by producing a Tetrapla at Alexandria, where he used it in his exegesis of Psalms. No knowledge of Hebrew would have been needed for this project, which involved only Greek versions. Then, at Caesarea, where he had access to new resources and faced new challenges from the city's vibrant Jewish community, he added the Hebrew columns.[61] This explanation need not exclude Origen's use of a preexisting Jewish transliteration, but it does avoid the need to hypothesize a Jewish synopsis. Instead it suggests that Jewish assistants whom Origen recruited at Caesarea carried out the task of correlating the new Hebrew columns with the preexisting Greek synopsis that Origen had made himself at Alexandria. This thesis also underpins the explanation that Clements offers for the arrangement of the columns. She sees their order as reflecting, in the first place, Origen's theological judgment that the text of

Theodotion, on the far right, was more "Christian" than the other two versions he arranged to the left of the Septuagint in his original Tetrapla. Second, the Hebrew columns were added alongside the other "Jewish" columns, that is, the translations of Aquila and Symmachus.[62] The larger picture is more complex: the evidence for a variety of multicolumn Bibles is inconclusive, and cannot be fused in a single neat explanation. Rather, it is perhaps best to interpret all of this material as suggesting that the Hexapla was not unique, as its cost and complexity might suggest, but spawned a range of imitations and adaptations intended for a variety of users. These may have included Origen himself, but they certainly did not end with him. Later Christian scholars, who copied and consulted multicolumn Bibles of all kinds, attributed the whole tradition to Origen as its intellectual father.

The question of the Tetrapla leads us to the second major problem that Origen would have faced in producing the Hexapla: the correlation of the Septuagint text of the fifth column with the other columns, wherever and whenever it was done. The Septuagint translations of several books differed radically from the Jewish tradition transmitted in Hebrew, which also lay behind the later Greek translations. As scholars today realize, in the wake of the discovery of the Dead Sea Scrolls, the Old Greek translators—who worked from the third century BCE on—relied on Hebrew base texts that differed at many points from the proto-Masoretic text that became standard among Jews by the end of the first century CE. Variant readings on the level of a single word, or even a phrase, would have presented no difficulties for Origen's project. But major omissions, insertions, and especially transpositions would have required special handling.

The book of Jeremiah provides the most extreme example of transposition. The second half of Jeremiah, chapters 25–51, contains two compositional units: the parable of the intoxicating cup (Jer. 25.15–45.5 in the Masoretic text), and a series of oracles against the nations (Jer. 46.1–51.64 in the Masoretic text). In the Septuagint, their order is reversed: the oracles against the nations come first (Jer. 25.14–31.44 Septuagint), then the parable of the cup (Jer. 32.1–51.35 Septuagint). Furthermore, the order in which the various nations are condemned differs between the two versions. In the Masoretic text, the nations are Egypt, Philistia, Moab, Ammon, Edom, Damascus, Kedar, Elam, and Babylon, while in the Septuagint they are Elam, Egypt, Babylon, Philistia, Edom, Ammon, Kedar, Damascus, and Moab.[63] Other books present similar, though lesser, differences in order. As we shall see, Origen was well aware of these problems.[64]

How did the Hexapla on Jeremiah cope with the transpositions in the second half of the book? If the goal of the Hexapla was to correlate parallel material for the two primary strands of the textual tradition, then rearrangement of one or the other would have been necessary. But the two traditions were not equally represented in the six columns of the Hexapla. Roughly speaking, four columns reflected the same text form that became the basis for the Masoretic text—the two Hebrew columns and the translations of Aquila and Symmachus. Only one, the Septuagint column, represented the alternative, with some support from the column of Theodotion to its right. Though in the absence of direct evidence we cannot really know, the more likely alternative is that the Septuagint text used in the fifth column of the Hexapla was rearranged. It makes sense to imagine this as a task undertaken before the copying of the Hexapla itself. To compile such a text for the fifth column would have required a careful, word-by-word comparison of the Septuagint with the other tradition, presumably via the medium of one of the translations.[65]

The notion that the fifth column was prepared in advance has implications for other questions scholars have raised concerning its contents. Did the fifth column include the critical signs, or were they inserted into a separate recension of the Septuagint, or both? Septuagint texts marked with asterisks, to show where material lacking in the Septuagint tradition had been added from the version of Theodotion, and obeli, to mark material present in the Septuagint but lacking in the later Hebrew tradition and the translations based on it, circulated in late antiquity. In his commentaries on the prophets, Jerome frequently refers to asterisks and obeli in the text of the Septuagint, and attributes them unequivocally to Origen. Elsewhere, too, he credits Origen with preparing a recension of the Septuagint marked with asterisks and obeli, and supplemented from Theodotion. In the *Letter to Africanus,* which we will discuss below, Origen actually says that he made such a version. Jerome seems to have found the Alexandrian critical signs in a freestanding text of the Septuagint. But many have concluded that the fifth column of the Hexapla was also marked with these signs, and supplemented from Theodotion.[66]

We think that this is unlikely, since a fifth column marked with critical signs and supplemented from the sixth column would have been both redundant and confusing: redundant, because where the Septuagint contained additional material lacking in the Hebrew and the *recentiores,* to leave the other five columns blank would have made the lack of a parallel to the Septuagint column abundantly clear, without the need for obeli marking the fifth column as well; confusing, because where the fifth column lacked material present in the others, to fill in the blank with the text of the sixth column would only have obscured the differences, even if the additions were marked with asterisks. Paul Kahle recognized this decades ago, and Jennifer Dines has now reasserted it.[67] The scholarly consensus, however, long rejected this interpretation, and focused instead on the chimera of a fifth column of the Hexapla furnished with the Alexandrian critical signs. No final certainty is possible on the question of whether Origen himself was responsible for a free-standing recension equipped with critical signs. But such a recension, as Clements argues, would fit well into a larger picture of Origen's philological project as a multifaceted effort, expressed in a range of specialized books produced over the course of decades.[68]

What, then, was the purpose of all this complex, laborious, and costly research? This question will prove difficult to answer. The evidence is scarce and ambiguous, even contradictory, and there has been no consensus as to its interpretation. Henry Swete, and others, thought that Origen believed that the Septuagint he knew had diverged from an original based on the same Hebrew text used by the *recentiores.* In their view, he attempted, misguidedly, to correct the Septuagint to reflect that Hebrew text more closely.[69] Nautin, by contrast, claimed that Origen created the Hexapla to assist him in reconstructing the original *Hebrew* text of the Old Testament—presumably, the Hebrew that had served as the base text of the Septuagint translations.[70] Others, such as Sebastian Brock, have focused on the help that Origen's textual researches furnished to Christians debating Jews over the interpretation of the Scriptures. Origen's work, according to Brock, served primarily to give Christians access to detailed information on the differences between their Greek Old Testament and the Hebrew Bible of the Jews.[71] Adam Kamesar believed that Origen's theory of biblical inspiration led him to seek to maximize the range of variant readings at his disposal, in order to expand the possibilities of exegesis.[72] Ruth Clements has provided the most satisfying interpretation to date. She argued that the Hexapla was part of a suite of scholarly tools, developed over the course of several decades, and answering to somewhat different purposes. The Hexapla, specifically, she sees as an attempt to subsume a version of the Hebrew tradition within the sphere of Christian truth, so as to turn that weapon against both internal Christian opponents and Jewish interlocutors at Caesarea.[73]

We agree with Clements that the purpose of the Hexapla can be appreciated only within the context of Origen's larger philological enterprise, and believe that her thesis suggests a more satisfactory description of the purpose of that work and the others that accompanied it. One of the central problems in the scholarly disputes over this issue has been the limited evidence and the difficulties of interpretation that it presents. Two passages from Origen's works, both from his late years at Caesarea—one from a letter he wrote to Julius Africanus, the other from his *Commentary on Matthew*—have been taken as referring to the Hexapla and explaining its purpose. But as Clements shows, these texts make more sense if seen as referring not only to the preparation of the Hexapla, but to the fashioning of a range of different research tools over the course of several decades.[74] What might those texts have included? The internal logic of the Hexapla, and the patristic testimonia that refer to it and to other products of Origen's philological labors, suggest that its creation involved a number of separate tasks. First, Origen had to prepare a special text of the Septuagint for insertion in the fifth column. Second, he had to create or obtain some form of synopsis, either drawing entirely on preexisting Jewish materials to correlate the Hebrew columns with the Greek translations, or first preparing the Greek synopsis, then relying on Jewish assistants to add the Hebrew columns. Finally, he eventually created a recension marked with the critical signs and supplemented from the translation of Theodotion, which came to circulate independently of the Hexapla itself. Origen's own statements, in the *Letter to Africanus* and the *Commentary on Matthew*, both reflect and illuminate this complex undertaking.

Julius Africanus, the Christian philologist, chronographer, and polymath, wrote to Origen to challenge his acceptance of the Greek additions to the book of Daniel as authoritative. With arguments very similar to those twentieth-century text critics used, Africanus contended that the story of Susannah could not have been a translation from the Hebrew, and therefore could not have been part of the original book of Daniel. Africanus identified two plays on words in the Greek text of Susannah that could have had no direct Hebrew equivalents. He also pointed out that the Hebrew texts in circulation among the Jews did not include the section on Susannah. The story, he contended, was a later interpolation in the Greek, and as such inauthentic.

Origen rejected Africanus's reasoning on every level. Though he acknowledged that the Jewish version of Daniel did not include the story of Susannah, and that the plays on words that Africanus cited depended on Greek vocabulary for their effect, he still postulated that a Hebrew original had once existed. Origen suggested that the Greek wordplay Africanus found so damning in the story of Susannah represented the attempt of the Septuagint translators to approximate similar effects in a lost Hebrew original. Furthermore, he maintained that the Hebrew text of Daniel in circulation among the Jews of his day was not reliable. In support of this claim, he noted numerous other divergences between the Greek of the Septuagint and the Hebrew and its corresponding versions, writing, "And in many others of the sacred books I found sometimes more in our copies than in the Hebrew, sometimes less. I shall adduce a few examples, since it is impossible to give them all." He catalogued the substantial differences between the Greek and Hebrew books of Esther, Job, and Jeremiah, writing of the latter, "in that book I found much transposition and variation in the readings of the prophecies." The next passage is of particular interest: Origen writes,

Other instances are to be found in Genesis, which I marked, so as to distinguish them, with the sign the Greeks call an obelus, just as on the other hand I marked with an asterisk those passages in our copies that are not found in the Hebrew. Why even speak of Exodus, where there is such variation in what is said about the tabernacle and its court, and the ark, and the garments of the high priest and the priests, that sometimes even the meaning does not seem similar? And, I suppose, when we notice such things, we should immediately reject as spurious the copies in use in our churches, and command our Christian brothers to throw away the sacred books they are now using, and to coax the Jews, and persuade them to give us copies that are untampered with, and free from forgery! Are we to believe that the same Providence which in the sacred Scriptures has taught all the churches of Christ, gave no thought to those bought with a price, for whom Christ died?[75]

Origen seems to expect this final question to be answered in the negative. As Clements emphasizes, in this passage Origen clearly expresses his belief that the Septuagint text in use among Christians had been providentially provided for them, and that it therefore embodied an independent expression of the divine inspiration of Scripture.[76] By contrast, he relegated the texts in the possession of the Jews to a lower level of authority.

In what follows, Origen accounts for the divergences between the versions of Daniel in a manner that he clearly intends to be exemplary. He concludes that the learned men among the Jews "hid from the knowledge of the people as many of the passages which contained any scandal against the elders, rulers, and judges, as they could, some of which have been preserved in uncanonical writings (Apocrypha)." That is to say, divergences between the Greek text of the church and the versions used by the Jews can be explained as the result of the Jews' deliberate corruption of their Scriptures. Such corruptions arose from the self-interested machinations of Jewish "elders," concerned to preserve their prestige against all rivals—not only Christians, but also potential critics among their own people.

In this context, Origen's creation of the Hexapla may at first seem more, rather than less, perplexing. If the Hebrew text and the Jewish versions that depended upon it and served to make it accessible represented a deliberately corrupted tradition, why did Origen bother to study them at all? Another passage of the letter makes at least one reason for his interest clear: it was in preparation for dispute with Jews—a situation that Origen faced regularly at this stage in his career, but that might have been less pressing for his interlocutor, Africanus—that Origen had undertaken his research into the Hebrew tradition.[77] Clements's interpretation of the letter to Africanus places particular emphasis on this possibility, which she fleshes out by reference to the growing literature documenting mutual influence between Origen and Jewish exegetes active at Caesarea during the mid-third century.[78] But Clements goes even further, and reconstructs with considerable plausibility the context in which Origen participated in public debates at Caesarea, perhaps in the city's Odeon, with Jewish scholars. As she shows, Origen refers explicitly to such debates, especially in late works contemporary with the letter to Africanus.[79]

The city of Caesarea, as we already know, had in Origen's day a population of perhaps 40,000 people. Lee Levine, whose work on Caesarea remains fundamental to appreciating the city's history and its people, has argued that as the result of a recent influx of population from the countryside, roughly equal numbers of Jews and Samaritans had joined the pagans who had long dwelt there, and whose presence was assured by the city's status as a regional center of the imperial administration.[80] But Levine may overestimate the Christian proportion of the city's population. If we draw instead upon the model of Christian growth proposed by Hopkins, then a generous calculation of the Christian population of Caesarea in Origen's day—using the figure of 2 percent of overall population that Keith Hopkins' model predicts for the year 250, then doubling that number to account for the concentration of Christians in cities, and for Caesarea's special status in Christian history—would yield a total of sixteen hundred Christians of all kinds resident in the city. This would have been a sizable community, but much smaller than Caesarea's population of Jews—rabbinic or otherwise—and Samaritans.

Of course, these are all hypothetical reconstructions, which should never be taken as more than merely possible. But whether or not we accept a lower estimate for the size of the Christian community, we should bear in mind that Judaism was at this time, a century after the Jewish revolt under Hadrian, fully recognized by the Roman authorities as a legal religion. By contrast, Christianity remained illegal, under the looming danger of persecution. Given later history, it is all too easy to interpret Christian polemic from the period before Constantine, especially that directed against Jews, through the distorting lens of a Christian triumphalism that threatens the rights and even the bodies of Jews in this world, not merely their hypothetical salvation in the next. But Origen did not foresee what would happen seventy years after his death. He lived and worked as an embattled representative of a tiny, obscure sect. When he died in 254, it was probably as a result of the abuse he had received from Roman officials enforcing Decius's short-lived religious reform of 250–251, whose requirement of universal sacrifice exempted Jews but fell heavily upon Christians. Against this background, Origen's public debates with Jews at Caesarea—and by extension, his entire career as a scholar—appear in a rather different light than that cast by previous scholarly intepretations, including Clements's.[81] His acute sense of the dangerous attraction that Jews, and their biblical manuscripts, held out to the Christians among whom he taught and preached seems less like theologically inspired paranoia than a realistic assessment of the situation.[82]

Origen's letter to Africanus, then, reveals one of the fundamental concerns that drove and shaped Origen's philological work: his desire to provide Christians, including himself, with tools to support the claims of their still-young revelation against learned Jewish debunkers. But it also sheds light on more concrete aspects of the project, albeit from a retrospective viewpoint, close to the end of Origen's career, that may distort the sequence of his earlier labors. The letter makes clear that Origen has conducted a careful comparison of the entire Septuagint text with the tradition in use among the Jews. By the time he wrote this passage, he had probably completed work on the Hexapla, for which such a comparison would have been a mere prerequisite. Does the letter to Africanus, nevertheless, look back to a first stage in Origen's textual labors, a comparative study of various texts and translations that would eventually produce the fifth column of the Hexapla? Even to give a hypothetical answer to this question, we will have to turn to a second passage that preserves a programmatic statement of Origen's on his philological work.

Apropos of a textual problem in the Gospel of Matthew

encountered in the course of his commentary on that book, Origen remarks:

> But now it is evident that much variation has arisen among the *antigrapha* [of Matthew], whether because of the carelessness of some of the copyists, or because of the daring of some rogues, or because of those who are unwilling to undertake the correction [*diorthosis*] of what has been written, or even because they add or remove things according to their own judgment in the process of correction [*diorthosis*]. Therefore, God willing, we have sought to heal the variation among the *antigrapha* of the Old Testament, using as a yardstick [*kriterion*] the other versions [*ekdoseis*]. For having cast them about the Septuagint, making a judgment [*krisin*] through the disagreement between the *antigrapha* on the basis of the remaining versions [*ekdoseis*] we preserved the agreement with them. On the one hand, we obelized those passages which did not appear in the Hebrew (not daring to remove them entirely), while on the other hand we adjoined [*prosethekamen*] some passages with asterisks, in order that it might be clear that they were not present in the Septuagint, adding them from the other versions [*ekdoseis*] in agreement with the Hebrew. He who wishes may attend to these additions.

As is clear from a close reading of this passage, and as Ruth Clements has argued, the textual labors to which Origen alludes involve several steps.[83] In the quest for evidence bearing on the form and purpose of the Hexapla, scholarship has focused on a single phrase, to the distortion of the meaning of the passage as a whole. When Origen writes that he "cast [the other versions] about the Septuagint," modern interpreters have seen an allusion to the form of the Hexapla, in which the Greek Bible of the church was surrounded on both sides by other texts.

While the passage seems to presuppose the existence of the Hexapla, and indeed to allude to it, it concentrates on other issues. Origen's primary focus is on the comparison of texts and the accumulation of variants, both between individual manuscripts of the Septuagint (the *antigrapha*) and between the Hebrew and the different translations, including the Septuagint (the *ekdoseis*). Thus while there are various *antigrapha* of the New Testament, referred to in the first sentence quoted, only for the Hebrew Scriptures does Origen speak of differing *ekdoseis*. The role of these *ekdoseis*—all of them, except the Septuagint itself, based on Hebrew texts similar to those in use among the Jews in Origen's day—in Origen's attempt to "heal" the Septuagint of the damage done by careless or malevolent copyists is clear. In attempting to adjudicate between variants among the manuscripts of the Septuagint at his disposal (the *antigrapha*), Origen used as a criterion the other translations, and perhaps the Hebrew itself. The individual readings that he selected, Origen claims, each had a basis in the text tradition of the Septuagint itself.

Again, it seems that in this late text Origen has conflated a number of separate stages in his textual researches, probably carried out over a period of decades, into a single operation. Although we are perhaps less confident than Clements that a history of these researches can be written, we concur with her analysis of the fundamental logic of Origen's textual project as a whole. As she emphasizes, Origen describes a multistage process here: first, the accumulation of variant readings found in different manuscripts of the Septuagint; second, perhaps, the creation of the Hexapla, in which the versions were "cast about" the corrected text of the Septuagint, so that it could be further emended by reference to the other versions, which collectively represented the Hebrew tradition; and third, the preparation of a special, marked and supplemented text of the Septuagint, whether as part of the Hexapla or, more likely, as a separate project.[84]

This entire undertaking, as the passage from the commentary on Matthew makes clear, was directed toward preserving the integrity of the Septuagint Greek Old Testament, the version that Origen regarded as divinely inspired and as providentially provided to the church. A second, and perhaps more central, purpose of Origen's textual research emerges here. Origen worked to provide Christians with textual resources that would allow them to debate Jews, on the basis of texts that the Jews themselves accepted. This is clear from what he writes to Africanus. But he was perhaps even more concerned to shore up the textual integrity of the Scriptures as they were interpreted within his own Christian community. As we will see, the scant remnants of Origen's exegesis—represented, for our purposes, almost entirely by the homilies that he preached at Caesarea, which have been transmitted largely in Latin translation but also, in a few cases, in the Greek original—reinforce this point.

John Wright analyzed Origen's use of Hexaplaric material in his homilies on Jeremiah, the only significant element of Origen's entire exegetical corpus on the Hebrew Scriptures to survive in the original Greek. He found that Origen used variants

among the translations assembled in the Hexapla in two different ways in his homilies: either to adjudicate between different
readings and arrive at a single text for comment, or to amplify
the meaning of the text, by allowing him to comment on both
readings. In the first case, Wright distinguished between two
different kinds of scholarly judgment. Sometimes, Origen uses
the other versions to decide upon a superior reading, among a
range of texts supported in the manuscript tradition of the Septuagint. In other cases, he chooses the text that best fits his
exegetical point.[85] Adam Kamesar, on the basis of a broader survey of the remnants of Origen's exegesis, also observed this latter
phenomenon. He attributed to Origen an "exegetical maxi-
malism" that treated the entire spectrum of Greek manuscripts
and versions of the Hebrew Bible as equally open to Christian
interpretation, though subsumed under the notional authority
of the Septuagint.[86]

Origen's willingness to intepret readings from the *recentiores*
even when they have no support within the Septuagint tradition
may seem to fly in the face of everything we have said about the
purpose of his philological work. If he set out, first, to secure a
correct text of the Septuagint for the use of the church, and second, to provide for his own use and that of his contemporaries a
means of accessing the Jewish biblical tradition in preparation
for disputes with Jews, then why did he feel free to employ
those same Jewish texts to support Christian meanings? Ruth
Clements has surely supplied a crucial part of the answer. Origen firmly believed that Scripture spoke at every point with the
voice of the *Logos,* which was Christ. On that basis he could appropriate even Jewish biblical texts and interpretations and subsume them within his own enterprise.[87]

But Origen's use of textual variants, and indeed his entire philological project, also make sense in a different way, when set against the background of the state of the Greek Bible as he would have encountered it, among the Jews and Christians of Egypt and Palestine in the first half of the third century. As Eugene Ulrich observed, Origen's own legacy, together with the disappearance of the Hexapla and the versions he compiled in it, has tended to obscure the true state of the biblical tradition in his time.[88] Only in the wake of the discoveries at Qumran, and at other sites in the Judean desert, has it become possible to appreciate the full complexity of the situation faced by students of the Bible in the third century. By selecting three translations identified with named individuals for use in the Hexapla, Origen conferred on them a semi-canonical status, as Jerome was perhaps the first to observe.[89] More recently, Dominique Barthélemy has exposed the distorting effect this choice has had on our notions of the relations between these translations and the larger world of Greek biblical texts in antiquity. Barthélemy has documented the existence of a range of biblical translations and of varying texts of those translations, a broad continuum of labile texts. The texts associated with Aquila, Symmachus, and Theodotion—and presumably those others that Origen assembled—emerged from this background and had been liable to dissolve back into it, until Origen singled them out.[90]

Scholars have also recognized that the Septuagint, far from being an independent, free-standing text, was subject throughout antiquity to correction against the Hebrew and, presumably, other translations. Indeed, the so-called Septuagint, as modern critics have long recognized, is in fact a rather haphazard collection of translations made at different times and under different conditions. The translators of the various books, who worked over the course of several centuries, approached translation in different ways, from literalism to free adaptation. Their work stands in widely different relations to the Hebrew tradition that was fixed by late antiquity. When we realize how messy the world of Greek biblical manuscripts available to Origen really was, we can appreciate that in selecting certain texts for presentation in his Hexapla, he must have been—again—attempting to represent in concise form some sense of the vast range of variation that he had encountered in his laborious work of collation. He could not have expected that the texts he selected would one day be seen as isolated mountain peaks, each connected with the labors of a particular, isolated individual, rather than as less prominent landmarks in a gentler, less sharply defined, but much richer landscape, where named translators were the exception and gradual, open-ended efforts at textual "improvement" were the rule.

Thus the Hexapla itself, elusive as it has proven to reconstruct and to interpret, stands in the path of the scholar who would gain access to the textual world in which Origen operated, as does the recension that great scholar produced. Only in its original context of almost unlimited textual and translational variety can we fully appreciate the nature and function of the Hexapla. At once selective and encyclopedic, it condensed for the reader fortunate enough to have access to such a costly research tool the results of a lifetime of study of the text of the Hebrew Scriptures in their Jewish and Christian versions, in both Greek and Hebrew. It provided a rich array of interpretive resources, which Origen's followers could deploy in very different, even diametrically opposed ways—but which nevertheless imposed principles of selection on what was otherwise a chaotic picture. Intellectually, then, as well as bibliographically and logistically, the Hexapla represented the state of the art in contemporary philology. Only Origen's Christianity, and the confrontation with an authoritative text in a non-Greek language, could have driven him to such an achievement.

The Hexapla was one of the greatest single monuments of Roman scholarship, and the first serious product of the application to Christian culture of the tools of Greek philology and criticism. Its complexity and sheer costliness demonstrate the resources that Origen could draw upon, both in terms of patronage and in terms of skilled labor. In this respect, it was a typical product of the philosophical, as well as the grammatical, culture of the first half of the third century, an era that largely continued the patterns of the so-called Second Sophistic of the previous century. Yet it also continued much older patterns. The tenacious concern for the details of an authoritative text that the Hexapla demonstrates emerged directly from interwoven traditions of grammatical and philosophical learning going back to the Hellenistic world. The scribes whose labor Origen commanded differed only in their specialized skills from those at the disposal of Philodemus in Campania in the first century BCE. Origen's success in acting the role of an authoritative purveyor of learning to the upper classes of his day, in the same way that philosophers and literary critics had to do, made the technical innovations of the Hexapla physically possible. His creation was not merely expensive; its design pushed the limits of third-century book technology. Without abundant support from private patrons, it could never have been made.

At the same time, the intellectual impetus behind the creation of the Hexapla drew upon yet another centuries-old tradition, that of Hellenistic Jewish biblical learning. Several of the translations, and perhaps also the transliteration, that it compiled were the products of the Greek-speaking synagogue. Its continued concern for the Hebrew original reflected ongoing reverence for the sacred language among Jews whose culture was otherwise wholly Greek. The very impulse to incorporate into the structures, both intellectual and physical, of Greek learning a barbarian text in its original language, can be understood only in the context of Origen's debt to Hellenistic Judaism.

In its fusion of Greek and Hellenized Jewish traditions of learning, the Hexapla exemplified the nascent Christian mode of scholarship. As an orthodox Christian, and a participant in the cosmopolitan culture of his day, Origen had to turn the burden of an authoritative literature drawn from outside the Greek cultural world into an advantage. Grammar and philosophy provided him with the analytical tools, and Hellenistic Jewish scholarship with the substantive traditions of learning that enabled him to do so. The technical feat of producing the Hexapla embodied the triumphant fusion of disparate traditions that Origen achieved in his intellectual program as a whole. In the next chapter, we will see that the Christian scholars who came after Origen appreciated his path-breaking innovations.

Eusebius's Chronicle:
History Made Visible

EUSEBIUS of Caesarea was Origen's best-known and most self-conscious successor. He has often been imagined as the direct inheritor of Origen's scholarly tradition, indeed as a kind of epigone. In fact, Eusebius went beyond his idolized predecessor on the conceptual level, by applying his formal innovations in book design and production to a range of problems of which Origen probably could not even have conceived. He also built an infrastructure for the production of learning, and of learned books, that far surpassed anything Origen could ever have imagined. This infrastructure was supported by forms of patronage that had never before been available to Christian scholars, and yielded an institutional legacy that survived Eusebius for several centuries.

Eusebius lived from around 260 to 339 CE. One of the most prolific and original Christian writers of the fourth century, he also served from 310 CE until his death as bishop of Caesarea. In that capacity he attended the councils of Nicea and Tyre and delivered important speeches at official occasions—for example, when Constantine dedicated his new church of the Holy Sepulchre at Jerusalem in 335 CE. Like Origen, he worked extensively on the text of the Bible, and as we will see he knew the Hexapla intimately. Like Origen too, he wrote extensive commentaries on the Bible. But he also produced a series of innovative scholarly and polemical works in which he mobilized the Bible, pagan writers, and documentary evidence to prove that a providential plan had guided mankind through world history.

In Chapters 1 and 2, we began with a profile of Origen's scholarly career and activities, and then examined the Hexapla. In Chapter 3, by contrast, we begin with one of Eusebius's most massive and influential works, his *Chronicle*, which he seems to have completed, in its first draft, in the years around 300 CE. We also reconstruct the local circumstances that enabled Eusebius to produce it, and concentrate on the ways in which he built on Origen's legacy. In Chapter 4 we will follow Eusebius's experiments in scholarship and book production through his career. We will try to reconstruct both his experiences as a young student and his accomplishments as a mature scholar.

Eusebius spent formative years working in Caesarea with the older Christian scholar Pamphilus, and he owed this living master, as well as Origen, a substantial intellectual debt. As we will see, he made a number of experiments in managing scribal book production, which embraced systematic work on the form of the New and Old Testament texts as well as the production of the *Chronicle*. In the middle years of his career, the 310s and 320s, Eusebius completed massive, anthological writings about the history and doctrine of the Church: the *Church History, Preparation for the Gospel,* and *Proof of the Gospel.* In writing these works Eusebius drew, as we will see, on what had become a massive, official collection of books and documents at Caesarea, and we will examine much of the surviving evidence about both this library and the new forms of scholarly work done there, much of which was made possible by its facilities.

Even in the last years of his career, Eusebius was still engaged in scribal and literary experiments, some of them closely connected with his status as bishop and his relationship with the emperor. In the 330s, for example, he produced massive pandect Bible manuscripts at Constantine's request. He also completed his *Onomasticon*, a commented list of biblical place names, and drafted but did not finish a *Life of Constantine* that made innovative use of official documents. Our concern, in both chapters, will be to bring out Eusebius's distinctive profile as scholar, writer, and impresario of research and book production. It will become clear that Eusebius's scholarship both shaped and was shaped by the institutions he created. A short concluding section will offer some comparisons that may help to set his enterprises into context.

In the decade or so after 300 CE, Eusebius decanted the varied pasts of ancient Assyria and Egypt, Israel and Persia, Greece and Rome into a single work in two books: his *Chronicle*.[1] When he composed this massive history, Eusebius did more than carry out a feat of rationalization and synthesis. He also created a new kind of physical object and devised new conventions for organizing information for storage and retrieval. Like a number of other enterprises in the imperial period and after, from Ptolemy's *Geography* to Justinian's codification of the Roman Law, the *Chronicle* required the creation of new textual and visual conventions that made it possible to fix a whole world on paper.[2] The history of scholarship on the *Chronicle* began in antiquity itself and continued in Byzantium. Petrarch revived it in western Europe, and the tradition of comparison and glossing that he began continues down to the present.[3] The work has attracted the attention of such fearless polymaths as Joseph Scaliger, Eduard Schwartz, Rudolf Helm, Jean Sirinelli, and Timothy Barnes, and continues to stimulate the interest of erudite and original scholars like Alden Mosshammer, William Adler, and Richard Burgess.[4] Their philological studies will frame and guide this analysis, as they will all future analyses, of the content of the *Chronicle*. But for all their varieties of method and style, none of them has examined the work primarily as a problem in the making of books. By treating Eusebius's book from this point of view, we can not only suggest some new perspectives on chronology, that dry subject, but also shed light on the intricate dialectical relationship between conventions of reading and writing on the one hand and more formal scholarly methods on the other, on the ways in which conditions of textual possibility inflected, and were inflected by, methods of textual scholarship, both in the ancient world and in later Christian traditions.

Eusebius's *Chronicle,* as is well known, consisted of two parts. In the first, or *Chronography,* he set out the scholarly basis of his work. He noted what chronologers call key synchronisms between Greek, Roman, and Jewish history—years to which he could connect dates from more than one kingdom and calendar. And he used these—notably the synchronism of Moses with Cecrops—as the grounds for arguing that Moses was older than any Greek writer.[5] Both the Jewish religion and its Christian offspring emerged from this argument as older than, and accordingly superior to, the traditions of the pagans. Eusebius also assembled a mass of raw material from a number of writers on the history of Chaldea, Assyria, Egypt, Israel, and Rome, and laid it out, in separate chapters.[6]

In the second part of his work, the *Canon*, or *Tables*, Eusebius, as he forthrightly declared, did something completely different. He decided that he could draw up a precise, coherent, and schematic chronicle of world history, at least from the time of the patriarch Abraham. This patriarch was the recipient of the second covenant, and thus an appropriate figure, typologically, to stand at the beginning of a history of Jews and Christians. He also would play a central role in "Eusebius' presentation of the Christian empire of Constantine as reviving the age of Abraham and the patriarchs."[7] So Eusebius reassembled in formal tables the basic chronological information about some nineteen states, Assyrian, Persian, Jewish, Athenian, Sicyonian, and so on, down to the Romans, that he had presented in separate chapters in book I. The *Canon* collated the years of rulers from the different realms a Christian needed to know about with those of the Hebrew patriarchs, starting from Abraham. In the blank spaces between the lists of dates, which Scaliger would christen *spatia historica*, Eusebius recorded the sorts of events that chronologers had recorded since the Hellenistic period: the creation of new technologies like the trireme, battles and portents, and the floruits of supposed gods and both supposed and real poets. The *Chronicle* thus grew into something like a comprehensive political, religious, and cultural history of the an-

Assyriorum	Hebraeorum		Atheniensiu
XLII	XXLIIII	occiseretroannis	II
XLIII	XXLIIII	Troianaccepsiui	III
XLIIII	XXX	tatiscumfuisse	IIII
		putantlicetiar	
XLIIII	XXXI	chilocusxxiii·o	(I)
XL	XXXII	Lyatpiademer	(II)
XLI	XXXIII	quincentesima	LIII
XLII	XXXIIII	Troianactuer	LIIII
XLIII	XXXU	sionisannum	LIIIII
XLIII	XXXUII	suffutet	X
XXIIII	XXXLII		XI
XXLI	XXXUIII		XII
XXLII	XXXLIIII		XIII
XXLIII	XXXUIIII		
		IIII	
	XLI·		XIIII
XXLIIII			

HEBRAEORUMREX
PRIMUSEXTRIBUIU
CADAUIDANN·XL

	I		XU
XXLIIII	II · y DAUIDPRIMUS		XUI
XLU	III EXTRIBUIUDA		XUII
XXLI	IIII REGNATAPUT		XUIIII
XXUII	U · hEBRACOS·		XUIIII
XXUIII	UI		XX
XXUIIII	UII HEBRAEORUMPONTIEX		XXI
XXUI			

285

Latinorum	Lacedemoniorum	Corinthiorum	Aegyptiorum
XX	XIII		XIII	XCIIII
XXI	XIIII		XIIII	XCU
XXII	XU		XU	XCUI
XXIII	XUI		XUI	XCUII
XXIIII	XUII	IONESPRO	XUII	XCUIIII
XXU	XUIIII	lugiathe.	XUIIII	XCUIIII
XXUI	XUIIII	NASSECON	XUIIII	C
XXUII	XX	TULERUN	XX	CI
XXUIII	XXI		XXI	CII
XXUIIII	XXII	pelopon	XXII	CIII
XXX	XXIII	Nenses	XXIII	CIIII
XXXI	XXIIII	CONTRA	XXIIII	CU
		ATHENAS		
LATINORUM·U·		DIMICAN		
LATINUSSILUI				
US·ANNIS·L·				
I	XXU	INCURSUS	XXU	CUI
		INASIAM		
		AMAZONU		
		PARITERCI		
		CIMMERI		
II	XXUI	ORUM	XXUI	CUII
III	XXUII		XXUII	CUIII
IIII	XXUIII		XXUIII	CUIIII
U	XXUIIII		XXUIIII	CX
UII	XXX		XXX	CXI
UIII	XXXI		XXXI	CXII
UIIII	XXXII		XXXII	CXIII

An opening from the chronological table of Eusebius, from the *Chronicle*, as translated by Jerome, in a manuscript of the fifth century CE. Bibliothèque Nationale, Paris, MS lat. 6400 B, fols. 8 verso and 285 recto.

cient world, one that served until the sixteenth century as the richest single source of information for anyone interested in the history of human culture.[8]

Eusebius, moreover, configured this text in ways that made it both informative and suggestive. He marked the tables off by decades, from the birth of Abraham, so the reader would always have chronological benchmarks by which he could find his place. The result was not only comprehensive, but also accessible, and rapidly so. The Christian student of the Bible or of classical texts could consult this universal timeline in order to set any given event or text into its widest possible historical context, quickly and with ease.

In the introduction to his tables, Eusebius lucidly explained how he had ordered his work, in terms that assumed the novelty of its form as well as the clarity of the historical lessons that it taught:

> To prevent the long list of numbers from causing any confusion, I have cut the entire mass of years into decades. Gathering these from the histories of individual peoples, I have set them across from each other, so that anyone may easily determine in which Greek or barbarian's time the Hebrew prophets and kings and priests were, and similarly which men of the different kingdoms were falsely seen as gods, which were heroes, which cities were founded when, and, from the ranks of illustrious men, who were philosophers, poets and important writers.[9]

As Eusebius explained in more lapidary fashion in book 1, "I will divide the periods of those who ruled each people into separate sections, and I will lay out the numbers of each one's years in the appropriate places across from one another, so that one can find out easily and quickly when any given person was."[10] As we will see below, the passionate interest in the spatial arrangement of texts for easy reference that Eusebius displayed here would remain a central theme throughout his life.

More important still, he arranged the tables of monarchies to teach one massive lesson. As all the other lists of rulers dwindled away and only the Roman one remained, as the multiple columns that recorded the early history of Greece and the Near East funneled down into one long, packed column devoted only to Rome, the *Chronicle* graphically proved that world history culminated in the contemporary Roman Empire. Significantly, the last rival kingdom to have a column of its own was that of the Jews. This ended, as Eusebius remarked, with the fall of Jerusalem to Vespasian, and the death of thousands of Jews, on the same day on which they had crucified Jesus—at once a clear sign of providential direction and the last step needed for the whole world to be open to Christianity.[11] This visual argument would have been all the more powerful and provocative if, as Richard Burgess has plausibly argued, Eusebius completed the work in the years 308–311, when it had become clear, even as the persecution continued, that none of the claimants to empire planned to make more martyrs.[12]

A stunningly effective visual display of information, the *Canon* resembles Charles Minard's famous statistical table of the French invasion of Russia in 1812, which traced the dwindling of the French army against movements in time, space, and temperature.[13] As a dynamic hieroglyph of the succession of kingdoms, the *Canon* located rulers and events more clearly than any prose account could. More important, it also embodied a particular notion of historical time—one in which every nation, even the pagan ones, had played a role in the larger drama of salvation history.[14] No one brought out the special visual qualities of Eusebius's work more vividly than the sixth-century scholar Cassiodorus, who described Eusebius's *Chronicle* as "an image of history"—in other words, a scholarly genre that combined form and content, *mise-en-page* and erudition, in a new way.[15] An impresario of scribal labor in his own right, Cassiodorus was one of the creators of the Western tradition of Christian scholarship. He could appreciate the earlier Christian scholar's achievement with a clarity that more recent critics have sometimes lacked.

Modern scholars have always noted that the *Canon* had a distinctive and remarkable tabular layout. But they have rarely inquired whether the world of book production that Eusebius knew offered any formal models for his work—at least in fields other than chronology. Timothy Barnes, that great questioner of widely accepted beliefs, has broken with convention in this as in so many other cases. He has noted that there was a vivid and powerful model for Eusebius's *Canon*—a model not for its content, but for its innovative layout—in Caesarea, where he lived and worked. Origen's Hexapla, as we have seen in detail, made innovative use of parallel columns to enable students of the Old Testament to move from version to version. Immense in size, fabulously expensive to produce, the multiple volumes of this great compilation were the most celebrated single possession of what, in Eusebius's time, became a great Christian library at Caesarea. Origen's Bible, laid out in columns, seems the obvious prototype for Eusebius's effort to lay out time in the same way.[16]

We believe that Professor Barnes is right to connect the *Can-*

on with the Hexapla. In fact, we believe that the Hexapla was the fundamental source for a whole series of innovations in chronological scholarship, which gave both books of the *Chronicle* their fundamental shape. But we will also argue that Eusebius's choice of a model was not merely a technical decision. It was one in a long series of brilliant and effective experiments in the processing of both information and texts, experiments by which he transformed the practice of scholarship. What made the *Canon* possible was Eusebius's ability to unite an innovative form of layout and book production with an innovative way of describing the past. Many of his later scholarly creations, as we will see, involved a similar, self-conscious emphasis on the interplay between content and design.

To appreciate what Origen's work meant for Eusebius, however, we must begin by setting the *Chronicle* against a wider backdrop—the field of chronology as it was practiced in the ancient world. Where Origen was very likely the first scholar, or at least the first Christian, to create a polyglot Bible, Eusebius knew many precedents for his work in pagan, Jewish, and Christian chronography. Only multiple comparisons between his *Chronicle* and earlier ones will enable us to identify his actual innovations. In this chapter, accordingly, we will move backward and forward between Eusebius's work and the traditions that he transformed.

The central achievement of the *Canon* lay in its vivid display of synchronisms—a technical term for the dating of a given event in multiple systems of chronological reckoning. Synchronisms in themselves were nothing new, but provided the foundation for ancient chronological scholarship. After the Sicilian scholar Timaeus introduced dating by Olympiads in the third century BCE and Eratosthenes and others adopted it, many chroniclers exerted themselves to work out which great events had fallen in the same year.[17] Astronomers and astrologers converted dates of astronomical observations reckoned in Roman or Athenian years, months, and days into dates in the Egyptian calendar, reckoned forward or backward from the accession of Nabonassar to the throne of Babylon on 26 February 747 BCE.

Censorinus, a Roman expert on calendars who wrote in the time of Africanus, dated the year in which he devised his birthday present for a friend, a book on natal days, in Roman terms, by the names of the consuls. But he showed at the same time that he could recompute his Roman dates in the Greek terms of the Olympiad system.[18] At the same time, he connected these already varied forms of historical reckoning to what he described as the cosmopolitan, artificial calendar of the astronomers, who used the neat 365-day years of the Egyptians to reckon the dates of celestial phenomena, and took Nabonassar's accession date as their standard epoch, or chronological baseline:

> For both we and the Egyptians record certain years, such as those they call years of Nabonassar, which start from the first year of his reign [747 BCE], and of which the present year is 986; and years of Philip, which are computed from the death of Alexander the Great [323 BCE] and, reckoned down to the present, make 562 years. But the beginning of these is always set at the first day of the month that the Egyptians call Thoth, and which fell this year on 26 June, but a hundred years ago, in the second consulate of the

emperor Antoninus Pius and Bruttius Praesens, fell on July 20, the time when the dog star rises [before dawn] in Egypt. (21.9–10)[19]

Censorinus also made clear that he based his comparative chronology on that of Varro, who "by collating the chronologies of different nations and computing eclipses and their intervals backward, established the clear truth" (21.5). From other evidence, we know that Varro actually carried out this project in collaboration with Lucius Tarrutius of Firmum, a diviner and astrologer who computed the dates of Romulus's conception and birth and the founding of Rome at the Roman scholar's request.[20] As we shall see, moreover, Christian apologists like Tatian and Clement and the most systematic Christian chronologer before Eusebius, Africanus, regularly employed synchronisms in their work.

As early as the third through first centuries BCE, Greek historians like Polybius and Diodorus came to see all the societies of the world as linked.[21] They traced the connections between national histories and set all of them into larger, cosmopolitan frames. In the same period, Jews, Egyptians, Chaldeans, and others raised the stakes of chronology by arguing that their cultures were older and more profound than that of the Greeks who had conquered them. Synchronisms mattered to these writers, not just for scholarly, but also for theological and ideological reasons. The realm of history, like the realm of prophecy, became a virtual battleground on which learning and imagination could avenge the defeats inflicted on Near Eastern peoples by Alexander, induce his successors to admire and take an interest in their new subjects, or even achieve both ends at once.[22] Some Greek and Roman writers also tried to master these swirling genealogies of individual peoples and inscribe them in well-defined universal histories of the entire human race.[23] All participants in these discussions about universal history cited documents, chronicles, and other written sources. Unlike political and military historians, they could not restrict their interests to recent times and rely solely on personal experience and eyewitness testimony. In many cases, their works had to do more than inform: they had to prevail, in a forensic contest against competing histories.

Berossos, born in Babylon between 330 and 323 BCE, and Manetho of Sebennytos in Egypt, who lived in the first half of the third century BCE, both responded as historians to the conquest of their nations by Alexander the Great. Both wrote accounts in Greek of their ancestors' mythical and historical traditions. Both drew on materials inaccessible to Greek writers, but framed them in new ways partly shaped by Greek historical traditions. It seems, for example, that Manetho drew his lists of Egyptian pharaohs from a document or documents like the so-called Royal Canon now in Turin, a list of the rulers of Egypt written in hieratic script in the thirteenth century BCE.[24] But he himself apparently devised the concept and term of "dynasty" as he arranged the names of rulers into groups and noted apparent discontinuities between these.[25]

Neither man's work provoked widespread response in his own day. Their long chronologies, and Berossos's elaborate account of the Flood and the origins of civilization, proved hard to integrate with the accounts of Ctesias and other Greeks. These writers connected the histories of peoples outside Greece and Rome to the relatively recent Trojan War, normally dated to the early twelfth century BCE. Ctesias, moreover, had conflated Assyrians with Babylonians—a confusion that Berossos would have set right, if anyone had used his work.[26] Even a polymath like the geographer Strabo made no effort to integrate these accounts, if he knew them, with his other evidence about the history of the Fertile Crescent.[27] In the first century BCE, two erudite compilers made epitomes of Berossos. Alexander Polyhistor, a Pergamene grammarian brought to Rome as a slave, and Juba, a scion of the Numidian royal house whom Augustus made the ruler of Mauretania, both had personal reasons to take an interest in the world outside Greece and Rome. Josephus used their work extensively in his polemical work against the Greek grammarian Apion. Manetho, for example, provided Josephus with reliable evidence that the Jews had come to and left Egypt almost a thousand years before the Trojan War. He took this testimony as all the more reliable since it came from an enemy of the Jews, who described them as evil and would not have invented anything in their favor.[28] Abydenus (second century CE), author of a *Chaldean History*, also drew on Berossos.[29] But the larger circulation and impact of these texts, if they had any, remain obscure.

The problem Berossos and Manetho posed was simple. They stated that their ancient records, carefully preserved by priestly annalists, covered periods of thousands—even tens and hundreds of thousands—of years. These claims were not wholly new. Every well-educated man remembered the Egyptian priest in Plato's *Timaeus*, who told Solon that "according to our sacred writings, our order of things has existed for 8,000 years," and promised to tell of "the laws of the citizens who lived 9,000 years ago."[30] Celsus, the pagan whose critique of Christianity provoked a long reply from Origen, argued that time was eternal and that many floods had taken place, not just the one Flood of the Hebrew Bible. Origen noted Celsus's reference to multiple floods. From it he plausibly inferred that Celsus would have cited "the dialogues of Plato about these matters," and dismissed such evidence as inferior to that of the "pure and pious soul of Moses."[31]

Origen's learned correspondent Julius Africanus took up the challenge presented by pagan critics like Celsus. He turned it into an opportunity not only to defend Christianity, but also to rework history as a whole in explicitly Christian terms. Africanus assembled a massive run of historical materials, Jewish, Christian, and pagan, into a chronological text in five books. The scale and method of his work are uncertain, and will remain so until the publication of the edition of its fragments now being prepared by William Adler and others. Yet the nineteenth-century edition of the fragments by M. J. Routh and the studies of the work by Heinrich Gelzer and later scholars, for all their inevitable faults, allow certain inferences.[32] Africanus treated chronology, as a number of his Hellenistic predecessors had, from a comparative and erudite standpoint. Like them, he felt the historian who traveled backward into the past walked on solid ground only until he reached the year 776 BCE, when the Greeks began to reckon time reliably, by Olympiads.

To give his work a firm foundation, Africanus emphasized synchronisms, the points where two separate chronological strands intersected, and the solid Hebrew narrative could underpin and illuminate the potentially wobblier Greek one: "I will take one Hebrew event that is simultaneous with an event recorded by Greeks and by sticking to it, while both adding and subtracting, and indicating which Greek or Persian or anyone else synchronized with that Hebrew event, I may perhaps achieve my goal." The Old Testament stated that Cyrus, king of Persia, began to send the Jews back to Palestine in the first year of his reign (Ezra 1:1–4). Diodorus and other historians and chronologers dated the first year of Cyrus to Olympiad 55, 1 (560/59 BCE): "Therefore the histories of the reign of Cyrus and of the end of the Captivity coincide." Like a master carpenter contemplating a neat joint, Africanus expressed his confidence that he could produce an equally smooth chronology down to his own time by continuing to follow "the Olympiad chronology" and using it to "fit the other histories to one another as well."[33] What Africanus provided—so far as we can tell from the scanty fragments that survive—was very much what he describes here: a narrative of biblical history to which he attached, so far as he could, contemporary events in the secular history of the Greeks and others.

Africanus's history, accordingly, dealt sparingly with the earlier centuries of recorded time, which he classified, as Diodorus and others had, as "mythistorical." Regarding the first millennium BCE and the first centuries of Christianity, Africanus offered more details:

> The Greek accounts of history are by no means accurate before the beginning of the Olympiads, but thoroughly confused and in total disagreement with one another. But there are many accurate accounts of events after this point, since the Greeks made their records of them every four

years, rather than at longer intervals. Hence I will give a rapid and selective account of the most famous mythical histories, down to the first Olympiad, but such remarkable events as took place later I shall join together in chronological order, the Hebrew with the Greek.[34]

Africanus also noted that he "narrated the history of the Hebrews in detail, while only touching on those of the Greeks." By this he seems to have meant that he treated Jewish history in a more elaborate and detailed way than Greek, even in the historical period. For all his learning, in other words, Africanus does not seem to have chronicled secular history with anything like Eusebius's passion for myriad dates and details unconnected in any obvious way to the biblical narrative.

The other fragments of Africanus's *Chronicle* confirm that its highest purpose was religious and apologetic. As a habitué of libraries in both Palestine and Rome, Africanus touched upon a wide range of texts and traditions. But he always did so from a Christian standpoint. Furthermore, he made clear that any element that threatened to disrupt the coherent structure he was building could be rejected without substantial discussion. Following earlier Christian apologists like Tatian, he insisted that the works of Moses were far older, like the history they recorded, than anything written by or known to a pagan.[35]

No wonder, then, that Africanus denounced the Egyptians for setting forth "outlandish chronological cycles and myriads of years," which they then tried to "reconcile . . . with the eight and nine thousand years that the Egyptian priests in Plato falsely enumerate to Solon."[36] As to the 30,000 years of history that the Phoenicians claimed to have recorded, or the 480,000

of the Chaldeans, "why," he asked, "should one even speak?"[37] It
was obvious, he thought, that the "more modest and moderate
teaching" of Moses, who set the Creation in the sixth millennium BCE, was correct.[38] Africanus, in other words, introduced
the texts of Berossos and Manetho into Christian chronology in
the manner of an eighteenth-century *philosophe* who inoculated
a healthy person with smallpox. He wished to protect his readers from the infectious pagan belief in the deep antiquity of the
world—a belief that could lend support to the popular view
that the Chaldeans and Egyptians had cultivated the sciences
for thousands of years.

But Africanus had more in mind than crafting a solid framework for the study of the Jewish and Christian past and denying
the pretensions of the pagans to greater antiquity than the Jews.
In his view, chronology should serve eschatology. It should determine not only when the Savior had arrived, but also when
the end of time itself would come and the Kingdom of God arrive on earth. To this end he exhaustively studied the prophecies
of Daniel, and did his best to prove that the actual life and
deeds of Jesus corresponded perfectly to what the prophet had
foretold about the seventy weeks of years that would precede the
end of history.[39]

Detailed computations made clear to the reader that the 475
solar years that lay between the twentieth year of Artaxerxes,
when he sent Nehemiah to build Jerusalem, and the birth of Jesus, amounted to 490 lunar years of the sort used by the Jews—
or 70 weeks of 7 years each, exactly as the prophet Daniel had
predicted (Daniel 9:24). More important still, Africanus found
as he investigated the history of the world that a simple, palpa-
bly meaningful structure underlay the apparent chaos of past

time and determined the timing of all great events. The Jews, he argued, "from their remaining Hebraic histories . . . have handed down a period of 5,500 years up to the advent of the Word of Salvation that was announced during the sovereignty of the Caesars."⁴⁰

The implications of this neat chronology were obvious—at least to someone who, like Africanus, believed that he could read the deeper meaning of history through its surface, as if he were explaining the hidden sense of a text. Creation took six days, and on the seventh God rested, creating the Sabbath. On the larger scale of history, Africanus inferred, time would last six days of a thousand years—or perhaps a bit less—to be followed by a cosmic Sabbath, the millennial rule of the Messiah and his saints. Since the Messiah had appeared at midpoint on history's last day, and Africanus himself was writing some two hundred years after that, the chief lesson chronology had to offer was clear. Quite simply, time itself would fairly soon be no more. For Africanus, in short, the primary task of historical chronology was to elucidate the future, in advance. To achieve this the chronologer must recreate a past whose duration was fixed and neat—not one that extended tens of thousands of years into the distant past.

As Eusebius shaped his diverse materials into the double form of chronographical encyclopedia and tables, he made clear that he rejected much of what Africanus had done with his sources. In the first place, he denounced the idea that chronology could yield precise predictions of the future:

> We must accept as true the word that the teacher spoke to his disciples: "It is not for you to know the hours or the

times, which the Lord has set in his own power" [Acts 1:7]. In my view, in uttering this brief statement He spoke, as God and ruler, not only about the end of time, but about all time, and did so in order to repress those who set themselves to work too boldly on empty investigations of this kind. And my discourse will use powerful evidence to confirm the master's view: that is, that we cannot derive a certain universal chronology from the Greeks or the barbarians or any other people, or even from the Hebrews themselves.[41]

Eusebius clearly took Jesus's admonitory phrase not only as a response to the errors of his disciples, but also as a condemnation of any effort to claim perfection and completeness for chronology.

History—for Eusebius as for Africanus—started with the expulsion of Adam from Paradise, since the time he and Eve spent in Eden was different in character and indeterminate in length.[42] Eusebius decided that so far as could be known, the start of Adam's normal life had taken place roughly 5,200 rather than 5,500 years before the Incarnation, as the chronology of the Septuagint suggested (other biblical versions offered different sums, as we will shortly see). By setting the Creation—or at least the start of history—closer to his own time than Africanus had, he effectively postponed the likely time of the Apocalypse even as he denied that anyone could know it in advance.

At the same time, Eusebius added much secular material to what Africanus had brought together. Where Africanus, like the pagan writers of the second sophistic, had emphasized older historical periods, Eusebius highlighted recent times as well, inserting lists of Christian bishops and notices of major events in

Roman history into his work.[43] More important, Eusebius insisted that not even he—to say nothing of the normal Christian reader—could solve all of the technical problems that chronology posed, or synchronize all the dates given in all the sources. In its form, the *Chronography* resembled the anthologies of earlier sources that had formed a part of Hellenistic Jewish literature, and that Africanus had already adapted to Christian ends.[44] Yet it also raised new questions, and together with the *Canon* it redefined the enterprise of Christian chronography. Just as eschatology drove Africanus to produce a neat, symmetrical image of time, the rejection of eschatology enabled Eusebius to articulate a radically different vision, at once complex and open, of the past.

The presence of Origen's Hexapla in Eusebius's library explains his central innovations, from the forms in which he cast his work to its most radical conclusions.[45] In the *Chronography*, to begin with, Eusebius made clear—as Africanus had not— that the surviving information about the ancient kingdoms of Egypt and Babyon could not be reconciled with the biblical account of human history. He told his readers he would be content if they learned from him "not to imagine, as others have, that they can master chronological computation with absolute certainty, and thus fool themselves."[46] Not even the Jews could appeal this judgment and claim that their records were absolutely clear and certain.

Eusebius directed this sharp passage against Africanus, and it amounted to a double blow, directed at his eschatology as well as his chronology. After all, it was only because Africanus believed that he could arrange all of history in a perfect, coherent timeline that he hoped to be able to predict the date when time would end. A Byzantine world chronicler of the early ninth century, George Syncellus, quoted the list of eras that Africanus drew up for the earliest centuries of human time—in essence, the history recorded in the first six chapters of Genesis:

Adam, when he was 230, begot Seth. And after living another 700 years, he died (that is a second death).

Seth, when he was 205, begot Enos: from Adam, then, up to the birth of Enos, there is a total of 435 years.

Enos, being 195, begot Kainan.

Kainan, at age 170, begot Maleleël.

Maleleël, at age 165, begot Jared.

Jared, at age 162, begot Enoch.

Enoch, being 165, begot Methusaleh. As one pleasing to God, he lived another 200 years and was not found.

Methusaleh, when he was 187, begot Lamech.

Lamech, being 188, begot Noah.[47]

Evidently, Africanus treated the dates when the patriarchs were born and when they begot their sons as the solid rungs of a ladder on which the chronologer could climb back to history's zero hour without ever missing a step.

Eusebius, by contrast, denied that the Bible could support a firm chronology, and provided detailed comparative tables that proved the point. In particular, he found that different versions of the genealogies in Genesis made the patriarchs beget their first sons at different ages, and that these divergences produced radically different chronologies for the period before the Flood. Eusebius listed three of these, each drawn from a different version of the Bible—the Septuagint, the Hebrew, and the Samaritan. And he noted that no two of them agreed. According to the Hebrew Bible, when Adam was 130, Seth was born; when Seth was 105, Enos was born, and so on. The sum of these intervals set the Flood in the year of the world 1656, and in this short chronology all seemed clear. But problems arose as soon as Eusebius considered the other versions. The Samaritan version offered a chronology of only 1,394 years, 349 years shorter than the Hebrew text. The Septuagint, by contrast, postponed the Flood to the year of the world 2262. The translators who produced this text made the interval between the birth of each patriarch and that of his son a hundred years longer than the Hebrew text did, possibly in response to the Egyptian and Chaldean claims to great antiquity that circulated in Alexandria, where the Septuagint took shape. When one follows the Septuagint computation rather than the Hebrew, world history becomes considerably longer: the interval between Creation and Incarnation lasts not around 4,000, but around 5,200 years.[48]

After tabulating these differences, Eusebius made clear that he himself preferred the Septuagint chronology, in which the periods that the various patriarchs lived before they begot their sons did not differ so radically as they did in the Hebrew text:

> In the above, the dates from Adam to Noah in the other versions of Scripture differ from the Septuagint in the length of time before each of the patriarchs begat a child. However, for the dates of Jared, Methusaleh, and Lamech, there is agreement with the Septuagint. On the basis of the areas where they agree, one can conclude that, for the dates of their predecessors, the reading in our version also offers a preferable chronology. From the greater period of time assigned to Jared and his successors, it is clear that the

chronology for their predecessors should also harmonize with the version of the Septuagint. For if, by the addition of a hundred years in the Hebrew text, the later generations born after them are found to be in chronological agreement with the Septuagint translation, would it not be that much more probable that their forefathers, from an earlier time, had much greater longevity than their descendants?[49]

Like Origen before him, he ascribed the chief differences, at least hypothetically, to the deliberate efforts of the Jews, who had altered the Hebrew text so that it supported their marital practices:

Now I observe that, for the total years of the life of each man, the sum of the years before and after procreation yields the same total according to the reading preserved in both the Hebrew and Septuagint version. And I notice that it is only the years before the begetting of the child that are compressed in the Jewish manuscripts. Therefore, I am inclined to suggest that this was perhaps the work of Jews who, in support of early marriage, ventured to compress and hasten the years before procreation. For if the men of most ancient times had lived long lives of many years, thereby arriving at marriage and procreation comparatively earlier, as the reading in their text shows, who would not take after them and imitate the practice of early marriage?[50]

For all Eusebius's confidence in the superiority of the Septuagint, however, he acknowledged that its chronology had obvious flaws. If the patriarch Methusaleh really lived 802 years after begetting his son, for example, he would have survived until the fourteenth year after the Flood. Yet the Bible clearly stated that the Flood wiped out "every living thing on the face of the earth . . . and only Noah was left, and those with him in the Ark" (Gen. 7:23). Eusebius was not the first to notice this discrepancy within the Septuagint text. Africanus had already postponed the date of the Flood from the year of the world (AM) 2242 to AM 2262 to allow time for Methusaleh's death. Eusebius rejected this solution.[51] But he himself could only propose to change the duration of Methusaleh's life, after he begot Lamech, from 802 to 782 years, "as is given in other copies."[52] Yet this change would have meant that Methusaleh died at the age of 949, while his grandfather, Jared, died at 962—in defiance of the widely held view that Methusaleh lived longer than any other man.[53]

When Eusebius denied that any certain chronology could be established for the Bible, he did not mean to call Revelation into question, any more than Africanus had. He noted with pleasure that the Chaldeans—that is, Berossos—also described a Flood, in terms that seemed to support the biblical account. General parallels like this one between pagan accounts of the ancient past and the Bible seem to have mattered more to Eusebius than what now seem—and what seemed in antiquity, at least to the many Jewish and Christian writers who resorted to abridgment, interpolation, and forgery in order to deal with them—flagrant divergences.[54] Eusebius even produced physical evidence to support the textual accounts of the universal Flood, bringing geology into the historical record in a way that recalled the theories of Xenophanes and adumbrated the efforts of Nicholas Steno and Johann Jakob Scheuchzer in later centuries:

And as to the Floodwaters' cresting above the highest of the mountains, we who are writing after the fact also have confirmation for its veracity from some people in our time who have personally examined fish discovered high up on the tallest peaks of Mount Libanos. For as some were cutting away stones there out of the mountains for their homes, they discovered various species of sea fish, which, it turned out, were congealed in mud in cavities in the mountains and remained up to this day in a kind of embalmed state. Therefore, the witness of the ancient tradition is confirmed by us, and with our own eyes at that.[55]

But Eusebius had a strong sense of responsibility to the facts as he knew them. In his view, they required him to admit that—as he put it in the introduction to his tables—he chose the chronology he followed only because the Septuagint appeared in more manuscripts than others, not because he could prove it was correct: "It has not escaped me that the periods of years are found in divergent forms in the Hebrew texts, and that these regularly appear higher or lower, as the translators believed to be correct, and we should follow the sum that is given credibility because it appears in the largest number of copies."[56] Biblical authority turned into human contingency even as Eusebius worked on the texts of Genesis in the Hexapla.[57]

Once Eusebius had decided that he could not plot the history of the world from Adam onward on a single line, he divided the past into two periods that he portrayed in sharply different ways—rather as an earlier Greek chronographer, long identified with Eratosthenes, had done long before when he distinguished between three kinds of past time, obscure, mythical, and historical, the last of them beginning with the fall of Troy.[58] Eusebius began the tables that formed book 2 of his *Chronicle,* as we have seen, after the Flood, with Ninus and Abraham. But he turned book 1 of the work into an anthology of supporting evidence, and in this he included, chapter after chapter, what Egyptians, Babylonians, Greeks, and others had to say about the whole course of history. Some of these accounts he could simply dismiss. As one who traced his own religion back to Moses, Eusebius found it easy, at least while writing as a historian, to treat the Greeks as ignorant. Like Africanus, he remembered the dialogue between Solon and the Egyptian priest in Plato's *Timaeus.* He felt certain that the Greeks, who lacked accurate written records kept by priests, were mere children when it came to knowledge of the distant past.[59]

Eusebius, moreover, had more than memories of Plato to sustain him in this attitude. Like Africanus, he folded versions of what Berossos and Manetho had written into his own work. The texts as Eusebius received them were naturally riven with errors and contradictions, the natural result of the long passage they had made through a whitewater rapids version of textual transmission which had left them battered and in part almost unrecognizable. What horrified Eusebius as he read them, however, was not the plethora of minor discrepancies that disfigured them but the core of their message. Naturally, he condemned these long chronologies as wild stories, mythical timelines that stretched so far back that they could not possibly be true: "Moreover, a good many quite mad histories of the Egyptians and Chaldeans are in circulation. The latter believe that their history amounts to more than 40,000 years. And the Egyptians weave all sorts of silly tales of their gods, and certain demigods, and also the spirits of the dead, and other, mortal kings. I am interested only in the truth; hence it is pointless for me to examine these matters in detail."[60] Since Eusebius rejected all efforts to draw up a complete history of the world, even the errors of these Near Eastern accounts had a limited positive value for him. They confirmed his efforts "to rebuke the vanity of the foolish chronologers."[61] But he could not leave the matter there. A reader who could believe Berossos's chronology, he mordantly commented, "must also believe the many other incredible things found there."[62]

Eusebius's horror is easy to understand. Any Christian who read Berossos's account of Babylonian origins, as preserved by Alexander Polyhistor, could be forgiven for feeling nausea and dread when he encountered this monstrous fish story:

But in the first year there appeared from the Erythraean Sea in a place adjacent to Babylonia a silly beast by the name of Oannes, just as Apollodorus also recorded, having the whole body of a fish, but under the head, another human head grew alongside under the head of the fish, and similarly human feet had grown out under the tail of the fish. It had a human voice. And its image is still preserved even now. He says that this beast spends its day with humans, taking no sustenance, and imparts to humanity the knowledge of letters and sciences and crafts of all types. It also teaches the founding of cities, and establishment of temples, the introduction of laws and land-measurement, and shows them seeds and the gathering of fruits, and in general it imparts to humanity all that pertains to the civilized life. From that time, nothing beyond this has been discovered. And with the setting of the sun, this creature

Oannes again submerges into the sea and spends the night in the sea. For it is amphibious.[63]

Every detail of this account—from its mention of Babylonian statues of the gods, to its account of the origins of the arts, which contradicted both the patriarchal stories in Genesis and the Hellenistic works on human inventors that Eusebius drew on, to its diabolic protagonist—was clearly unacceptable from Eusebius's standpoint. Nothing would have seemed easier than to dismiss the entire work of Berossos, and that of Manetho, as pure pagan fantasies. No wonder that Africanus did not hesitate to reject them in his own, strongly apologetic work.[64]

Yet as Eusebius examined these texts more closely, he found himself strongly tempted to reconsider their evidence. An agonized paragraph reflects his struggle to reconcile conflicting desires. On the one hand, he longed to reject the Chaldeans' long chronology without further ado. On the other, he hoped to interpret it in a way that bore some relation to biblical chronology, without suggesting that it could be accepted as it stood: "But if anyone should persuade himself to believe that the Chaldeans, who recorded this immensely long chronology, were somehow right, then by the same token he would have to believe their other deceptive tales. But if this chronology completely exceeds the bounds of nature, and is implausible in itself—for all that it could be understood in a different way—if, then, anyone persuades himself to believe this, he will carry on and not accept those accounts of chronology without testing them."[65]

In later comments Eusebius clarified what he had in mind with this tortuous sequence of throat-clearings and qualifications. He was rejecting what he saw as the obvious way to deal with reports of historical periods that stretched back too far for scholarly comfort. The standard toolkit of the late antique chronologer included just the implement that Eusebius seemingly needed. Long before he wrote, more than one pagan scholar—most notoriously Cicero—had treated the long chronologies of ancient Near Eastern history with scathing skepticism.[66] These writers offered a short, sharp way to deal with claims to a multi-millennial past. Censorinus, whom we have met before, noted in 238 CE that some maintained "that in Egypt the earliest year was only one month long."[67] This suggestion, in turn, was not new, and it seems that an astronomer, rather than an antiquary, had been the first to venture it, centuries before. In his commentary on the *Timaeus,* Proclus noted that "if what Eudoxus says is true, and the Egyptians called the month a year, then the sum of all these many years would not be surprising."[68] When Africanus criticized as "inclining . . . to the mythical" Egyptian efforts to reconcile the myriads of years claimed by some for Egyptian history with the 8,000 or 9,000 years claimed by the priest in the *Timaeus,* he probably had in mind these pagan efforts, both ancient and recent, to save the credit of Egyptian chronology by reducing its length.[69]

Late antique chronologers of every stripe, moreover, often proved more than willing to amputate facts or dates that they could not accommodate in their neat, providential systems. Ardashir (180–239 CE), the first Sasanian ruler of Persia, feared the power of ancient prophecy. Zoroaster had lived, he thought, 300 years before Alexander, and Alexander 513 years before Ardashir. And Zoroaster had predicted that the empire and religion of Iran would last 1,000 years. "In order to mesh Sasanian pretension with Mazdean prophecy, Ardashir excised some two and a half centuries from Iranian history."[70] To postpone the doom that threatened his descendants, Ardashir proclaimed that he had acceded to the throne in the year 260, rather than 513, of Alexander. A little later in the third century CE, Yose ben Halaphta and other rabbis in Babylon laid out what would eventually become the standard chronological system of rabbinical Judaism. Yose took no account of nonbiblical sources, if he knew them, for the Persian period, and held that prophecy ended not with Ezra and the reconstruction of the Hebrew Scriptures, after the return from the Babylonian Exile, but with Alexander the Great. To bring the last prophets, who predicted the rebuilding of the Temple, as close as possible to Alexander in time, he abridged the history of Persia to a mere 54 years, and that of Media and Persia as a whole to 210 years in all. Yose insisted that these kingdoms had had no rulers other than the ones explicitly mentioned in Scripture: "You find only two Persian kings, Cyrus and Darius, and for Media Darius and Ahasuerus."[71] In each case a history too long for present purposes was abridged, arbitrarily and without justification. Chronology, in this mode, turned into a bed of Procrustes, where excess data were simply excised, rather than an open-ended, comparative field of study, the results of which could occasionally challenge the basic assumptions of its practitioners.

Unlike Africanus, Eusebius was clearly tempted to solve his problems by accepting Eudoxus's attractive assumption and applying it to Berossus and Manetho. "One could perhaps rightly wonder," Eusebius suggested, "whether their accounts are somehow true." When Berossos wrote that 10 Babylonian kings had ruled for 120 *saroi,* or periods of 3,600 years, he might not be making the insane claim that they had literally lived 430,00 so-lar years. "Perhaps . . . the *saroi* do not refer to the number of years that I thought, but to some shorter interval. For the earli-est Egyptians spoke of 'lunar years'—that is, they called the days of the month, 30 in all, a year . . . It seems right and proper that the so-called *saros* of the Chaldeans has a similar meaning."[72]

As Eusebius confronted Manetho's long chronology of Egyp-tian history, he adopted the same suggestion, far more deci-sively: "The Egyptians used to call a year what we now call a month."[73] He thus reduced the 24,900 years during which, in Manetho's account, gods, demigods and the spirits of the dead had ruled Egypt to 24,900 "lunar years, which are 2,206 solar years."[74] In a later note, he offered a second, supplementary sug-gestion, this time geopolitical rather than chronological in the strict sense. Perhaps, Eusebius surmised, some of the dynasties that Manetho listed as if in one continuous sequence had ac-tually ruled at the same time, in different Egyptian regions.[75]

This idea was undoubtedly ingenious. In the mid-seven-teenth century, when G. J. Vossius reinvented the notion that a number of dynasties had ruled simultaneously in different parts of Egypt, his theory helped many Christian chronologers deal with the excessive antiquity of the Egyptians.[76] But the very fact that Eusebius felt he had to put this second argument forward shows how clearly he saw that his first effort at the reduction of Egyptian chronology could not solve all of the problems that confronted him. The data seemingly still implied, after all, that the kingdom of Egypt had existed before the Flood, and that Manetho had known about its history from some extra-biblical source. Though Eusebius claimed that his shorter chronology of antediluvian history matched "the Hebrew chronology," moreover, he was deliberately trying to confuse a point. For only the Septuagint chronology, not that of the Hebrew or Samaritan text, could accommodate even his shortened Egyptian prehistory.

Eusebius, in other words, allowed different, and quite divergent, voices to speak in the first book of his chronology. Though he suggested ways of harmonizing what they said, he also admitted, at least implicitly, that he could neither wholeheartedly reject nor perfectly explain their testimony. The Alexandrian chronologers Panodorus and Annanius, writing early in the fifth century, rebuked him for this failure.[77] Yet they too found themselves accepting what the later Byzantine chronologer George Syncellus would call the "fantasies" of Berossos, "namely that there were rulers in Babylon before the Flood," and of Manetho, "who manufactured an analogous fantasy about a dynasty of Egyptian kings before the Flood."[78]

Nothing was more distinctive in Eusebius's approach than the Bakhtinian openness that he showed here, his willingness to turn his early books into so odd a conversation among priests of several nations and to accept that their Pinteresque dialogue necessarily ended in uncertainty. Like Origen, he produced not only a synthesis, but also a polyglot collection of research materials from which other scholars could draw what conclusions they liked. Like Origen, too, he took foreign traditions very seriously even when he set out to show that they were wrong on vital points. If Eusebius's enterprise looked back to Africanus, his attitude and his practices looked back to Origen.

Both before and after Eusebius wrote, Christian chronologers normally assumed that they could and should provide a full account of the history of the world. Orosius, for example, who composed his world history about a century after Eusebius, criticized pagan chronologers for starting from Ninus—more or less as Eusebius did—rather than from the Creation:

> Almost all the learned Greeks and Romans who have offered written accounts of the history of kings and peoples have started from Ninus, son of Belus, king of the Assyrians. Though in their blindness they wish it to be believed that world and man had no beginning, they still use him to define the starting-point of reigns and wars, as if the human race had lived like animals until then, and only then awoke, as if struck for the first time by a sort of new providence. I have decided to begin my account of human misery from the beginning of human sinfulness, at least briefly.[79]

Pagan chronologers dismissed the earliest centuries of history as lost in the mists of darkness and myth. Christian chronologers need not—must not—agree.

Eusebius firmly believed that the Septuagint chronology of the Bible offered the one true key to world history. But he resisted all temptations to exclude discordant ingredients from the rich crazy salad of his first book, or even to claim that he could offer a firm chronology from the Creation to the Flood. Instead, he framed a deliberately modest approach, couched in the dry, ascetic language of scholarly self-denial. In his preface to the *Canon,* he offered his reader only two general results, one negative and one explicitly tentative: "first, that no one will fool himself into imagining, as those others have, that he can achieve absolute certainty in chronological computation; and second, that everyone will know this is only intended as matter for debate." Every sensible student of the field, he concluded, must accept a state of doubt and uncertainty.[80] In Eusebius's hands, the Christian world chronicle metamorphosed into a treasury of non-Western, non-Jewish, non-Christian accounts of ancient history and myth—one that proved a Pandora's box of insoluble problems and irreconcilable discrepancies when Joseph Scaliger finally prized it open again, 1,300 years later.[81]

In its Greek form, as Hervé Inglebert has pointed out, Eusebius's work resembled both the universal history of Polybius, with its effort to follow the movements of great events comprehensively across the Mediterranean, and that of Diodorus, with its efforts to accommodate multiple, conflicting accounts of early human history.[82] Inglebert suggests that Eusebius discussed the discrepancies between the different biblical chronologies in order both to remove the footings from eschatological predictions "and to justify his own decision to start with Abraham, on whom the different chronologies agreed."[83] It would be more accurate to say that Eusebius's knowledge of the discrepancies forced him to start with Abraham rather than the Creation—but also enabled him to find a way to set off an earlier, mythical time in a separate account.[84]

One simple, local fact explains why Africanus—a skilled philologist who knew that the Greek and Hebrew texts of the Old Testament differed substantially—found it possible to ignore the divergences between the different biblical texts in this context, while Eusebius did not. Africanus, who had no opportunity to consult Origen's Hexapla, believed in the integrity of the Septuagint chronology.[85] Eusebius, who consulted the Hexapla regularly in the course of his efforts to improve copies of the

Greek bible and may even have corrected a copy of Origen's work, did not share his predecessor's optimism even though he too preferred the Septuagint and its chronology.

The Syro-Hexaplar, a Syriac translation of the Septuagint text from the fifth column of the Hexapla, made at Alexandria in 615–617 CE by Paul of Tella, offers particularly striking evidence about what Eusebius found when he studied Origen's great edition. Paul based his version on Hexaplaric manuscripts corrected by Eusebius, as a number of Syriac colophons clearly show.[86] Subscriptions preserved in later manuscripts also reveal that someone unknown—perhaps Origen himself—collated the Hexapla for Exodus and Numbers with the Samaritan text, and that Eusebius knew and annotated manuscripts that contained some of the notes in question.[87] Since the remains of the *Chronicle* show that Eusebius also compared the Septuagint text of Genesis to the Samaritan text, it seems likely that the entire Pentateuch in the Caesarean copy of the Hexapla was collated against, or perhaps even had an extra column drawn from, the Samaritan text. Unlike pagan scholars, Eusebius could not simply relegate the earliest stages of history to the realm of "mythical time" and go on his way rejoicing, even if he could relegate the earliest histories of the pagans to his first book. But he also could not use them to frame a single, coherent chronicle, since the mysteriously conflicting numbers in the parallel columns of Hebrew, Samaritan, and Septuagint text made clear, begetting by begetting, that biblical chronologies differed radically.[88]

Reading the Hexapla column against column, in other words, taught Eusebius to compare texts word by word. And the evidence that Eusebius turned up as he did so forced him to admit that no single authoritative chronology of the world could be drawn from the Old Testament. Eusebius read the Hexapla as Origen had meant it to be read: as a treasury of exegetical materials, some of them perplexing, rather than an effort to provide a stable, perfect text of the Bible. By doing so, he turned chronology from a fixed, perfect armature for the history of the world into an open, hotly debated discipline. This step provoked a series of controversies that would not be resolved for centuries.

Yet Eusebius's bold approach had one crucial advantage, at least from his standpoint. It established the need for chronologers, as the only experts capable of adjudicating these difficult and obvious problems for Christian readers. The example of the Hexapla thus enabled Eusebius—as it had originally enabled Origen—to redefine the nature of Christian scholarship. The chronologer had to have an expert command of diverse records and traditions, of divergent calendars and terminologies. Chronology, far from being a way to make the ancient past neat and familiar, became a guide to the cosmopolitan variety of traditions that Christian historiography needed to take into account.

We return to book 2 of the *Chronicle,* now that we have confirmed the suggestion from which we began: that the Hexapla played a central role in Eusebius's reframing of world history. This point is vital, for students of ancient chronography have debated for decades about the originality of Eusebius's *Canon* and its place in the chronological tradition. Historical tables had existed, to be sure, for centuries, as had historical synchronisms—a tool that Herodotus applied in a number of different ways.[89] Lists of Olympic victors, Argive priestesses of Hera, and Spartan kings circulated in fifth-century Athens. Comparison of the fragments of these early works with that of Eusebius confirms both the originality of his enterprise and the impact that the Hexapla had on the way he finally framed it.

A fifth-century chronographer and ethnographer, Hellanicus of Lesbos, apparently made the series of Argive priestesses of Hera into "a chronological backbone for his attempt to write 'universal history.'"[90] His work does not survive as a whole, and what we know about it comes from Thucydides and other later writers.[91] Thucydides sharply criticized Hellanicus's method. After all, he explained, it was impossible to be accurate if one fixed events simply to particular priests or magistrates, without establishing when during the particular individual's term in office they fell.[92] His own method, which dated events to successive winters and summers, yielded greater precision. To judge by this critique, Hellanicus's work was laid out in an abstract, almost genealogical way, year by year, and fixed the events it recorded only to the names of individual priestesses and other officials, not to their precise places in the calendar year.

Despite Thucydides's negative verdict, the annalistic framework, with its approximate synchronisms, remained standard in chronology for centuries to come. In the third and second centuries BCE, Eratosthenes and other chronologers compiled list-like chronicles that resembled that of Eusebius in some respects—for example, in the considerable space they accorded to poets and inventors. Early sections of the *Chronicle* drew heavily on these compilations. Some of the Hellenistic lists assumed material form. The Parian Chronicle, for example, entries first found in which resurface in Eusebius's work, was inscribed on marble around 264–63 BCE.[93] Polybius mentions in passing other chronological tables that were apparently posted

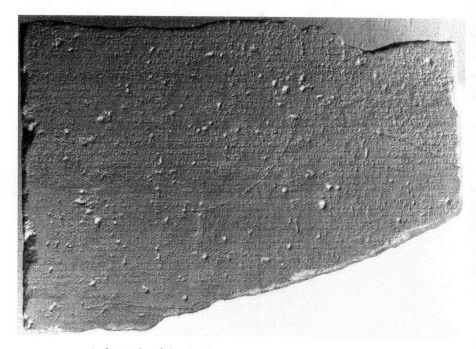

A chronicle of the third century BCE: the Parian Chronicle.

on city walls.[94] Other lists circulated in the literature of astronomy. Ptolemy's *Canon* of Babylonian kings from Nabonassar to his own time was transmitted with manuscripts of his *Handy Tables,* and would eventually be integrated with Christian chronology by the Alexandrian scholar Panodorus.[95]

Some modern scholars believe that Hellenistic chronographers drew up elaborate synchronistic tables, centuries before Eusebius. They base this view primarily on a passage in Polybius's histories, in which he praised Timaeus for comparing the years of the ephors with the kings of Sparta, and the archons of Athens with the Argive priestesses of Hera and the victors at the Olympic games.[96] From this testimony David Asheri inferred that Timaeus devised "a single or a double synchronistic table, possibly with vertical columns according to various local eponyms and with two panhellenic standards, the Olympiads and the Argive priestesses. By reading such a table horizontally from left to right, one could obtain a wide Hellenic synchronization at a glance." He credited Timaeus, accordingly, with "the invention of the multiple synchronistic table and its graphic form."[97] Yet not a scrap of this reconstructed table survives, and the form that Asheri ascribed to it seems to be a backward reconstruction from Eusebius. And there is no evidence to suggest that Timaeus, or any other early chronologers, anticipated Eusebius's ingenious effort to make book 2 of his *Chronicle* a literal "time map"—a visual narrative whose plotline no reader could miss.[98] Polybius, moreover, described Timaeus as "making comparisons" between the various lists, a phrase that suggests critical discussions of individual synchronisms rather than full tables. Rudolf Helm argued in 1924 that none of the earlier tables, varied as they were, anticipated Eusebius's effort at comprehensiveness or his emphasis on the synchronicity of events in so many different kingdoms and societies. In 1979, Alden Moshammer confirmed that Eusebius, for all his debts to earlier chronographers, had devised the form of his *Canon* himself.[99] These arguments still seem cogent.[100]

True, the literature of Latin scholarship may have included one fairly precise formal precedent for the *Chronicle*. Cicero's friend Atticus drew up a list of Athenian archons matched with Roman consuls, which served as a timeline to which he attached literary and other materials. He entitled this the *Liber annalis*. Only fragments of this work survive. But in his dialogue *Brutus,* Cicero portrays himself, Brutus, and Atticus discussing the work. Cicero claims that Atticus's book had excited him so much that it more or less revived him from the dead (*Brutus* 3.13). Brutus asks for clarification: "Do you mean that book in which he covered the entire past, succinctly, and, in my view, very precisely?" "That's the one I mean," Cicero replies, "that's the book that saved me" (3.14). Then Atticus breaks in. Welcome though he finds Cicero's enthusiasm, he remarks, he wonders just what feature of his work was so new and useful as Cicero claims. "The book," Cicero answers, "both offered much that was new to me, and proved handy, in just the way that I needed, so that I saw all the events that happened in the past, drawn up in their chronological ranks, in one single view" (4.15).[101]

Cicero's enthusiastic description of the *Liber annalis* as a sort of historical Roman legion, every fact marshaled in sequence and presenting arms, gives a sense of the excitement with which formal innovations of the sort Eusebius devised could inspire ancient readers. To judge from the *Brutus,* Atticus's book lined up the lives of the poets and the works they wrote with the dates of particular consuls. The facts and dates that Cicero presumably drew from the *Liber annalis* imply that Atticus and his sources did their share of synchronizing, and that their work offered readers much the sort of information that generations would derive from Eusebius's *Chronicle.*[102] But Eusebius probably had little or no direct knowledge of the antiquarian achievements of Atticus and his colleagues. They wrote their works in Latin rather than Greek, and these were probably limited in their circulation to Rome itself by the sheer difficulty of reproducing such complex texts.[103]

The evidence suggests, in sum, that book 2 of the *Chronicle* represented a dramatic formal innovation. Eusebius made mistakes, some of them grave, and even more silent approximations, which were required if he was to adjust the uneven periods of rulers' actual reigns to his larger annalistic system. He also drew heavily on lists assembled by both earlier and more recent chronographers.[104] But his tables amounted to a stunningly original work of scholarship—one that situated dozens of rulers and bishops named in varied lists in years of Abraham and, after 776 BCE, Olympic years as well.[105] Though not continually popular, book 2 provoked lively discussions in the fifth century and later. Once edited, translated into Latin, and brought up to date by Jerome, Eusebius's tables provided the model for Latin world chronicles for centuries to come.[106] Translations into Armenian and Syriac spread the text's influence.[107] Even in the early seventeenth century, when Scaliger wanted to create a new structure for universal history, he set out to do so by reconstructing Eusebius's work.[108]

In an age of manuscripts, producing a text with such an intricate form posed immense practical difficulties. To put it more bluntly: in a world in which laundry lists were not yet proverbial, it took a kind of genius to make history into one. Jerome, in the preface to his Latin version, eloquently evoked the complexity and foreignness of the *Canon:* "it has barbarous names, things unknown to the Latins, dates too complex to unravel, lines interwoven with both the events and the numbers, so that it is almost harder to work out the order of the text to be read than to arrive at knowledge of its content."[109] It is no coincidence that Atticus—someone who specialized in the production of books, though he was not a book dealer or publisher in any modern sense—seems to have been the one scholar before Eusebius to try to draw up comparably elaborate synchronistic tables.[110]

Over the centuries, relatively few Christian chronologers rivaled Eusebius's ability to hold data and theses that contradicted one another in a productive if delicate balance. Many followed the model he offered in book 2, the *Canon,* which seemed to trace a cogent providential story across the centuries and politely ignored such problems as the apparent existence of Egyptian dynasties before the Flood. When Jerome adapted the *Chronicle* in Latin, moreover, he ignored the first book. The brief introduction to the *Canon* in his version skipped past the problems raised by early history. In the West, accordingly, many Christian chronologers believed, as Orosius did, that they could extend Eusebius's work backward, dating all events and following all the paths of providential history right back to Adam.

In the Greek East, however, Eusebius's whole book continued to provoke debate. A century after Eusebius completed the first version of the *Chronicle,* the Alexandrian scholars Annianus and Panodorus tried to reconcile his materials with both the Bible and Ptolemy's precisely dated list of kings. Four hundred years after them, the chronicler George Syncellus struggled with the same problems. Byzantine scholars never forgot that Egyptian and Chaldean chronology posed serious problems. Though Joseph Scaliger had little respect for Eusebius, the system he recreated from the materials that Syncellus and others preserved bore a strong resemblance to the *Chronicle,* both in its tolerance for diverse materials and long chronologies and in its willingness to accept strains and contradictions. The Christian library of Caesarea, evidently, was no *hortus conclusus.*

The combination of enterprises that enabled Eusebius to produce the *Chronicle*—bold scholarship productively yoked to innovative book design—reappears again and again in the course of his career. Now that we have seen Eusebius intensively at work on a relatively early project, we have become familiar with his general approach. We are ready to turn to the larger environment that he worked in, and in turn helped to transform, in Caesarea, and to follow his methods and creations as they evolved from his formative years in the late third century through the first four decades of the fourth.

4

Eusebius at Caesarea: A Christian Impresario of the Codex

I T was in Caesarea that Eusebius learned to be a scholar; in Caesarea, too, that he created new literary forms and institutions. In this chapter we follow the complex interplay between the man and his environment. Our concern will be to tease out the ways in which each shaped, and was shaped by, the other. As we will see, Eusebius built a unique institution, and worked out genuinely new ways to organize scribal labor. But the methods that he forged for correcting the text of the Bible and for wielding documents to create new forms of historical and polemical text—methods central to his achievement as a scholar—rested in important ways on precedents that Eusebius knew, as he knew the Hexapla, from the start of his career.

The Caesarea in which Eusebius read the Hexapla and created the *Chronicle* was a major center for the production, as well as the consumption, of Jewish and Christian books. Many of the former, as well as the latter, were written and studied in Greek.[1]

At the end of the third century, a wealthy Christian presbyter, Pamphilus, settled in the city and began to accumulate a library of sacred works. The collection that he built, and that his protégé Eusebius, the eventual bishop of the city, presumably continued to expand, became so famous in later antiquity that it was described, with some exaggeration, as the Christian equivalent of the library of Alexandria.[2] A native of Berytus, Pamphilus studied with the Alexandrian Christian philosopher Pierius, himself a follower of Origen. Eusebius, Pamphilus's disciple, informs us that his mentor devoted not only his fortune, but also his own labor as a copyist, to building his rich library of Christian books. In 310, under the reign of Maximinus, and only fourteen years before Constantine took control of the entire empire, Pamphilus died in one of the final waves of the persecutions initiated by Diocletian.[3] His books survived him, however, and Eusebius used both some of these texts and the methods he had learned from Pamphilus to transform Caesarea into a new center of Christian scholarship.

It is not easy to reconstruct Pamphilus's library, or his working methods, in detail. Some scholars have held that he simply continued an enterprise begun by Origen, and that Eusebius in turn took up the reins when Pamphilus met his martyr's death by decapitation on 16 February 310.[4] Others—most recently René Amacker and Eric Junod, the editors of the *Apology for Origen* that Pamphilus wrote in collaboration with Eusebius— have argued that the library at Caesarea probably did not have a continuous institutional history. We agree with them.[5] Certain facts seem clear. Origen left the Hexapla and other works behind in Caesarea. Pamphilus created a basically Christian collection, which centered on Origen but may also have contained pagan texts. Eusebius in his turn built up a massive library, including some of what Origen and Pamphilus left behind, which seems eventually to have become part of the episcopal library of Caesarea. Beyond that the scanty evidence does not allow us to go, though it has provided plentiful nourishment for speculation in the past.[6]

The sources for Pamphilus's life and work fall into several quite discrete categories, each requiring an analysis of its own, and they offer no information on such elementary points as his year of birth. Taken together, the various pieces of evidence support a number of inferences: that Pamphilus had a solid classical education and built a substantial Christian library; that he trained a number of other young men in disciplines of the book, in ways that did much to form his star pupil, Eusebius; and that his enterprises, though organically connected to those that flourished before and after him in Caesarea, also differed from them in vital ways.

The full life of Pamphilus that Eusebius wrote, in three books, is almost entirely lost.[7] But fragmentary evidence from and about it, and two other major ancient accounts of his life and work, survive. Eusebius, in *The Martyrs of Palestine,* identifies Pamphilus as the descendant of a noble family, and emphasizes both his mastery of Greek culture and the Bible and the charismatic charm that attracted young men to work and suffer with him. Jerome, in *De viris illustribus,* emphasizes the passion for Origen that led Pamphilus to copy out the greater part of Origen's works in his own hand.[8]

One well-known quotation from Eusebius's biography, preserved in Jerome's polemical work against Rufinus, offers a vivid sketch of Pamphilus's central activities. Eusebius, in this context, ascribed to him a very particular view of scholarship, as an enterprise that was not only collective, but also literally selfless:

> Pamphilus was a friend to all who studied. If he saw that some lacked the basic necessities of life, he generously gave as much as he could. He also eagerly distributed copies of the sacred scriptures, not only to be read, but also to be kept, and not only to men, but also to those women who had shown him that they were devoted to reading. Accordingly, he prepared many codices, so that he could give them out to those who wanted them whenever the need arose. So deep was his humility, however, that he wrote nothing of his own composition, except the letters that he now and then sent to friends. But he was most zealous in reading the treatises of the ancient writers and devoted himself to intensive meditation about them.[9]

The portrait is affecting, and much further evidence, as we will see, confirms Eusebius's emphasis on the Christian core of his teacher's scholarly activities—just as recent work confirms that Christian women read and exchanged biblical and other texts.[10]

Yet the supernaturally humble figure Eusebius depicts is distorted in at least one vital respect. The statement that Pamphilus "wrote nothing of his own" is false, at lest in its literal sense. No one knew this better, moreover, than Eusebius himself, since the two men collaborated, during Pamphilus's last years, in composing the first five books of a defense of Origen. They were driven to write this "because of the fault-finders," as Eusebius himself noted—that is, by the many clerics who attacked the two men's hero, Origen.[11] Part of their defense of

Origen survives, in a Latin translation by Rufinus. Even Jerome, who in the heat of controversy tried to expose the work in question as a forgery, eventually admitted that Pamphilus had written it.[12] We will see below that the methods used in this book are highly relevant to those Eusebius applied in his own scholarly enterprises.[13] And this was not the only case in which Pamphilus engaged in scholarly activities of a more varied and technical kind than reading homilies and copying manuscripts.

On one point, all the evidence agrees: Pamphilus collected books. He did more than amass them, moreover; he also set them into order and drew up some sort of catalogue. Both Eusebius and Jerome used the library Pamphilus assembled, and their statements on its contents match better than those on the authorship of the *Apology*. In book 6 of his *Church History*, which deals with Origen, Eusebius noted that he did not need to give a catalogue of Origen's works. It would take too much space, he argued. Moreover, "I recorded it in full in my account of the life of our contemporary, the holy martyr Pamphilus. There, in order to show how zealous he was for holy things, I offered as evidence the catalogues of the library that he assembled of the works of Origen and other Christian writers. From these, anyone who wishes can gain the fullest possible knowledge of the works of Origen that have come down to us."[14] This passage suggests that Pamphilus both collected Origen's works and drew up formal catalogues of them in the Alexandrian fashion.

Jerome confirms that interpretation, and expands somewhat on it. True, he wrote the letter in which he remarked that Pamphilus "found a great many" of Origen's works "and left us a catalogue *[indicem]* of his discoveries" before he came to Palestine. At this point Jerome depended on Eusebius for his knowledge of Pamphilus.[15] But Jerome's brief note on Pamphilus in *De viris illustribus,* written when he knew the library of Caesarea at first hand, records that "the presbyter Pamphilus burned with so much love of the divine library [Scripture], that he copied the greater part of Origen's works, as preserved down to the present in the library at Caesarea, in his own hand."[16] Presumably, too, it was from Pamphilus that Eusebius derived his habit of collecting Origen's letters, arranging them "in separate roll containers" to protect them, and listing them.[17]

It also seems clear that this collection was Pamphilus's own project. Origen may well have brought a substantial working collection of books to Caesarea, and the Hexapla certainly formed part of it there. He also had stocks of texts by Philo and others that he, like Eusebius, knew at first hand. Origen's letter to Pope Fabian, which we have already examined, shows how much time he and his benefactor Ambrose dedicated to the preeminently bookish task of correcting manuscripts. But no evidence suggests that Origen set special store by copying his own or anyone else's books, or that he compiled formal catalogues of his holdings. Pamphilus had to chase down and collect Origen's writings—clear evidence that they had not been systematically collected and preserved by their author. To this extent at least, Pamphilus emerges as a distinct figure—an eager intellectual disciple who spent much of his capital and his immense energies on preserving the works of an earlier Christian writer.

The wider boundaries of Pamphilus's activities as collector and copyist remain somewhat indistinct. Jerome, for example, owned twenty-five manuscripts *(volumina)* with Origen's commentary on the Minor Prophets, "written in Pamphilus's hand."

He described these books as a possession that filled him with as much joy as if he had the wealth of Croesus.[18] We have no way of knowing whether they were duplicates, produced by Pamphilus for some friend or benefactor, or strays from the collection at Caesarea. One bit of evidence, moreover, hints both that Pamphilus did not limit himself to collecting Origen, and that at least some of his manuscripts of other texts came from the collection of his favorite author. The acts of a supposed council held by the apostles in Antioch bear the title: "The holy martyr Pamphilus's copy of the acts of the synod of the apostles in Antioch, that is, part of the canons of the synod, as found in the library of Origen."[19] It is at least possible that other prizes and pyrites in Pamphilus's collection came to Caesarea in Origen's time, passed through his hands, and inspired forgers and librarians to claim this exalted provenance for their books.

In one vital respect at least, Pamphilus followed Origen's lead as a scholar. As collector and scribe, he occupied himself intensively with the Bible. Ancient scholars who corrected manuscripts regularly entered notes, normally at the end of books or sections, in which they identified themselves and briefly—all too briefly—described what they had done to them. Normally these survive only in copies, often made hundreds of years after the activities they describe. Many manuscripts of the Greek Old and New Testaments, as well as copies of the Syro-Hexaplar, have subscriptions, and a fair number of these short and sometimes cryptic texts mention Pamphilus and his associates.[20] Two of the most informative appear in one of the three great fourth-century manuscripts of the Greek Bible, the Codex Sinaiticus. Both derive from earlier manuscripts that no longer exist, and describe the steps that Pamphilus and others took to correct them. The shorter one, copied at the end of II Esdras in Sinaiticus sometime between the fifth and the seventh century, reads: "Collated against a very old copy corrected by the hand of the holy martyr Pamphilus. At the end of his copy appears an autograph attestation, which reads as follows: 'Copied and corrected from the Hexapla of Origen. Antoninus collated; I, Pamphilus, corrected.'"[21] The longer one, added by the same hand at the end of Esther, offers even more information: "Copied and corrected from the Hexapla of Origen, as corrected by his own hand. Antoninus, the confessor, collated; I, Pamphilus, corrected the volume in prison. . . . And if it is be not bumptious to say so, it would not be easy to find a copy that comes close to this copy."[22] Several other colophons, some in manuscripts of the Greek Bible and others in manuscripts of the Syro-Hexaplaric text, record that Pamphilus and Eusebius worked together on the correction of texts of IV Kingdoms, Proverbs, Ecclesiastes, the Minor Prophets, Isaiah, and Ezekiel.[23]

These texts, of course, do not yield their secrets lightly. They were entered in the manuscripts centuries after Pamphilus, by scholars trying to emend their own copies of the biblical text, and it is not always clear which parts of the subscriptions come from the lost manuscripts of Pamphilus and which were added by their readers. Was it Pamphilus or the much later scribe who copied his subscriptions into Sinaiticus who wrote: "And if it be not bumptious to say so, it would not be easy to find a copy that comes close to this copy"? Learned opinion differs.[24] When subscriptions report a given scholar's statement that "I corrected" (Latin *emendavi*) a text, moreover, they indicate a process normally limited to one occasion and one book. In most cases, classical subscriptions record one or more particular schol-

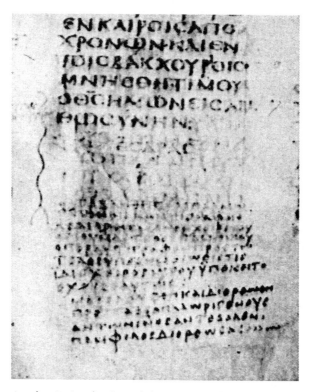

A subscription by Pamphilus as entered in the Codex Sinaiticus, reproduced from the facsimile, *Codex sinaiticvs petropolitanvs et Friderico-Avgvstanvs lipsiensis. The Old Testament preserved in the public library of Petrograd, in the library of the Society of ancient literature in Petrograd, and in the library of the University of Leipzig, now reproduced in facsimile from photographs by Helen and Kirsopp Lake, with a description and introduction to the history of the Codex by Kirsopp Lake* (Oxford: Clarendon Press, 1922).

ars' effort to improve a given manuscript, by checking it against the original from which it was copied, by collating it against another manuscript, or by conjecture. In some cases Christian scholars, bent on preserving the integrity of a sacred text, went further, identifying the particular text that they had used as a standard. By doing so they showed that they had carried out their work as Irenaeus—in a famous subscription preserved by Eusebius, and thus known in Caesarea—demanded Christian literati should: "I call upon you, who will copy this book, to swear by our lord Jesus Christ, and by his glorious advent, when he comes to judge the living and the dead, that you will collate what you transcribe and and correct it against this exemplar from which you transcribe it. And in the same way you will also transcribe this oath and put it in the exemplar."[25] Eusebius cited this passage as exemplary. Modern readers, he said, would profit by seeing the "really zealous concern of the ancient, truly holy men"—the way, that is, in which they had blended piety and precision.[26] (*HE* 5.20.3).

This seems to have been more or less the way in which Pamphilus and his friends approached their textual work on the Bible. But the details remain a fruitful field for elaborate reconstructions that rest precariously, like inverted pyramids, on a very small basis of evidence. One standard interpretation holds that Pamphilus, or he and Eusebius, produced a recension of the Septuagint based on the fifth column of the Hexapla, which they used as a standard.[27] A variation on this, which we proposed above, holds that Origen himself produced such a recension. Pamphilus and Eusebius might have taken this as their standard. One could conjecture, without too much strain, that when the two men claimed to have collated copies of the Old

Testament books against the Hexapla, they actually meant that they had used a recension of the Septuagint derived from it. Or one could take the subscriptions literally and assume that Pamphilus and his helpers used the Hexapla itself as their standard.[28]

But exactly what Pamphilus did to the manuscripts of Ezra, IV Kingdoms, and other biblical books that he corrected remains unclear. Perhaps he drew individual corrections for particular, well-known controversial passages from Origen's work. Or perhaps he actually collated each manuscript from beginning to end with the Hexapla, or with a single manuscript that contained the so-called Hexaplaric signs added by Origen to certain texts: obeli, or dashes, to identify words and phrases in the Septuagint that had no counterpart in the Hebrew, and asterisks to identify lacunae in the Septuagint that had been filled in from other sources. The terminology that Pamphilus and Eusebius used leaves vital details of their work in obscurity.[29]

Jerome remarked in his preface to *Chronicles* that three versions of the Septuagint were especially influential in the Christian world: that of Hesychius, which was popular in Egypt; that of Lucian the martyr, which found approval from Constantinople to Antioch, and a third, Palestinian text, "drawn up by Origen and disseminated by Eusebius and Pamphilus."[30] Modern scholars have modified this neat picture of three recensions, each created by a third-century martyr. Instead of a Hesychian recension, they identify a group of manuscripts as "Alexandrian" or "Egyptian." They refer to the "Lucianic" text, more generally, as "Antiochene." True, contemporary textual critics still see the work of Origen, Pamphilus, and Eusebius as "an unambigu-

ous work of planned revision."[31] But we may never know what
precise impact the activities of Pamphilus and Eusebius had
on this third family of manuscripts. Over time, a recension
based on the Hexapla "dominated the field." But as scribes
omitted or mistranscribed the critical marks, the distinctions
that Origen—and, presumably, Eusebius and Pamphilus—tried
to preserve between the Septuagint and other versions "became
blurred so that what now passed for 'the LXX' was in fact a
badly corrupted text."[32]

In these circumstances, it makes little sense to try to describe
the way in which Pamphilus and Eusebius worked with a level
of vividness and precision that the sources by their nature ren-
der spurious. If Pamphilus's methods of collation and philological goals remain obscure, the flavor and texture of his everyday
practices as a scholar emerge clearly from the subscriptions. It
was a collaborative and specialized enterprise. Normally, Pamphilus and one other man worked together. The subscriptions
in Sinaiticus, for example, say, in the voice of Pamphilus, that
one Antoninus *antebalen,* while Pamphilus *diorthosa. Anti-
ballein,* in this context, is a technical term for collation, and
diorthoun for correction. In each case, Antoninus examined the
Hexapla (or another base text), while Pamphilus corrected the
new manuscript. As a number of scholars have shown, moreover, this process must have been oral—like most collaboration
between scholars or writers and their secretaries in the ancient
world.[33] In a process that reversed the normal methods of authorship—in which the author spoke while a secretary wrote
down what he said—Antoninus read the base text aloud, while
Pamphilus followed and entered corrections in the new text. It

seems likely that the young men who worked with Pamphilus began by reading aloud and only later, if ever, actually corrected manuscripts on their own.

It is all the more suggestive, then, that when it came to IV Kingdoms, according to the Syro-Hexaplar, Pamphilus did the collating, while Eusebius corrected the text and wrote the colophon.[34] Perhaps the older man chose the humbler task out of humility and respect for a specially gifted pupil. More likely he did so in order to oversee the younger man's first efforts to prepare a new manuscript for sacred reading. If so, the collaborative work recorded in the colophons amounted to an apprenticeship in textual criticism.

Over time, Pamphilus acknowledged Eusebius as a full colleague. A number of the colophons record that "Pamphilus and Eusebius corrected" or "accurately corrected" a given book or section of the Bible. Eusebius must have had this painstaking collaborative effort to control and improve the sources of religious truth in mind when he quoted the *Little Labyrinth*. This pamphlet denounced the Theodotians, the followers of Theodotus the Tanner, who had "critically revised" the Septuagint and the New Testament. The biblical texts that these heretics used varied so much as to condemn them: "If anyone wishes to gather the texts of each of them and to compare them with one another, he would find great discrepancies among them. For the copies of Asclepiades [i.e., those with his subscription] do not agree with those of Theodotus."[35] The critic went on to say that the clearest evidence of the Theodotians' crime lay in the carelessness with which they had produced their biblical texts. The fact that the Theodotians could not identify, much less produce, the sources from which they worked proved that they had arbitrarily changed their texts: "they cannot deny that they committed this crime, since the copies are written in their own hand. And they did not receive the Scriptures in this form from those by whom they were instructed, and they cannot produce any exemplars from which they made their copies."[36] (*HE* 5.28.18). The true Christian scholar made clear in a colophon just what he had done to the sacred texts, and in whose company—or so at least Eusebius demanded in this polemical context, though his practices rarely if ever lived up to so high a standard.[37]

A range of evidence shows that Pamphilus collected and corrected manuscripts of the New Testament as well as the Old. Jerome thought, as many others have, that the original text of the Gospel of Matthew was in Hebrew, and that the Greek text in circulation was a translation by someone unknown. He noted that "the Hebrew itself has been preserved until the present day in the library at Caesarea, which Pamphilus the martyr so diligently created."[38] Eusebius made elaborate efforts to establish the canon of New Testament books, which he laid out in the *Church History*. These attempts to pigeonhole the sacred texts may well have rested on precedents set by Pamphilus, who must certainly have reflected at some point about the contents of the Christian segments of the "sacred Scriptures" that he gave away.[39] The mysterious Euthalius, who edited the book of Acts and the Pauline Epistles, dividing them into chapters and equipping them with a biography and bibliography of Paul and a list of Old Testament quotations, claimed to have done some of his work in Caesarea, where he collated his text of Paul against a manuscript written by Pamphilus himself.[40] Though it is anything but clear whether Pamphilus contributed much to the "Caesarean" recension of the New Testament reconstructed by modern critics, it seems certain that he applied his standard methods of collation and correction to the Gospels and other New Testament texts.[41]

Pamphilus, in other words, taught his younger associates to correct manuscripts of the Bible in the course of close and protracted periods of joint work. These went on not only throughout the Great Persecution, in what must have been difficult conditions, but also, famously, in confinement, during the period from 5 November 307, when Pamphilus was arrested and imprisoned, until his death in 310.[42] The scholium to Esther reproduced in the Codex Sinaiticus states this explicitly: "Antoninus, the confessor, collated, and I, Pamphilus, corrected the volume in prison, by the favor and enlargement of God." Pamphilus probably viewed this collaborative effort as far more than a set of lessons in the techniques of textual criticism. Correcting and copying central Christian texts was a religious act. Origen and Ambrose, as we have seen, treated their joint work of correction as a form of Christian asceticism, which they pursued with passion. Jerome described the texts of Origen that Pamphilus wrote as the relics of a holy martyr: "If it is happiness to possess one letter by a martyr, how much the more so to have thousands of lines, which he [Pamphilus] seems to me to have marked with the traces of his blood?"[43]

The young men whom Pamphilus chose for their mastery of Greek culture and initiated into the textual study of the Bible found that they had joined a sacred community. Antoninus, who helped Pamphilus correct biblical manuscripts in prison, was martyred before him. So were the brothers Apphianus and Aedesius.[44] In Apphianus's case, Eusebius describes what seems almost a natural transition from biblical study to martyrdom: "And after he had been with us and had been drilled in holy studies and had taken part in lessons on the sacred Scriptures by the great martyr Pamphilus, he attained a virtuous state that was far from ordinary. Once he had prepared himself in this way for the perfection of martyrdom [as the next part of the discourse will show], all who saw were amazed, all who heard were full of wonder at his boldness, his freedom of speech, his constancy, his self-control, his words to the judge, his replies, and, beyond all these, his daring."[45] Study of the Bible with Pamphilus enabled Apphianus to lead the highest form of virtuous life—one characterized by the freedom of speech, prudence, and courage that had marked the wise man since Socrates, and that sometimes brought both pagan and Christian saints into conflict with political authority.

Like Apphianus, whose studies at Berytus had given him a command of Greek culture without corrupting him, Aedesius mastered Greek learning before Pamphilus initiated him into Christian scholarship: "Even before his brother felt the love of God, his dedication to philosophy put him in the lead. For he studied all sorts of things, and mastered not only Greek *paideia,* but Roman as well. And he shared Pamphilus's way of life for a long time."[46] Evidently, collaborative work on the Bible formed an organic part of a deeper and richer spiritual relationship, one in which Pamphilus offered his young disciples much more than training in the use of a set of technical tools.

Late in life, at the Council of Tyre in 335, Eusebius would find himself under attack for having failed to become a martyr with Pamphilus and his friends. Pottamon, who had been in prison with Eusebius, had himself lost an eye there. He reproached Eusebius for escaping "alive and without mutilation," and accused him of having made sacrifice as Roman officials demanded.[47] The criticism is harsh, and no further evidence supports it. Yet even Eusebius apparently felt a certain unworthiness as he contemplated the courage of another of Pamphilus's helpers, Porphyry. Not yet eighteen, Porphyry appeared before the judge and demanded the bodies of Pamphilus and his fellows for burial. His reward was brutal and immediate. Porphyry died before his friends in a slow fire, after being tortured, torn, and abraded with haircloths. Eusebius—who made clear by calling himself "Pamphili" that he took his teacher as a spiritual father—showed how much he admired *il miglior fabbro* when he described Porphyry as "a true nursling of Pamphilus, not yet eighteen . He had become a master of the art of penmanship, and his moderation and manners were beyond praise, as was proper for the disciple of such a man."[48] The truest form of discipleship would have led Eusebius, like Porphyry, not to the episcopal throne but to the fire.

Even after resisting the temptations of heroism, however, Eusebius followed in the scholarly path of his master. He applied the editorial techniques, explicit and tacit, that he learned from Pamphilus throughout his life. From the start of his career, however, Eusebius did more than ransack the materials and apply the methods that Pamphilus had used. Many of his earliest innovations had to do with the forms, as much as the content, of the books he created. Eusebius learned from the Hexapla, as we have seen, that a tabular presentation could make information take on radically new meanings. He applied this lesson to a number of problems. What first made Eusebius's approach to book-making distinctively different from that of Pamphilus was the ingenuity with which he applied Origen's provocative expedient—the use of tabular format to enable quick comparisons across the pages of a codex—to a variety of textual problems and tasks. He devised elegant new tools that made the most important texts accessible to readers. These texts brought his compilatory energy and imaginative sense of page design into play in highly creative ways, while at the same time engaging the precedents set by Origen and Pamphilus.

Like Origen, Eusebius felt himself to be confronted by multiple sacred texts that somehow had to be studied together, and he found new ways to synchronize them—just as he synchronized histories in his *Chronicle*. Earlier Christian writers had tried to find ways to make it easier to compare the accounts of Jesus's life and teachings in the four Gospels. Ammonius, for example, broke up the Gospels of Mark, Luke, and John and arranged extracts from them next to the parallel passages in Matthew. But this method, as Eusebius complained in a famous letter to one Carpianus, shattered the texts, making it impossible to read them in their integrity: "the continuous thread of the other three is necessarily broken, preventing a consecutive reading."

To avoid fragmenting the biblical texts, Eusebius devised a radically different approach. He divided the Gospels into numbered sections. Then he drew up ten tables, which listed parallel or related passages, first in all four Gospels, then in any three of them, then in any two, and finally set out those found in only one system. A simple, elegant system of numerical cues enabled the reader to move immediately from any passage to any parallel in any of the four Gospels:

A set of Eusebius's canon tables, showing parallel passages from the Four Gospels, from a Byzantine manuscript. Princeton University Library, MS Garrett 2.

A section of Gospel text, showing Eusebius's canon numbers on the left margin. In the bottom three cases, the bottom number indicates the table to be consulted; the top one designates the section of text beside it. Princeton University Library, MS Garrett 2, fol. 127 recto.

Before each section of the four Gospels stands a number in the margin, beginning with the first, then the second and third, and proceeding in order throughout until the end of the books. And underneath each number is marked a note in red, indicating in which of the ten canons the number occurs. (For example, if it is 1, it is clear that it is in the first canon; if 2, in the second; and so on as far as 10.) Hence, if you were to open any one of the four Gospels, and wish to light upon any chapter whatever, to know who else has said similar things and to find the relevant passages in which they treated of similar things, then find the number marked against the passage which you have before you, look for it in the canon which the note in red has suggested, and you will immediately learn from the headings at the start of the canon how many and which have said similar things. If you then find the numbers of the other Gospels parallel with the number which you have before you in the canon, and look for them in the appropriate places of each Gospel, you will find those passages which say similar things.[49]

Eusebius's canon tables, often dazzlingly illuminated, became a standard feature of New Testament manuscripts in a number of languages and cultures.[50]

Another tabular device, his *pinax* of the Psalms, had the opposite effect. One of the techniques of classical grammatical scholarship that Origen regularly applied to the interpretation of the Bible involved identifying the *prosopon,* or persona, who was speaking in any given passage.[51] Eusebius applied this principle systematically in his *Psalm Tables,* which dissected the Book of Psalms into the work of a series of individual speakers or authors, not all of whom Eusebius felt he could identify. This *pinax* proved considerably less popular than the Canon Tables, perhaps because he left it as a bare scholarly tool unaccompanied by clear instructions for users, unlike the Canon Tables.[52] Perhaps, however, like book 1 of the *Chronicle,* this work marked so strenuous an effort to hold contrasting views in productive tension that it made some readers uncomfortable.

But as a great specialist on early Christian books and scholarship, James O'Donnell, has pointed out, the triumphantly successful Canon Tables were extraordinarily original and effective information retrieval devices: the world's first hot links. They enabled readers not simply to rely on memory or to use rearranged texts of the bible, but to turn the four Gospels into a single web of cross-commentary—to move from text to text as easily as one could move from kingdom to kingdom in the *Canon.*[53] When Eusebius modeled his *Canon* on the Hexapla, he was not carrying off an isolated feat of sophisticated *mise-en-page.* Rather, he was revealing what would become a persistent strain in his work on texts: an effort to configure them, using layout, colors of ink, and other visual clues to lead readers through them rapidly and effectively. In Eusebius's introduction to his *Canon,* he proudly described how he had laid out parallel blocks of events in parallel columns for chronological clarity and easy reference. The same sensibility, the same concern for textual integrity and readers' comfort, inspired his Canon Tables. One of Eusebius's most intelligent and persistent students, Jerome, paid tribute to the master's design sense in a prominent way. Eusebius had his scribes use red ink to mark the divisions of the Gospels. Jerome had the annals of the different kingdoms in the *Canon* written in different inks, a Eusebian trick designed to make the work even easier to consult.[54] No early creator of codices understood more vividly than Eusebius the possibilities that the new form of the book created for effective display of texts and information.

Eusebius's ability to produce the *Chronicle* and the *Canon* and *Psalm Tables*—complex and demanding works, which required elaborate page layout, coordinated use of red and black ink, and continual attention to nontextual detail—reveal something vital about the culture of the library at Caesarea. The textual evidence about Pamphilus portrays him as carrying out his own scribal work, copying Origen and collating biblical manuscripts in his own hand. Evidently, however, the diocesan complex of buildings as it emerged under Eusebius's episcopate housed something resembling a staff of scribes trained well enough to follow complex directions and produce nontraditional texts. This infrastructure played a central role in many of Eusebius's projects.

If Eusebius's passionate interest in *mise-en-page* has largely escaped the attention of scholars, another central feature of his scholarly work in the next period of his life, the 310s and 320s, has fascinated them for decades. Long ago, Arnaldo Momigliano pointed out, drawing on Eduard Schwartz, that Eusebius made the direct quotation of documents, literary and archival, a central feature of his history of the church.[55] This became a lasting characteristic, one that sharply distinguished ecclesiastical from civil history, which usually took the form of a narrative uninterrupted by direct quotations.[56] More recently, Michael Hollerich has noted that many of Eusebius's works—theological ones as well as historical—took the form of mosaics, fashioned

A leaf from the chronological table of Eusebius, as translated by Jerome, in a manuscript of the fifth century CE. Note the visible underscoring that enabled the scribe to enter the complex text evenly and legibly. Bibliothèque Nationale, Paris, MS lat. 6400 B, fol. 289 recto.

from excerpts from earlier sources. He has portrayed Eusebius's career, in fact, as one long adventure in systematic quotation.[57]

These judgments reflect Eusebius's own statements about his methods. He emphasized more than once that the novelty of his approach to many subjects lay in his reliance on source research and his profuse citation of original texts. In the introduction to the *Chronicle,* for example, he emphasized that his work rested on systematic excerpting of a vast range of sources:

> I have gone through the varied historical works of the ancients, including the reports of the Chaldeans and Assyrians, the detailed accounts of the Egyptians, and the narratives that the Greeks present as certain—as if that were possible. These contained the dates of kings and Olympiads, that is, athletic games, and certain outstanding deeds done by barbarians and Greeks, brave men and cowards, as well as their marvelous armies, military leaders, wise men, heroes, poets, historians, and philosophers. I thought it would be proper to put all of this down in the briefest possible form, so far as it is really useful and relevant, and to add to the aforementioned the ancient history and chronology of the Hebrews, transmitted by the sacred scriptures. [58]

In his preface to the *Church History,* similarly, Eusebius claimed that his work was radically novel, and that it consisted in the creation of a particular kind of anthology:

> We are the first to attempt this enterprise, as if we were traveling on a deserted, unused road. We pray God to guide us and grant that we have the power of the Lord to

help us, for we cannot find even the bare footprints of men who have gone down the same road before us, except some small indications, through which they have left us partial accounts of their times, each doing so in his own way. . . . Accordingly, we have gathered from the scattered records everything that we believe will be relevant to the present subject, and culled, so to speak from intellectual meadows, everything the ancient writers said that is appropriate to it. We will try by using a historical approach to make them into a coherent whole.[59]

Citing passages like these, scholars have long noted that Eusebius practiced an intensely book-based form of learning. Only in a major Christian collection like that of Pachomius's monastery, partially represented by the Dishna papers, a varied collection found in Egypt, near Nag Hammadi, or that in Caesarea— a collection that included biblical texts, early Christian writings, and a fair number of pagan texts as well—could the *Chronicle* have been produced.[60] That sufficiently explains why "the documentary and archival character" of Eusebius's work, as it took shape in the bookish surroundings we have come to know, makes his writings "treasure troves for scholars on the trail of lost or fragmentary works."[61]

In fact, Eusebius's method, as well as his library, had particular, local roots in Caesarea. For Pamphilus did more than correct and meditate over the contents of his library. He thought hard about how to apply his books effectively in a polemic against Christian adversaries. Origen's enemies, Pamphilus noted, told other Christians not even to read his writings, as if they lacked the good moneychanger's knack for telling good specie from bad.[62] In fact, however, their attacks missed virtually all their marks. These critics claimed that humble Christians were treating Origen himself as a saint and his writings as sacred. Even when they found errors in Origen's works, moreover, they ignored one vital fact. Origen, who realized the mystery and obscurity of the Scriptures, often gave more than one interpretation at a time, allowing the *prudens lector* to choose the best one.[63] (*Ap. Or.* 3). Given these facts, Pamphilus confessed himself at a loss to understand the critics' motives, especially when some of the most savage among them appropriated Origen's ideas and claimed credit for them while reviling him, while others only repeated the critiques, and revealed under interrogation that they had not read Origen's books themselves.[64]

In order to mount the most compelling possible defense, Pamphilus compiled a long series of extracts from what he identified as Origen's chief works:

> Therefore, we have decided to work in the following way: to make our defense not with our own words or arguments, but with his own words, by which he attests, in his own language, that these objections that are made to him are actually foreign to him. For if we tried to make this claim in our own words, the suspicion might arise that we were concealing any errors on his part out of love for him. But when we use the words of the accused, and defend him against all the objections of his accusers in his own words, not with our own argument, what possible pretext can be left for attacking him—except for those who are moved not by desire for the truth, but by a sort of perverse desire to find fault? And since he is now the subject of our discourse, who can serve as a stronger witness on behalf of a dead man with his judges than his own works?[65]

Eusebius and Pamphilus "toiled together" on this work, as Eusebius later recalled.[66] Pamphilus laid out more than seventy quotations from Origen, interspersed with comments of his own, in just the first book (all that survives) of his *Apology* for his hero.[67] Evidently, then, he saw and used his library not only as a source for Christian teachings, but also as an arsenal for theological arguments. Pamphilus devoted some of his last months on earth to compiling these proof texts systematically for his Christian brothers, who were suffering in the Palestinian copper mines at Phaeno.[68] It seems likely that Pamphilus's library included earlier polemical works that served as his models, such as Josephus's polemical treatise *Against Apion*. And it seems certain that a young scholar could learn a vital lesson, as he sat at Pamphilus's side. Citation, at least when practiced systematically, could become "une méthode d'exposition, qui correspond à une forme de pensée."[69] Eusebius—who completed the *Apology for Origen* after Pamphilus's death—learned the uses of *bricolage* from his beloved master. Pamphilus, not Eusebius, first taught the vital lesson that excerpting could form the core of an effective technique for polemical writing.

One passage in Eusebius's *Church History*—a passage at which we have already looked, while examining the Hexapla—makes clear how deeply he took these principles to heart, and how elegantly he put them to use. In his description of the Hexapla, Eusebius indicated with notable precision how Origen had identified the manuscripts of the different versions he compiled:

With regard to these, on account of their obscurity (not knowing whose in the world they were) he merely indicated this: that the one he found in Nicopolis near

Actium, and the other in such other place. On the other hand, in the Hexapla of the Psalms, after the four well-known editions, he placed beside them not only a fifth but also a sixth and a seventh translation; and in the case of one of these he has indicated again that it was found at Jericho in a jar in the time of Antoninus the son of Severus.[70]

In this passage, as Giovanni Mercati showed long ago, Eusebius adapted—and slightly simplified—information also preserved in a separately transmitted mass of notes.

Probably a remnant of Eusebius's working materials, this text contains the exact words in which Origen described some of his versions and their sources:

> Concerning the fifth and sixth edition further.
>
> The fifth edition which I found in Nicopolis near Actium. The marginal notes in it show how far (another similar text) differs from it.
>
> The sixth edition which was found together with other Hebrew and Greek books in a jar near Jericho in the time of the reign of Antoninus [ms.: Antonius] the son of Severus.
>
> The translator of the fifth edition, having separated the 10th (Psalm) from the 9th, dividing it into two, goes on with the addition of one until the 69th (Psalm), then, joining the 70th to the 69th, he puts the numbers like those in our MSS, until the 113th (Psalm). From there, by joining some and dividing again others, he concludes with the 148th (Psalm).[71]

It took one of the greatest modern students of Eusebius, Eduard Schwartz, to work out the exact identity of these paragraphs.

They were, in fact, the subscriptions that Origen left at the end of each column in the Hexapla of the Psalms: hence the first-person description ("which I found") of the provenance of the fifth "edition." Though Eusebius omitted certain technical details, on the whole he reproduced the subscriptions precisely in his text—so precisely that he even put the verb to find *(heurein)* in the active voice in his description of the fifth "edition," and in the passive in his description of the sixth, exactly as Origen had.[72] From this detail—and many others—we can gain at least some impression of both the formal knowledge of biblical scholarship and the tacit mastery of text processing that Eusebius gained as he worked with Pamphilus, observing and taking part in his everyday regimen.

Yet here, as in his experiments in *mise-en-page,* Eusebius abstracted and built upon the lessons of his master. What Pamphilus devised as a particular technique designed to expose the malevolence of Christian opponents, Eusebius generalized into the most effective way to prove central theses about Christianity, in works directed against pagans, Jews, and other Christians. Pamphilus's work, moreover, rested on the works of Origen alone. And here too the differences are striking. Pamphilus's library, we suggest, began as a kind of relic collection, devoted to the memory of the confessor Origen and to the preservation, correction, and transmission of the text of the sacred Scriptures.

Over time, Eusebius, and later Jerome, began to describe this library in other terms as well: as a massive repository of texts, pagan, Jewish, and Christian, any and all of which the Christian reader might need to consult, excerpt, or copy. Jerome—admittedly before he saw the later diocesan library—claimed that Pamphilus deliberately set himself up as a Christian competitor to the creators of other great textual repositories: "the blessed

martyr Pamphilus . . . since he wished to match Demetrius
of Phalerum and Peisistratus in his zeal for the sacred library,
searched the whole world for images of the true intellects, and
their eternal monuments. He showed special zeal for the books
of Origen, and dedicated them to the library at Caesarea."[73]
In fact, however, it seems to have been Eusebius, more than
Pamphilus, who made the library the sort of collection that
challenged comparison with the most famous examples in the
Mediterranean world. We turn to the institution he built up.

As Eusebius rose to the rank of bishop and specialized in the
production of works based on excerpts, the library seems to
have developed in two complementary ways. Functions became
more specialized, in ways that left the library's new master less
involved in the physical making of books than Pamphilus had
been. Though Eusebius, like Pamphilus, left subscriptions that
attest to his work as a redactor of the Scriptures, later readers in
Caesarea did not lavish praise on his personal industry as a
scribe. Rather, the evidence portrays him as a deft entrepreneur,
a manager of others' systematic scribal labor. Eusebius's administrative talent underpinned his innovations in *mise-en-page.*
When, in the *Chronicle,* he devised a written armature for the
history of the world, he must already have known that local
scribes could produce clear and legible copies of this difficult,
complex new text. That alone helps to explain why he dared to
create a work of this kind.

The arc of Eusebius's career in the church probably detached
him from the preparation and coloring of papyri or skins, but
also enabled him to expand his skilled scribal work force. Unlike Origen, Eusebius became a bishop. Presumably he super-

vised a numerous clergy of presbyters, deacons, and others, some of whom could readily have served him as scribes. As a bishop, he probably also had independent access to funds that could pay for supplies and labor, as Origen had not. The sheer number of Christians in the empire had increased massively—exactly how massively we do not know—since Origen's day. Eusebius could undertake complex and costly projects to an extent that previous generations of Christian scholars could not have dreamt of. Accordingly, the activities of collecting, cataloguing, and text production carried out in the library seem to have grown in scale and intensity. Like Philodemus before him, Eusebius constructed a remarkably full apparatus of sources, meticulously designed to help him reconstruct in minute historical detail the development of the tradition to which he had pledged allegiance.[74]

The meticulous recent work of Andrew Carriker, who has reconstructed the library by close analysis of the sources of Eusebius's major works, reveals just how broad and solid a base of sources he worked from—and suggests how widely he must have cast his net for books. Where earlier scholars toiled to show that Eusebius more often used compendia and intermediary sources than the originals, Carriker argues that he had, and directly used, a massive run of pagan and Christian sources—a collection far larger than his teacher Pamphilus, or even his much admired Origen, would have needed. Working above all from Eusebius's own writings, Carriker makes clear that Eusebius extended into new fields the same kinds of collecting activities in which Pamphilus had specialized. The materials he added to the library included further accounts of martyrdoms, and a great many letters of Origen, which he catalogued as he had done the collection of Philo.[75] Eusebius also used massive amounts of ancient Near Eastern historiography and Middle Platonist philosophy, some of it in the form of epitomes but much of it in the originals. Exactly how much of this material belonged to the diocesan library itself is hard to say.[76]

Fragmentary evidence enables us to follow Eusebius on at least a few of his trips into the archives. He observed in his account of Origen's youth that "at that time [the second decade of the third century] there flourished many eloquent clergymen, and it is easy to find the letters which they inscribed to one another, which are still extant. They have been preserved down to our time in the library at Aelia [Jerusalem], which was fitted out by Alexander, who was then in charge of the church there. From it we have been able to gather the materials for the foundation of this work."[77] Eusebius then went on to list quite a range of materials that he evidently found in Jerusalem: "varied elegant writings," as well as letters, by Beryllus; unspecified works by Hippolytus; and a dialogue by Gaius that discussed the canon of Paul's letters.[78] Though vivid, these details do not quite satisfy. Did Eusebius have copies of these documents made and deposited in Caesarea? We do not know.

In some cases Eusebius clearly relied on materials in his own collections, as some revealing mistakes in dating show. He dated the martyrdoms of Pionius and Metrodorus, who died during the Decian persecution in 250 CE, for example, to the same time as that of the "marvelous and apostolic Polycarp," who was actually martyred in 155 CE or slightly later. Eusebius synchronized other crowd-pleasing death scenes as well, such as those of the Decian martyrs Carpus and Papylas, with that of Polycarp—all, evidently, because he worked from a single collection of *Acts* in which the texts that described their deaths appeared together.[79] Eusebius described this source as "the martyrdoms of the ancients that we have collected" and mentioned that a particular text, the martyrdon of Pionius, had been inserted into it.[80] In this and other cases, the fragmentary evidence reveals that Eusebius worked through his collections in Caesarea, text by text, following in his narrative the sometimes random order in which sources appeared in the library's boxes of rolls and codices.[81] Under the sidewalk, the beach: under the bumpy surface of the *Church History* lie the buried remains of dozens of material texts that Eusebius collected, copied, excerpted, and sometimes manipulated in arbitrary ways.

Tiny but telling clues suggest something of the range and diversity of the non-Christian texts in the library. An eleventh-century manuscript in the Österreichische National Bibliothek in Vienna, theol. gr. 29, contains half of Philo's work *On the Creation of the Universe*. It also boasts a *pinax,* or table of contents, listing eight other works by Philo, which no longer survive in Greek. Another note in the manuscript, to be discussed below, shows that it derives from a copy in the library of Caesarea. The *pinax* gives an impressive sense of the scale and quality of the collections of Philo that Eusebius assembled. The list of Philo's works that he drew up and inserted in his *Church History* confirms this impression—even though all of these materials taken together do not suffice to establish exactly which works of Philo were there.[82] Other evidence suggests—though the point cannot be proved beyond a doubt—that the library also contained a substantial collection of the philosophical, historical, rhetorical, and poetic works by pagan authors on which Eusebius drew so heavily in his apologetic works.[83]

Eusebius's eclectic enterprise as a collector was certainly not unique. George of Cappadocia, a slightly later bishop, compiled so rich a collection of books both "philosophical" and "Galilean" that Julian the Apostate took personal action to obtain them after George was lynched in Alexandria in 361.[84] But contemporary comments and later legends alike attest that Eusebius collected on an unusually grand scale. What Eusebius created, moreover, was more than a collection of books. It was also a center for their production—and it seems to have become a larger and more efficient one after Eusebius became bishop of Caesarea in 314. As bishop, Eusebius specialized in producing works that required massive help from collaborators. These works sometimes refer explicitly to the processes that brought them into being. In the *Preparation for the Gospel,* a work from this second period, Eusebius again and again introduces a quotation from an ancient source with a formula like *labon anagnothi* (taking this, read it). His language comes from the courtrooms of the day, in which advocates used formulas like this when calling on a "clerk or secretary to read the affidavit of a witness."[85] But it also reveals a particular social situation and set of institutions. Karl Mras, the editor of the *Preparation,* sketches these:

This massive compilation of extracts could hardly have taken shape without the collaboration of secretaries. In my view, the best way to imagine the situation is as follows. Eusebius sits on his episcopal throne, surrounded by his deacons, who are also secretaries (shorthand writers), in the diocesan library at Caesarea. Commands like "taking this, read it" . . . are naturally directed at the reader. But nothing stops us from assuming that they also applied to the deacons who surrounded Eusebius. What one deacon read aloud, the next one copied down. And at the conclusion of each reading, Eusebius offered his own commentary, which sometimes expanded into homilies, and which were also written down.[86]

Internal evidence confirms the core of this dazzlingly vivid, if slightly romanticized, conjectural narrative. As bishop, Eusebius continued to revise his early works, the *Chronicle* and the *Church History*. Both in the process of composition and in the course of these revisions, many errors and inconsistencies crept into his work. Often Eusebius himself omitted or distorted vital facts because he saw history as "an apologetic tool to promote and vindicate the truth of Christianity and the person and policies of Constantine and his sons."[87] Often, however, his slips are just that: errors and inconsistencies that seem to play no role in his larger arguments. In the second book of the *Church History*, for example, Eusebius remarked that Hegesippus, who came just after the Apostles, gave the most accurate account of the martyrdom of James the Just.[88] In the fourth book, however, he corrected himself twice, setting Hegesippus first under the emperor Hadrian (117–138), then under Antoninus Pius (138–161) or Marcus Aurelius (161–180), only to go off cheerfully leaving the attentive reader to weep in frustration, unable to determine even the generation in which Hegesippus wrote.[89] Errors like this—like the majority of Eusebius's dozens of abridged and sometimes mutilated quotations—did not contribute anything to the arguments he wished to make.

For the last century and more, scholars have used such inconsistencies to argue that Eusebius produced a number of editions of both the *Chronicle* and the *Church History* (three of the former, at last count). Yet a busy bishop could not have carried out even minor revisions in so many different books. Think in terms of an intellectual production line; of a bishop who could command subordinates to produce new books or revise old ones, and the whole story becomes far more plausible. The inconsistencies that reveal the change from one edition to another also reveal the necessary pressures and slippages of collaboration, even when managed by an impresario of learning as energetic and skillful as Eusebius. To produce these immense compilations, as to draw up copies of the *Canon* and equip sets of the Gospels with canon tables, Eusebius had to mobilize a flock of secretaries and notaries. This simple fact helps to explain why his extracts from extant sources are often faulty, and why they sometimes contradict his own descriptions and introductions.[90]

Like a great German professor, Eusebius relied on assistants to realize his massive research project. Like a great professor, he taught them his new techniques—like that of adding chapter headings, which, as Barnes suggests, they very likely applied to the Bible as well as to the sections of Eusebius's own writings.[91] And like a great professor, he self-consciously proclaimed the novelty of his methods, not only in set-pieces like the preface to the *Church History* already quoted, but throughout his massive oeuvre.[92] Eusebius readily admitted that his work resembled a mosaic, a collection of fragments gathered from other sources. Deftly altering an allusion to Clement of Alexandria's *Stromateis*—perhaps the most prominent and elaborate work of similar character by one of his predecessors—he advertised that, like a sedulous Sicilian bee, he had mastered the craft of reusing the works of his predecessors in his own, original way.[93] In fact,

Eusebius boasted that the collage-like character of the work represented one of its chief novelties.[94]

By 320 or so, we would argue, Eusebius's workplace must have become a substantial research institution, at once an archive, a library, and a scriptorium. Staffed by specialist scribes and notaries who worked with their bishop on a wide range of projects, it seems to have offered a wealth of holdings organized by author and perhaps by other categories. Boxes kept at least some of the rolls from harm, and bindings performed the same service for codices. The institution apparently suffered after Eusebius's death. Jerome, presumably drawing on an intermediary source, noted in *De viris illustribus* that Euzoios, Arianizing bishop of Caesarea from ca. 376 to ca. 379, "set out to restore the library of Origen and Pamphilus, which was deteriorating badly, by transferring it to parchment codices"—that is, he had the library's holdings copied from papyrus rolls and codices into parchment codices, no doubt an expensive and demanding process.[95] The Vienna manuscript of Philo's treatise *On the Creation of the World* contains a brief note, written in the form of a cross, that neatly confirms this account: "Bishop Euzoios had new copies made in codices."[96] Evidently, Eusebius had built something larger and more lasting than any of his predecessors—a collection so large and varied that it proved hard to keep up. That perhaps explains why imaginative scribes devised Caesarean provenances for texts written even after this time. As the Alexandrian library became a symbol of Greek culture and scholarship, that of Caesarea had become a massive symbol of Christian erudition, a library of the mind.

By the end of Eusebius's career, his abilities as a bookman became famous—so famous that they enabled him to reconfigure existing forms of literary and documentary culture in yet another highly original and productive way. As Constantine built the Eastern empire, the world around Eusebius changed, and his position in Caesarea offered him new opportunities. As always, he seized them. At some point after 335, when Eusebius returned from Constantinople to Caesarea, Constantine wrote to him to ask for help in producing Bibles for Constantinople. In his life of Constantine, Eusebius quotes the letter, word for word. The emperor begins by describing the situation in his new capital: "In the city which bears our name by the sustaining providence of the Savior God a great mass of people has attached itself to the most holy Church, so that with everything there enjoying great growth it is particularly fitting that more churches should be established." Then he asks Eusebius to fill the need by providing "fifty volumes with ornamental leather bindings, easily legible and convenient for portable use, to be copied by skilled calligraphists well trained in the art, copies that is of the Divine Scriptures, the provision and use of which you well know to be necessary for reading in church."[97]

Producing fifty Bibles—or even fifty New Testaments— would have been a formidable task. It required, in the first place, a massive blood sacrifice, since a large parchment codex might consume the skins of one hundred or more cows. Constantine clearly knew as much, and did not expect a bishop— even the bishop of a rich city—to have access to so vast a quantity of parchment at one time. Rather, he explained, the *rationalis* (financial officer) of the diocese of Oriens would provide parchment (and, perhaps, ink and other supplies as well): "Written instructions have been sent by our Clemency to the man who is in charge of the diocese that he see to the supply of all the materials needed to produce them."[98] Later in the document Constantine also promised the use of "two public vehicles"—the carts of the *cursus velox,* or express service—to transport the copies to Constantinople.[99] Eusebius, for his part, evidently knew how to mobilize the skilled labor that the task demanded: "The preparation of the written volumes with utmost speed," Constantine explained, "shall be the task of your Diligence."[100] The emperor suggested that one of Eusebius's deacons might accompany the books, and would be suitably rewarded for doing so. Evidently the bishop suited his action to his patron's words. "Immediate action followed," he wrote, "as we sent him threes and fours in richly wrought bindings."[101] (*VC* 4.37.1).

Constantine's letter and Eusebius's account of his response have occasioned much debate among historians of the church and of the Christian book. Many have wondered what Eusebius meant when he said that he sent the emperor "threes and fours" *(trissa kai tetrassa):* books laid out in three or four columns; books copied in quires with three or four bifolia per quire; or three or four copies at a time?[102] Scholars have also debated whether, when Constantine asked for "fifty *somatia* of the Sacred Scriptures," he wanted complete Bibles, which would have represented an innovation, or sets of the four Gospels, which had begun to be produced regularly in the third century.[103] Recently, the late T. C. Skeat revived the old suggestion that two of the extant fourth-century pandect Bibles might have been among the volumes that Eusebius produced. These monumental codices, one almost intact, the other in a sadly fragmentary condition, are now known as Vaticanus (or Codex B, in the terminology of New Testament textual criticism) and Sinaiticus

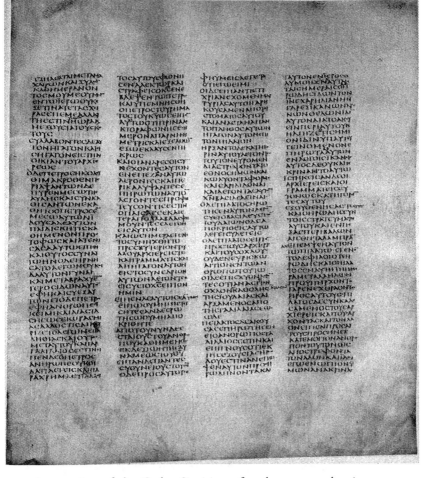

An opening of the Codex Sinaiticus, fourth century, showing two pages of the Gospel of Luke. British Library Add. MS 43725, ff. 244v.– 245.

(Codex ?). Both rank among the most impressive products of fourth-century book culture. If they were indeed produced at Caesarea under Eusebius' supervision—a hypothesis that seems tempting, though by no means proven—they would provide striking evidence that he commanded the services of numerous skillful scribes.[104]

Perhaps doubting that Eusebius could have accomplished such a task, some scholars have sought other interpretations for Constantine's request, and other provenances for the two fourth-century pandects: perhaps they were written at Alexandria under Athanasius, in response to a request from the emperor Constantius. But a number of arguments add up to a strong, if circumstantial, case in favor of identifying the two pandects as volumes produced by Eusebius in response to Constantine's command. Paleographical analysis indicates that the two codices came from the same scriptorium, which was probably in either Caesarea or Alexandria. Their magnificence argues strongly for imperial patronage. But it is the sophistication of the two pandects' *mise-en-page* that suggests most strongly that they might have originated in Caesarea under Eusebius, in the same scriptorium that invented and reproduced so many major innovations in the application of the column to the display of Christian text.

Each of these codices employs varying arrangements of multiple columns per page to display different kinds of text. Prose books of the Bible are written in three columns per page in Vaticanus, while Sinaiticus, uniquely, presents four. The Psalms and other poetic texts, on the other hand, are laid out two columns per page and arranged *per cola et commata* rather than without respect to word divisions, as ancient books were usually written. T. C. Skeat, moreover, ingeniously suggested that even the differences in the two manuscripts' layout are revealing. Perhaps, he conjectured, producing these manuscripts turned out to be so demanding and expensive that Eusebius, after starting on the grand scale with the Codex Sinaiticus, actually broke off work on that manuscript to produce the Codex Vaticanus, in a format that would consume only half as much parchment as the larger one.[105] In one of his very last writings, Skeat evoked Constantine and other members of his household, examining the great manuscripts that Eusebius had produced—and reiterated his view that "Vaticanus is the sole survivor of that historical occasion."[106] Whatever their actual provenance, these two magnificent products of fourth-century book culture powerfully suggest the heights that Eusebius's scriptorium, under Constantine's patronage, could have reached.

A second experiment, perhaps even bolder than the *Chronicle* itself, seems to have represented an earlier effort on Eusebius's part to meld ecclesiastical scholarship with official information processing. According to Jerome, Eusebius completed his *Onomasticon,* a detailed gazeteer of Palestine, at some point after he put the finishing touches to the *Church History*—probably, it now seems, in the 320s.[107] In the prefatory letter to this ambitious work Eusebius promised his readers a fund of information: "I shall set out the cities and villages contained in Holy Scripture in the ancestral tongue, designating what places they are, and how we name them, whether similarly to the ancients or differently." As usual, he also planned to marshal this immense amount of information in reader-friendly, easily accessible form: "So, from the whole divinely-inspired Scripture, I shall collect the names that are sought, and set each one down in alphabetical order, for easy retrieval of names when they happen to occur here and there in the readings." He even set out to add substantial visual aids: "a map of ancient Judaea from the whole book, dividing the allotted territories of the twelve tribes," and an image of Jerusalem with a plan of the Temple.[108]

This complex project—which, if carried out, was not fully preserved—drew on cartography and manuscript illustration, as well as Eusebius's beloved systematic tables, to make a vast amount of detail easily accessible. Like Eusebius's other projects, it clearly began in the realm of ecclesiastical learning. But like so many of his other efforts, the *Onomasticon* soon transcended its origins. It seems certain that Eusebius gathered some of his information in the field, as he visited sites in the course of his travels.[109] He assured readers that he would produce his plan of the Temple "after comparison with the existing remains of the sites"—a clear promise that he would carry out an antiquarian investigation at first hand, and a powerful testimony to the way that travel writing and antiquarian scholarship stimulated and supported each other, in the ancient world as in the early modern period.[110]

But the *Onomasticon* also offers a great deal of precise information that Eusebius would have found it hard to gather on his own. He gave the distances between dozens of cities in "miles" (numbers of mileposts). More strikingly still, he noted the positions of a number of Roman garrisons.[111] It seems more likely that this precise information was collected and filed by the imperial government and its armies than by ecclesiastics. Systematic pilgrimage to the Holy Land had barely begun when Eusebius wrote: he may have hoped to encourage pilgrims with his book. But Roman officials and military commanders had amassed and stored geographical information for centuries, ever since the Augustan *cursus publicus* took responsibility for arranging the movements of officials and their families.[112] "In the provincial capital of Caesarea," as Peter Thomsen noted long ago, "Eusebius would have had easy access to official itineraries, either in the form of the itineraries that we have [such as the Antonine] or in that of maps"[113] made after Constantine reorganized the eastern part of the empire. It seems likely that Eusebius, like the compiler of the Peutinger map a few decades later, did pioneer work as he translated these materials into a new form for Christian use. And it is certain that two decades or so after he began work on the *Chronicle,* Eusebius was still experimenting with format and *mise-en-page,* and still redefining Christian scholarship. By his choices and his omissions, he laid out a vision of Palestine as sacred space that forms a fascinating, if less elaborate, counterpart to the *Chronicle*'s ordering of time.[114] In this case too, as in the *Chronicle,* he laid down the outlines for a secular, even millennial project. More than a thousand years later, the most erudite antiquaries in Catholic and Protestant Europe were still trying to establish detailed Christian geographies and chorographies of the Holy Land.[115]

One last work of Eusebius's, a text that we have already examined in passing, proved that he could and did collect, and sometimes publish, documents produced in the imperial chancery. None of his books was more innovative in form; none has proved more controversial in modern scholarship than the *Life of Constantine* that he left unfinished when he died in 339 CE.[116] An imperial panegyric, the *Life* challenged convention in many ways, not least by omitting the sorts of battlefield triumphs for which emperors were normally and effusively praised. Like Porphyry, who quoted primary sources in his life of Plotinus, and Philostratus, who quoted letters in his life of Apollonius of Tyana, Eusebius stuffed his work on the first Christian emperor with primary sources: in this case, some fifteen imperial documents, from 324 on. Some were originals signed by the emperor, some were Latin copies that Eusebius apparently translated (though scholarly controversy rages on this point). Some of them, like the emperor's letter asking for fifty Bibles, Eusebius received in his official capacity. Some were perhaps provided by a friendly official, such as the imperial notary Marianus.[117]

More than once, Eusebius explicitly stated that he had far more documents at his disposal than he had space to quote. He regretted this fact, since the omitted texts vividly expressed the emperor's piety and love of the Church.[118] At one point, Eusebius expressed the hope that "there may be an opportunity to assemble these in a special collection, so as not to disrupt the sequence of our present account." This amounted to a proposal for something like an anthology of Constantine's legislation regarding the Christian church, a work that would have been even more documentary in its texture and flavor than the *Life* or the *Church History*.[119] Nothing in Eusebius's earlier work adumbrates the range and depth of the documentation to which he now had access. It seems clear that government archives had preserved, and now supplied, a substantial portion of this material.[120]

Eusebius did not always reproduce the documents exactly, and he sometimes drew tendentious inferences that could not be verified, since in a number of cases he cited documents, but did not quote them word for word.[121] But these flaws, as we have seen, marked nothing new in his work, and in this case too could have resulted in part from the poorly coordinated efforts of collaborators. Certainly there is no reason to accuse him of general bad faith, as many students of the *Life of Constantine* have done. Centuries of effort by scholarly skeptics have failed to show that Eusebius sytematically falsified these texts. One of the documents he cited, moreover, has turned up on a papyrus.[122] As before, Eusebius created a new literary form by enriching narrative with the creations of late antique documentary culture: "Eusebius was an innovative writer in many other spheres, and the very task of writing about a Christian emperor presented new problems and called for new solutions."[123] As before, his work exercised a vast influence on later readers and writers, but found little direct imitation.

Eusebius's comprehensive enterprise had more than one parallel. Scholars in many traditions worked extensively on texts that they considered profound, holy, or at least vital for practical purposes. They drew up canons, corrected texts, and added visual aids. Sometimes they even employed disciplined crews of scribes to produce effectively uniform texts. A look at some of their projects will make clear that the imperial age and late antiquity saw many efforts to compile and organize traditions, some of which required substantial expense and ingenious organizational efforts. But it will also highlight the originality of Eusebius's work in Caesarea.

Epicureans, for example, took a strong interest in questions of textual criticism. Demetrius of Laconia (2nd century BCE) "distinguished between reliable editions of Epicurus and corrupt and interpolated copies, and within the school he defended criteria for determining the original statements of the Master."[124] The library of Philodemus boasted a number of Demetrius's works, and showed a similar inspiration: at its core were copies of most or all of the thirty-seven books of Epicurus's great work *On Nature,* sometimes multiple ones. Preserving and correcting these and other classic texts was clearly a central part of Philodemus's "cultural project," which also involved massive efforts to reconstruct the history of philosophy over the centuries.[125]

Another pagan philosopher much closer to Eusebius in time and space, Porphyry, came closer to Pamphilus and Eusebius alike in his editorial activities, which reflected his concern for the condition and legibility of manuscripts. He made clear in his *Life of Plotinus,* which he wrote as an introduction to his teachers works, that he had extensive knowledge of Plotinus's works, from the earliest ones on, in the original manuscripts:

> When Plotinus wrote something, he could not stand to look at it again, or even to read and go through it, because his sight did not serve him well in reading. When he wrote, he did not aim at beauty when he formed the letters, nor did he divide the syllables clearly, or pay attention to spelling, but he kept his mind fixed on the sense, and he astonished all of us by continuing to do this until his death.[126]

More important, as we have already seen, Porphyry noted that he had redacted Plotinus's core texts personally, adding the sorts of aids for the reader that Eusebius and his scribes added to the texts of the Bible..[127] Porphyry's editorial reach may have exceeded his grasp. Though he describes what sounds like a table of contents for the *Enneads*, this list does not survive in the manuscript tradition and may never have existed. It is not clear what form Porphyry's prefatory summaries took, or if he drew them up as systematically as he claimed.[128] Nonetheless, it seems clear that he undertook efforts quite similar to those that Pamphilus would undertake for Origen and the Bible, and Eusebius for many more texts. Eusebius certainly knew about this editorial enterprise.

Members of other philosophical schools as well took a serious interest in the details of script and layout. The late Aristotelian commentator Simplicius, for example, remarked in his commentary on the *Categories* that "we commonly write the *diple* and the *koronis* beside the margins of the text; these signify nothing by themselves, but signify something with the written text."[129] The manuscripts of Simplicius's commentators often have the *diple*, or small cross, placed in the margin. Christian Wildberg has shown that these indicated word-for-word quotations—a practice that editors of the philosophical fragments quoted by Simplicius have often ignored, to their cost.[130]

More generally, scholars working in any number of textual traditions during the first centuries of the Christian era made systematic efforts to correct and standardize authoritative texts. Controversy surrounds the date and nature of the processes that established the canon of the Hebrew Bible of Torah, Nevi'im and Ketuvim. Nonetheless Talmudic evidence suggests that particular individuals were officially paid during the Second Temple period to examine and correct texts of the Bible.[131] The New Testament was also redacted at some point into a coherent whole studded with cross references. The Mishna, or Jewish code of law, was edited by Yehuda ha-Nasi (d. 217 CE) and his contemporaries.[132] And the Palestinian Talmud and its even more complex cousin, the Babylonian Talmud, that immense and magnificent mosaic of sources, were probably redacted a number of times, as modern analysis shows, and became all the richer for the multiple voices that were allowed to speak on their pages.[133]

One of the grandest of all these projects, as well as the most systematic in execution, was the codification of the Roman law that began under Diocletian. The creation of the Theodosian Code between ca. 429 and 438 CE marked one high point in this process, which culminated in the compilation of the first three sections of the *Corpus* of Roman law, at the command of the emperor Justinian, between 527 and 535 CE. Consider just one segment of Justinian's enterprise, the *Digest*, or *Pandects*. In December 530 Justinian ordered that more than 1,500 controversial *libri*, works written by older lawyers but still considered authoritative in the courts, be condensed into 50 books. These were to present all the usable material, pruned of obsolete matter and organized by subject headings. A committee of elite lawyers headed by Tribonian accepted this charge. They completed the *Digest*, or *Pandects*, a massive compilation of more than 9,000 passages that had to be excerpted from the original works, reordered, and redacted, in December 533. To carry out this project on the fast track they employed some thirty-nine "scriptores," a team that even Eusebius would have envied.

Still closer to Eusebius is a Christian enterprise that Richard Rouse and Charles McNelis have recently reconstructed, one based in the North Africa of the fourth or fifth century. The Donatists, as is well known, felt special contempt for the "traditores" who had given up copies of the Sacred Scriptures to their persecutors. It is not surprising, then, that Donatist scholars drew up stichometry figures—apparently exact measurements, cast in artificial units of sixteen syllables—for the books of the Old and New Testaments and the works of Cyprian, a North African theologian whom they regarded as one of their own. The author of the Cyprian list made clear that he was trying to stabilize what he regarded as the true text, one superior to those commercially available in Italy: "Because the index of verses in Rome is not clearly given, and because in other places too, as a result of greed, they do not preserve it in full, I have gone through the books one by one, counting sixteen syllables per line, and have appended to each book the number of Vergilian hexameters [conventionally taken as sixteen syllables long] it contains."[134]

A particularly striking parallel to Eusebius's masterly management of scribal book production comes from the pagan world of Roman law. A manuscript commentary on Ulpian's *libri ad Sabinum,* probably written not long before the codification of the *Corpus juris* by Justinian, preserves fragments of lectures. Partly technical, partly fluid and colloquial—at one point the lecturer exclaims "beautiful!" to emphasize the power of a nice point of law—these notes give a vivid sense of day-to-day practices in the legal classroom. The teacher instructs his students, in one passage, to "skip 50 lines, down to 'et cum res venit'"; in another, to "skip 10 lines, down to 'aliis quoque modis'"; in still another, to "skip 25 lines, down to 'tutelam.'"[135] These stray remarks, possibly recorded in one of the lecture halls of the great law school at Berytus, seem to refer to standardized manuscript copies of Ulpian's work—codices through which the teacher led his students, focusing their attention on selected passages.[136] Like their successors in the great Italian law schools of the Middle Ages, the Roman jurists may have commissioned particular scribes or stationers to produce uniform textbooks.[137]

In scale and influence, Eusebius's achievements as a self-conscious, articulate impresario of manuscript publication remain historically distinctive. It took both Eusebius's extensive experience with systems of text retrieval and reference, and the unique resources for research assistance and scribal reproduction that he enjoyed in Caesarea, to make possible the production of his chronological tables and a great many of his other works. Eusebius's multiple new ways of representing the past involved much more than the routine rewriting of old texts. They represented as brilliant, and as radical, a set of new methods for the organization and retrieval of information as the nineteenth-century card catalogue and filing system would in their turn. If the chronological questions Eusebius and his anonymous helpers put were traditional, the answers he found glittered with methodological and formal novelty. And the very fact that some of his chief successes lay in the visual display of chronological information helps to explain both why Eusebius decided to create this new form of history and how he was able to succeed. Only in Caesarea, only in the hands of Eusebius, who gradually forged a new kind of working environment there for both the study and the production of sacred books, could this long series of tables, maps, and literary mosaics have taken their startling new shapes. Attention to the dialectical relation between the library and scriptorium and the books produced there can reveal much that no internal analysis of Eusebius's work, however probing, will ever explain.

A final point has to do with the world outside Eusebius's library. It seems likely that his elegant books served a particular purpose in the economy of relations between Caesarea and its emperor. When Eusebius drafted the *Chronicle,* its vision of all of history culminating in the Roman Empire was only an alluring prophecy—at least from the Christian standpoint. But Constantine's accession turned prophecy into history. By making special books that drew on his scholarly efforts to celebrate Constantine's achievement and to serve his needs, Eusebius won the interest and gratitude of his ruler. Scholarship enabled him to attain the results that effective eloquence—which he also possessed—had won for the provincial elites of earlier centuries. His scholarship and his neat demonstration that only he could clarify the disorderly and threatening realms of competing chronologies, genealogies, and histories made him a particularly deserving object of patronage—especially when he couched his results in so novel and attractive a physical form.

The formation of the library at Caesarea by Pamphilus, who devoted his personal wealth to the acquisition of Christian books, was in itself nothing new. What came afterward was revolutionary. We have already described Eusebius's favorable relations with the emperor; other producers of Christian books were to receive comparable patronage later in the century. This alone was an immense transformation. Imperial patronage outweighed many times over the support that any private patron could have offered. The role of the emperor as patron, and his overwhelming preeminence in that capacity, formed essential elements of imperial rule, established earlier by Augustus and intensified in the transformation of principate into dominate in the late third century. It proved essential to Eusebius's achievement in its final form. The new scholarship of Caesarea rested, in short, not only on the peculiar resources available there, but also on the larger transformation of East Roman society that took place in the late third and fourth centuries.

Coda:
Caesarea in History
and Tradition

ORIGEN, Pamphilus, and Eusebius, we have argued, forged their innovations in producing and designing works of Christian learning in different historical contexts, which partly explain both the limitations and the successes of their careers. Origen operated within a traditional model of personal patronage. His close relationship with Ambrose mirrored those that had supported the efforts of bookish philosophers at least since the beginning of the period of Roman domination of the Mediterrancan world. Eusebius began his career in a similar context, under the spiritual and scholarly tutelage of Pamphilus. But he then took advantage of changes in the internal structure of the Christian church, and of the epochal novelty of a Christian emperor ready to patronize specifically Christian scholars, to build a new infrastructure for learning.

Still, both men's most strikingly innovative works—the *Hexapla* and the *Chronicle*—reflect a common understanding of the nature of Christian truth. This vision, we suggest, was the fundamental driving force behind their need to make such strange and complex books. These massive compilations made creative use both of the codex—originally used primarily as a note-book—and of complex columnar formats—found previously, if at all, in administrative documents and accounts, rather than in works of learning. By adopting these expedients, the two men managed to incorporate the traditions of barbarians, both phys-ically and conceptually, within a schema both Greek and Chris-tian, subordinating them to Christian truth, but not erasing, or even softening the edges, of their otherness.

These texts would have been a startling sight for contempo-rary readers, particularly the Hexapla with its first, unintelligible columns: Hebrew letters, read from left to right, followed by a word-for-word Greek transliteration that would have been only slightly less daunting. The *Chronicle,* though even more visually impressive, might have been a bit less intimidating at first. At least it did not physically incorporate a foreign language or a non-Greek writing system. But the conceptual structure of the *Chronicle*—founded, as was its innovative arrangement, on what Eusebius had learned from studying Origen's Hexapla—posed an even sharper threat to a cozy, inward-looking mental-ity that assumed the superiority of Greek culture to all that was other. The two-part organization of the *Chronicle* implicitly ad-mitted that the problems presented by primeval history were in-soluble. It also set barbarian traditions alongside those of the Greeks and their *soi-disant* cultural heirs, the Romans, in the tables of the *Canon.* Eusebius's cosmopolitan history reduced Greek learning to one voice among many, none of them clearly authoritative. Indeed, if any tradition dominated Eusebius's ap-proach to world history, it was the barbarian one of the Jews, as represented by the chronology of the Old Testament. Rather than domesticate this foreign mass through some kind of *translatio Graeca,* the core of the *Chronicle,* which dealt with pre-Roman, pre-Christian history, used the most sophisticated tools of Greek learning to subordinate that very tradition to one that came from outside it. Both language and history, these two books suggested, were irreducibly polyglot, as seen from a Christian standpoint that did justice both to orthodox theology and to the textual record.

Both Origen and Eusebius adopted this new attitude toward barbarian learning because they took seriously the fundamental problem that orthodox Christianity created for itself when it decided, in the late second century, to incorporate the Jewish Scriptures within the nascent Christian biblical canon. By doing so, Christianity introduced alien elements—barbarian and non-Christian—into its very fabric. The new church founded itself on a tradition that it could never fully incorporate or reduce to sameness. Of course, many Christians, learned and otherwise, saw no serious problem here. Origen's own Platonizing allegory of the Old Testament offered a solution to part of the difficulty that was to have a powerful influence on the Church's reading of Hebrew Scripture across the millennia that followed. Nevertheless, the tradition of Christian scholarship founded at Caesarea also found more direct intellectual heirs, scholars who continued to worry at this problem in just the ways that Origen and Eusebius had: by studying Hebrew, by conversing with Jews and converts, by taking seriously the learning of those outside their own cultures, and, above all, by making rich, complex, and innovative books.

One of the first to take up this challenge was Jerome of

Stridon, who put Origen's Hexapla to a use its maker had surely never intended: as a crib to support his production of a new Latin Old Testament translated from the Hebrew, and of extensive commentaries on the Hebrew prophets. In Jerome's biblical scholarship, the Greek translations compiled in the Hexapla served to defend his new version against the authority of the Septuagint, until that time the universally accepted Old Testament of the church. Working in Bethlehem at the end of the fourth and the beginning of the fifth centuries, Jerome had access to the full riches of the library that Eusebius had created at Caesarea, where successive bishops had treasured and maintained it as the chief ornament of their see. Jerome himself, moreover, followed central strands of the Caesarean tradition in learning. He was perhaps the only Christian in late antiquity who could justly claim, as he proudly did, the title of *vir trilinguis*—at least in the sense that his scholarship moved with assurance, if not always without error, among Hebrew, Greek, and Latin.

Jerome's books show none of the formal novelty of the *Hexapla* and the *Chronicle,* and only intermittent efforts to emulate their cosmopolitan spirit. He clearly appreciated the formal innovations that his predecessors made. After all, he translated both book 2 of Eusebius's *Chronicle,* the *Canon,* and Eusebius's work on the geography of Palestine. He even reformatted the *Chronicle,* in a way that Eusebius might have appreciated. Jerome instructed future scribes to follow his own practice and assign a particular color to each kingdom, to be used consistently, page after page. Showing his customary distaste for excessive expenditure on elaborate books, Jerome assured readers that he had devised this labor-intensive improvement on the original not "to give the eyes mindless delight" but to distinguish the dynasty lists, "which are so close to one another that they are almost intermingled."[1] Yet Jerome also amputated almost the entire first book of Eusebius's *Chronicle,* along with the deeper chronological questions that it raised, and reproduced none of the visual materials that Eusebius had added to his text on the place names of Palestine.

But on another level, Jerome's commentaries on the Prophets admitted the polyglot nature of the Christian tradition into their very heart, perhaps even more deeply than did the works of Origen and Eusebius. He systematically incorporated elements of Jewish biblical exegesis in his comments and placed a biblical text founded ultimately on Jewish manuscripts in the position of final authority. By doing so Jerome endowed his commentaries with an internal complexity different from that of the Hexapla and the *Chronicle,* but at least as profound. Jerome helped to provide the Western church with its own Latin Bible—and thus to make it, for centuries, effectively independent of Greek and Hebrew traditions. But he also bequeathed to it an ideal of trilingual scholarship that would turn out to be highly provocative and productive in later centuries.

The model of Christian scholarship that Origen, Pamphilus, and Eusebius had created underwent many further changes. In some cases, the similarities between later developments and the precedents we have examined did not reflect any direct historical filiation. When medieval biblical scholars used elaborate designs and systems of marginal signs to fix the biblical history of the world in their and their readers' memories, they were using the possibilities of scribal book production as creatively as Origen and Eusebius had, and for similar ends, but had no idea that they were applying a model forged in Caesarea.[2] The same seems to have been true of the theologians and encyclopedists who, in the thirteenth century and after, drew up section headings, indexes, and other devices to make their compilations readily accessible to busy preachers searching for the right biblical passage, gloss, or *exemplum*.[3] In the same manner, the Christian biblical scholars who began, in the thirteenth century and after, to study rabbinical commentaries and the Talmud, and developed complex and partley contradictory attitudes toward Jewish learning, did so because they found themselves confronting living Jews and trying to convert them, not because they remembered Origen.[4]

Still, the practices and institutions of scholarship founded in third- and fourth-century Caesarea became something more than a single thread in the historical tapestry of Christian erudition. In the fifteenth and sixteenth centuries, when humanists like Valla and Erasmus insisted that the Vulgate Latin Bible must be corrected against the Greek New Testament, they saw themselves as following in the footsteps of the scholars of ancient Caesarea. Erasmus, who himself published the first Greek-Latin edition of the New Testament in 1514, numbered Origen and Eusebius, as well as Jerome, among his predecessors in the reformatting of the Bible. He believed that both Origen and Eusebius had had a hand in devising the canon tables—clear evidence that he connected both with the formal arrangement of the Biblical text.[5]

Though scholars have rightly seen that Erasmus modeled his persona as a scholar on Jerome, he owed Origen a great deal as well—much of it highly substantive.[6] For him, as for many contemporary and later biblical scholars. "Origen's Hexapla, with its parallel columnar disposition of different Hebrew and Greek versions of the Bible, provided the model for how scholarship could elucidate sacred meaning."[7] Erasmus's two-column New Testament, which offered the Greek text to readers as a check on his own new Latin version, was a modest tribute to the ancient man of steel. Hebrew scholars offered much grander ones. Cardinal Ximenes, impresario of a team of scholars based in Alcalá de Henares, looked back to Origen when he organized the production of the first of several stately polyglot Bibles—editions that laid out the text of the Old Testament, as well as the New, as Origen had, column by column. In Ximenes's Bible the Hebrew Old Testament and the Septuagint flanked the Vulgate, while the Aramaic Targum of Onkelos appeared at the foot of the page, with a Latin translation of its own. The cardinal found this arrangement worrying, and compared the Latin text in the central column to Christ, crucified between two thieves.[8]

Many later Christian Hebraists shared his view, and mastered Jewish learning only to snipe at the whimsy and pedantry of Jewish scholarship, but the foreign genie had clearly escaped the Christian bottle. A series of polyglot Bibles, climaxing in the great London edition of 1653–1657, made clear how wide the range of ancient versions was, and how many problems they posed for anyone who hoped to maintain the perfection of a particular text of the Old Testament.[9] Hebraists, many of them more open-minded than Ximenes, mastered many different Jewish methods of biblical interpretation, from the rationalistic to the Kabbalistic. Many scholars taught, and many more learned, Hebrew at schools and universities, and a vast range of Jewish texts were translated into Latin—all because the early modern successors of Origen realized that they could not edit or explicate the Christian Scriptures without acknowledging that they contained central elements alien to Christianity.[10]

Christian chronologers, similarly, would reenact the struggles of Africanus and Eusebius. In the late sixteenth and seventeenth centuries, it became clear both that the different texts of the Old Testament offered divergent chronologies and that other ancient traditions flatly contradicted the Bible. Erudite chronologers from Gerardus Mercator and Joseph Scaliger down to James Ussher and Isaac Vossius did their best to lay out the sources and reconcile their differences. In the end, however, they found the task as impossible as Eusebius had—especially since they had to confront new information from the Americas and China that seemed reliable and broke the bounds of biblical chronology. In many ways, their knowledge of the older traditions of Egypt and Babylon, which they owed to Eusebius, prepared them as well as anything could have to try to assimilate this new information into the inherited framework of biblical time.[11] Christian chronology remained—and remains—recognizably the enterprise of Africanus and Eusebius, permanently suspended between a basic faith in the reliability of the Bible and a commitment to do justice to nonbiblical sources as well.

The models created in Caesarea proved even more prominent in other traditions. Again and again, ecclesiastical history was defined by its profuse quotation of written authorities. Eusebius, as Rosamond McKitterick has written, "constructed the Christian past in terms of books and authors."[12] Bede—to name only one of his emulators—did exactly the same when he filled whole chapters of his *Ecclesiastical History of the British Nation* with excerpts from Adamnan's book on the Holy Land and the Abbot Ceolfrid's exhaustive letter on the observance of

Easter.[13] The need to assemble, assess, and excerpt documents had consequences on the institutional as well as the textual level. Again and again, the demands of ecclesiastical scholarship, which could not serve its polemical purposes unless it rested on massive textual foundations, forced scholars to look for substantial, long-lsting income streams and, if they found support, to create collaborative research centers.

In the 1550s, when Matthias Flacius Ilyricus and Caspar von Nidbruck set out to produce the first Protestant history of the church at Magdeburg, they created something like a research institute for ecclesiastical history. Its members—who included young scribes and more experienced scholars, each with his own specialized job—hunted down, collected, and assessed masses of manuscript and printed evidence, excerpted from it everything that seemed vital, and distilled from their notes the so-called *Magdeburg Centuries*.[14] Physically weighty and apparently erudite, the *Centuries* demanded a response from Catholic scholars, determined to prove that history and tradition both stood on the side of Mother Church. Cesare Baronio, whose *Annales* represented the most elaborate Catholic effort to regain the historical high ground, ransacked the greatest existing library—that of the Vatican, where he served as prefect—for evidence to use against Flacius and his team. He too found it necessary to enlist collaborators, though he played down their role in the final product. Many other Catholic scholars flanked him.[15]

Whatever their disagreements on ancient liturgies or the role of art in the early church, all ecclesiastical historians saw their task as collective and defined it as hunting, gathering, and collecting the documents. They were the rightful heirs of Eusebius, who first defined the scale and character of ecclesiastical erudi-

tion, and who first made the history of the church a collaborative enterprise, long before the institutional supports on which
early modern church historians relied had come into existence.
"The monks," as Arnaldo Momigliano wrote of the Benedictines of Saint Germain des Près, "were working co-operatively.
Their team spirit became a legend. The healthy and the sick,
the young and the old were made to contribute to the work of
the house; and proof-reading was the most usual occupational
therapy."[16] A similar form of collaboration—and a similar form
of work discipline—flourished in the house of the Benedictines' enemies, the Jesuit Bollandists, in Antwerp. The Protestant scholars of Leiden and Cambridge, too, aspired to match
the Catholics' ability to find and mobilize talent—as Richard
Bentley did when he put the most learned and intelligent young
M.A.'s in his university in charge of the Cambridge University
Press's editions of the classics and the Bible.[17]

On both the Protestant and the Catholic side, new forms of
scholarship were regularly accompanied, and sometimes made
possible, by new forms of technical publication. Flacius and his
collaborators not only compiled elaborate notes on the supposed heretics who had preserved the truth through the dark
centuries of the Middle Ages, but also published a bibliography
of their writings, the *Catalogus testium veritatis,* in 1556. And
they produced edition after edition of the heretical pamphlets
and liturgies that Catholic Inquisitors had failed to suppress
with fire and sword. For all their historical range and graphic
content, however, even these publications fell short in grandeur
and originality of the great Catholic works on paleography,
Jean Mabillon's *De re diplomatica* and Bernard de Montfaucon's
Palaeographia Graeca, in both of which numerous facsimiles

illustrated the development of scripts and gave readers who lacked the Paris Benedictines' easy access to ancient sources a way to learn what really ancient documents looked like.

By no means all of those who created these institutions and their practices remembered what they owed to the Greek scholars of the early church. And some of those who did, like Baronio, insisted on their debts for polemical rather than substantive reasons. The link to the patristic past was for them merely part of the claim they staked to represent the church's central, secular tradition against innovators who, for example, ventured to show that Josephus sometimes contradicted Eusebius—and seemed often to be right when he did so. Yet the goals, and even the practices, first pursued in Caesarea would continue to define major sectors of Christian learning for almost two millennia. Petrarch spent much of his life engaged in a colloquy with Augustine, who served as his model of a Christian scholar deeply engaged with the study of the classics.[18] Erasmus—who drew up his own new Latin version of the New Testament and devoted much of his life to creating new forms of biblical commentary—often presented himself as a modern counterpart to Jerome.[19] But the model of ecclesiastical learning that took shape in the library at Caesarea shaped the whole, millennial tradition of Christian scholarship, in subtle but vital ways. In many respects, we are still the heirs of Origen and Eusebius.

ABBREVIATIONS

BIBLIOGRAPHY

NOTES

ACKNOWLEDGMENTS

INDEX

Abbreviations

BT	Babylonian Talmud
CCSL	Corpus Christianorum Series Latina (Turnhout: Brepols, 1953–)
CSEL	Corpus Scriptorum Eccliesiasticorum Latinorum
DE	Eusebius, *Demonstratio evangelica*
FrGrHist	*Die Fragmente der griechischen Historiker,* ed. Felix Jacoby (Berlin, 1923–; Leiden, 1958)
GCS	Die griechischen christlichen Schriftsteller der ersten [drei] Jahrhunderte
HE	Eusebius, *Historia ecclesiastica*
LCL	Loeb Classical Library
NPNF	Nicene and Pre-Nicene Fathers
OLD	*Oxford Latin Dictionary*
PE	Eusebius, *Praeparatio evangelica*
PG	*Patrologiae cursus completus: Series Graecas,* ed. J.-P. Minge (Paris: 1844–1864)
P. Herc.	*Papyri Herculanenses*
PL	*Patrologiae cursus completus: Series Latina,* ed. J.-P. Minge (Paris: 1857–1866)
RE	*Real-Encyclopädie der classischen Altertums-Wissenschaft,* ed. A. Fr. von Paul, rev. G. Wissowa et al. (Stuttgart: 1894–1980)
VC	Eusebius, *Vita Constantini*

Bibliography

Primary Sources

Africanus, Sextus Julius. 1971. *Les Cestes*. Ed. R. Vieillefond. Florence: Sansoni; Paris: Didier.

Berossos. 1978. *Babyloniaca*. Tr. and ed. S. M. Burstein. Malibu: Undena.

Chaeremon. 1984. *Chaeremon, Egyptian Priest and Stoic Philosopher: The Fragments Collected and Translated with Explanatory Notes*. Ed. Pieter Willem van der Horst. Leiden: E. J. Brill.

Cornutus, Lucius Annaeus. 1881. *Theologiae graecae compendium*. Ed. Carolus Lang. Leipzig: Teubner.

Eusebius. 1818a. *Chronicorum canonum libri duo*. Ed. Angelo Mai and Johannes Zohrab. Milan: Regiis typis.

———1818b. *Chronicon bipartitum*. 2 vols. Ed. Johannes Baptista Aucher. Venice: Typis coenobii PP. Armenorum in insula S. Lazari.

———1903. *Evangelicae praeparationis libri XV*. 4 vols. Ed. E. H. Gifford. Oxford: Oxford University Press.

———1903–1909. *Kirchengeschichte*. 3 vols. Ed. Eduard Schwartz. GCS. Leipzig: Hinrichs.

————1904. *Das Onomastikon der biblischen Ortsnamen.* Ed. Erich Klostermann. Leipzig: Hinrichs.

————1911. *Die Chronik des Eusebius aus dem armenischen übersetzt.* Ed. and tr. J. Karst. GCS 20. Leipzig: Hinrichs.

————1923. *Chronici canones.* Tr. Jerome, ed. J. K. Fotheringham. Oxford: Clarendon Press.

————1927. *The Ecclesiastical History and the Martyrs of Palestine.* Tr. Hugh Lawlor and John Oulton. I, London: S.P.C.K.

————1975. *Der Jesajakommentar.* Ed. Joseph Ziegler. GCS. Berlin: Akademie-Verlag.

————1984. *Die Chronik des Hieronymus.* eEd. Rudolf Helm. GCS 47. Berlin: Akademie-Verlag.

————2003. *Palestine in the Fourth Century A.D.: The Onomasticon by Eusebius of Caesarea.* Tr. G. S. P. Freeman-Grenville, ed. Joan Taylor. Jerusalem: Carta.

Eusebius and Pamphilus. 2002. *Apologie pour Origène.* 2 vols. Ed. René Amacker and Eric Junod. Sources Chrétiennes. Paris: Les Editions du Cerf.

Funk, Francis Xaver (ed.). 1905. *Didascalia et constitutiones apostolorum.* 2 vols. Paderborn: Ferdinand Schöningh

George Syncellus. 1984. *Ecloga chronographica.* Ed. Alden Mosshammer. Leipzig: Teubner.

————2002. *The Chronography of George Synkellos: A Byzantine Chronicle of Universal History from the Creation.* Ed. and tr. William Adler and Paul Tuffin. Oxford: Oxford University Press.

Gregory Thaumaturgus. 1969. *Remerciement à Origène.* Tr. Henri Crouzel. Paris: Editions du Cerf.

Hippolytus. 1986. *Refutatio omnium haeresium.* Ed. Miroslav Marcovich. Berlin and New York: De Gruyter.

Jerome. 1895. *De viris inlustribus.* Ed. Carl Albrecht Bernoulli. Freiburg i.B. and Leipzig: J. C. B. Mohr.

————1910–1918) *Epistulae.* 3 vols. Ed. Isidorus Hilberg, CSEL, Vienna: Tempsky; Leipzig: Freytag.

————1982., *Contra Rufinum*. Ed. Pierre Lardet. CC, Series Latina. Tournhout: Brepols.

————1983. *Apologie contre Rufin*. Ed. and tr. Pierre Lardet. Paris: Editions du Cerf.

————1999. *On Illustrious Men*. Tr. Thomas Halton. Washington, D.C.: Catholic University of America Press.

Lasserre, F. (ed.). 1966. *Die Fragmente des Eudoxus des Knidos*. Berlin: de Gruyter.

Neoplatonic Saints: The Lives of Plotinus and Proclus by their Students. 2000. Tr. Mark Edwards. Liverpool: Liverpool University Press.

Origen. 1953 [1965]. *Contra Celsum*. Tr. and ed. Henry Chadwick. Cambridge: Cambridge University Press.

————1969. "La lettre d'Origène à Grégoire," in Gregory Thaumaturgus 1969, 186–195.

Philo. 1896–1930. *Opera quae supersunt*. 7 vols. in 5. Ed. L. Cohn and P. Wendland. Berlin: Reimer.

Philo of Byblos. 1981. *The Phoenician History*. Ed. Harold W Attridge and Robert A Oden. Washington, D.C.: Catholic Biblical Association of America.

Plotinus. 1966–1988. *Enneads*. Rev. text and tr. by A. H. Armstrong. 6 vols. Cambridge: Harvard University Press.

————1991. *The Ennead*. Tr. Stephen Mackenna and John Dillon. London; Penguin.

Polydore Vergil. 2002. *On Discovery*. Ed. and tr. Brian Copenhaver. Cambridge: Harvard University Press.

Porphyry. 1966. "The Life of Plotinus," in Plotinus 1966–1988, I, 1–90.

————1969. *The Cave of the Nymphs in the Odyssey: A Rev. Text with Translation by Seminar Classics 609, State University of New York at Buffalo*. Arethusa Monographs 1. Buffalo: Dept. of Classics, State University of New York at Buffalo.

————1983. *On the Cave of the Nymphs*. Tr. Robert Lamberton. Barrytown, N.Y.: Station Hill Press.

————1994). *Porphyry's Against the Christians: The Literary Remains.* Ed. R. Joseph Hoffmann. Amherst, N.Y.: Prometheus Books.

Proclus. 1903. *In Platonis Timaeum commentaria.* 2 vols. Ed. E. Diehl. Leipzig: Teubner.

Riccobono, Antonio, et al. (eds.). 1909. *Fontes iuris romani antejustiniani.* 2 vols. Florence: Barbèra.

Routh, Martin Joseph. 1814–1818. *Reliquiae sacrae; sive, Auctorum fere jam perditorum secundi tertiique saeculi fragmenta, quae supersunt. Accedunt epistolae synodicae et canonicae Nicaeno Concilio antiquiores.* 5 vols. Oxford: Typis Academicis.

Scherer, Jean. 1956. *Extraits des livres I et II du Contre Celse d'Origène d'après le papyrus no. 88747 du Musée du Caire.* Cairo: Institut français d'Archéologie Orientale.

Seder Olam. 1998. *Seder Olam: The Rabbinic View of Biblical Chronology.* Ed. and tr. Heinrich Guggenheimer. Northvale, N.J.: Jason Aronson.

Suetonius. 1979. *Suetonio De Poetis e Biografi Minori.* Ed. Augusto Rostagni. New York: Arno Press.

Tatian. 1982.. *Oratio ad Graecos and Fragments.* Ed. Mollie Whittaker. Oxford: Clarendon Press.

Tcherikover, Victor, and Alexander Fuks (eds.). 1957–1964. *Corpus papyrorum Judaicarum.* 3 vols. Cambridge: Published for the Magnes Press, Hebrew University, by Harvard University Press.

Verburgghe, Gerald, and John Wickersham. 1996. *Berossos and Manetho Introduced and Translated: Native Traditions in Ancient Mesopotamia and Egypt.* Ann Arbor: University of Michigan Press.

Secondary Sources

Adler, William. 1989. *Time Immemorial.* Washington, D.C.: Dumbarton Oaks.

————1992. "The *Chronicle* of Eusebius and Its Legacy." In Attridge and Hata (eds.) 1992, 467—-491.

————2003. "The Chronology of Africanus." Seminar, Princeton University.

Aho, John Arvid. 2002. "Using References in the Work of Eusebius of Caesarea (ca. 26-339) to Understand the Collection of the Library of Caesarea." Ph.D. diss., University of Texas.

Allen, P. S., H. M. Allen, and H. W. Garrod (eds.). 1906–1958. *Opus epistolarum D. Erasmi Roterodami*. 12 vols. Oxford: Clarendon Press.

Alonso-Nuñez, J. M. 1990. "The Emergence of Universal Historiography from the Fourth to the Second Centuries B.C." In *Purposes of History*, ed. H. Verdin et al. Leuven: n.p.

Amarante, Licia, Giuliana Auriello, and Rita Pappalardo. 1995. *Indici del papiri ercolanesi in "Cronache ercolanesi," 1971–1995*. Naples: G. Macchiaroli.

Anderson, Graham. 1976. *Lucian: Theme and Variation in the Second Sophistic*. Supplements to *Mnemosyne* 41. Leiden: Brill.

————1986. *Philostratus, Biography, and Belles Lettres in the Third Century AD*. London: Croom Helm.

————1993. *The Second Sophistic: A Cultural Phenomenon in the Roman Empire*. London: Routledge.

Archibald, Sasha, and Daniel Rosenberg. 2004. "A Timeline of Timelines." *Cabinet* 13.

Armstrong, David, ed. 2004. *Vergil, Philodemus, and the Augustans*. Austin: University of Texas Press.

Arnold, Klaus. 1991. *Johannes Trithemius (1462-1516)*, 2nd ed. Quellen und Forschungen zur Geschichte des Bistums und Hochstifts Würzburg, vol. 23. Würzburg: Kommissionsverlag F. Schöningh.

Attridge, Harold, and Gohei Hata (eds.). 1992. *Eusebius, Christianity, and Judaism*. Leiden: Brill.

Baars, W. 1968. *New Syro-Hexaplaric Texts Edited, Commented upon, and Compared with the Septuagint*. Leiden: Brill.

Bagnall, Roger. 1992. "An Owner of Literary Papyri." *Classical Philology* 87:137-140.

Barclay, John M. G. 1996. *Jews in the Mediterranean Diaspora: From Alexander to Trajan (323 BCE-117 CE)*. Edinburgh: T&T Clark.

Barnes, Timothy. 1975. "The Composition of Eusebius' *Onomasticon*." *Journal of Theological Studies* 26:412-415.

————1981. *Constantine and Eusebius*. Cambridge: Harvard University Press.

————1989. "Panegyric, History, and Hagiography in Eusebius's *Life of Constantine*." In *The Making of Orthodoxy: Essays in Honour of Henry Chadwick*, ed. Rowan Williams,. 94–123. Cambridge: Cambridge University Press.

————1994. "Scholarship or Propaganda: Porphyry *Against the Christians* and Its Historical Setting," *Bulletin of the Institute of Classical Studies* 39:53-65.

Barret-Kriegel, Blandine. 1988. *Jean Mabillon*. Paris: P.U.F.

Barthélemy, Dominique. 1963. *Les devanciers d'Aquila; première publication intégrale du texte des fragments du Dodécaprophéton trouvés dans le désert de Juda*. Leiden: Brill.

————1967. "Est-ce Hoshaya Rabba qui censura le 'Commentaire Allégorique?' A partir des retouches faites aux citations bibliques, étude sur la tradition textuelle du Commentaire Allégorique de Philon." *Philon d'Alexandrie,* Colloques nationaux du Centre National de la Recherche Scientifique, Lyon, 11–15 September 1966, 45–78. Paris: Editions du Centre National de la Recherche Scientifique. Repr. in Barthélemey 1978, 140–173.

————1971. "Eusèbe, la Septante, et 'les autres.'" *La Bible et les Pères*, Colloque de Strasbourg, 1–3 October 1969, 51–65. Paris: Presses Universitaires de France. , Repr. in Barthélemy 1978, 179–193.

————1972. "Origène et le texte de l'Ancien Testament." In *Epektasis. Mélanges patristiques offerts au Cardinal Jean Daniélou*, 247–261. Paris: Beauchesne. Repr. in Barthélemy 1978, 203–217.

————1978. *Etudes d'histoire du texte de l'Ancien Testament*. Orbis Biblicus et Orientalis 21. Fribourg: Editions Universitaires Fribourg; Göttingen: Vandenhoeck & Ruprecht.

Barton, Tamsyn. 1994a. *Ancient Astrology.* London: Routledge.

————1994b. *Power and Knowledge: Astrology, Physiognomics, and Medicine under the Roman Empire.* Ann Arbor: University of Michigan Press.

Battles, Matthew. 2003. *Library: An Unquiet History.* New York: Norton.

Bauer, Walter, Robert Kraft, and Gerhard Krodel (eds.). 1934; tr. 1971. *Orthodoxy and Heresy in Earliest Christianity.* Philadelphia: Fortress Press.

Baumgarten, Albert I. 1981. *The* Phoenician History *of Philo of Byblos: A Commentary.* Leiden: Brill.

Baynes, Norman. 1938. "Eusebius and the Christian Empire." In *Mélanges Bidez,* 13–18. Brussels: Université Libre de Bruxelles. Repr. in Baynes 1955, 168–172.

————1955. *Byzantine Studies and Other Essays.* London: University of London, the Athlone Press.

————1972. *Constantine the Great and the Christian Church,* 2nd ed., with a preface by Henry Chadwick. London: Oxford University Press.

Beard, Mary, John North, and Simon Price. 1998. *Religions of Rome.* Vol. I: *A History.* Cambridge: Cambridge University Press.

Beatrice, Pier Franco. 1992. "Porphyry's Judgment on Origen." In Daly (ed.) 1992, 351–367.

Beggs, M. R. 1998. "From Kingdom to Nation: The Transformation of a Metaphor in Eusebius' Historia Ecclesiastica." Ph.D. diss., Notre Dame.

Bentley, Jerry. 1983. *Humanists and Holy Writ: New Testament Scholarship in the Renaissance.* Princeton: Princeton University Press.

Bickerman, Elias. 1976–1986. *Studies in Jewish and Christian History.* 3 vols. Leiden: Brill.

Billanovich, Giuseppe. 1954. *Un nuovo esempio delle scoperte e delle letture del Petrarca: L' "Eusebio-Girolamo-PseudoProspero."* Schriften und Vorträge des Petrarca-Instituts Köln, 3. Krefeld: Scherpe.

Bisbee, Gary. 1988. *Pre-Decian Acts of Martys and Commentarii.* Harvard Dissertations in Religion, 22. Philadelphia: Fortress.

Blanchard, Alain (ed.). 1989. *Les débuts du Codex: Actes de la journée d'étude organisée à Paris les 3 et 4 juillet 1985 par l'Institut de Papyrologie de la Sorbonne et l'Institut de Recherche et d'Histoire des Textes.* Turnhout: Brepols.

Blanck, Horst. 1992. *Das Buch in der Antike.* Munich: Beck.

Blank, David. 1998. "Versionen oder Zwillinge? Zu den Handschriften von Philodems *Rhetorik.*" In Most (ed.) 1998, 123–140.

Boffo, Laura. 1995. "Ancora una volta sugli 'archivi' nel mondo greco: conservazione e pubblicazione' epigrafica." *Athenaeum* 83: 91–130.

Bonfil, Robert. 1988. "How Golden Was the Age of the Renaissance in Jewish Historiography?" *History and Theory, Beiheft* 27: *Essays in Jewish Historiography,* 78–102.

Borg, Barbara (ed.). 2004. *Paideia: The World of the Second Sophistic.* Berlin: Walter de Gruyter.

Botfield, Beriah (ed.). 1861. *Prefaces to the First Editions of the Greek and Roman Classics and the Sacred Scriptures.* London: Bohn.

Bourdieu, Pierre. 1977. *Outline of a Theory of Practice.* Cambridge: Cambridge University Press.

Bowersock, Glen. 1969. *Greek Sophists in the Roman Empire.* Oxford: Clarendon Press.

———2002. "Philosophy in the Second Sophistic" In *Philosophy and Power in the Graeco-Roman World: Essays in Honour of Miriam Griffin,* ed. Miriam T. Griffin, Gillian Clark, and Tessa Rajak. Oxford: Oxford University Press.

Bowersock, Glenn (ed.). 1974. *Approaches to the Second Sophistic: Papers Presented at the 105th Annual Meeting of the American Philological Association.* University Park, Penn.: American Philological Association.

Bowman, Glenn (1999), "'Mapping History's Redemption': Eschatology and Topography in the *Itinerarium Burdigalense.*" In Levine (ed.) 1999, 163–187.

Brann, Noel. 1999. *Trithemius and Magical Theology: A Chapter in the Controversy over Occult Studies in Early Modern Europe.* Albany: State University of New York Press.

Brent, Allen. 1995. *Hippolytus and the Roman Church in the Third Century: Communities in Tension before the Emergence of a Monarch-Bishop.* Leiden: Brill.

Brock, Sebastian. 1970. "Origen's Aims as a Textual Critic of the Old Testament," *Studia Patristica* 10:215–218. Repr. in *Studies in the Septuagint: Origins, Recensions, and Interpretations,* ed. Sidney Jellicoe, 343–346. New York: Ktav.

Brown, Peter. 1992. *Power and Persuasion in Late Antiquity: Towards a Christian Empire.* The Curti Lectures, 1988. Madison: University of Wisconsin Press.

Brüll, Nahum. 1876. "Die Entstehungsgeschichte des babylonischen Talmuds als Schriftwerk." *Jahrbücher für jüdische Geschichte und Literatur* 2:1–123.

Buell, Denise Kimber. 1999. *Making Christians: Clement of Alexandria and the Rhetoric of Legitimacy.* Princeton: Princeton University Press.

Burgess, R. W. 1997. "The Dates and Editions of Eusebius's *Chronici canones* and *Historia ecclesiastica*." *Journal of Theological Studies* n.s. 48: 471–504.

Burgess, R. W., with the assistance of Witold Witakowski. 1999. *Studies in Eusebian and Post-Eusebian Chronology. Historia.* Einzelschriften, 135. Stuttgart: Steiner.

Burnett, Stephen. 1996. *From Christian Hebraism to Jewish Studies: Johannes Buxtorf (1564-1629) and Hebrew Learning in the Seventeenth Century.* Leiden: Brill.

Butler, Shane. 2002. *The Hand of Cicero.* London: Routledge.

Cadiou, R. 1932. "Dictionnaires antiques dans l'oeuvre d'Origène." *Révue des Études Grecques* 45:271–285.

Caltabiano, Matilde. 1996. *Litterarum lumen: ambienti culturali e libri tra il iv e il v secolo.* Rome: Institutum Patristicum Augustinianum.

Cameron, Alan. 1992. "Filocalus and Melania." *Classical Philology* 87:140-144.

———2004. *Greek Mythography in the Roman World.* Oxford: Oxford University Press.

Cameron, Averil. 1983. "Eusebius of Caesarea and the Rethinking of History." In *Tria Corda: Scritti in onore di Arnaldo Momigliano,* ed. Emilio Gabba, 71–88. Como: New Press.

———1991. *Christianity and the Rhetoric of Empire: The Development of Christian Discourse.* Berkeley: University of California Press.

Cameron Averil, and Stuart Hall (eds.). 1999. *Eusebius: Life of Constantine.* Oxford: Clarendon Press.

Carotenuto, Erica. 2001. *Tradizione e innovazione nella* Historia ecclesiastica *di Eusebio di Cesarea.* Naples: Il Mulino.

Carriker, Andrew. 2003. *The Library of Eusebius of Caesarea.* Leiden: Brill.

Carruthers, Mary. 1990. *The Book of Memory: A Study of Memory in Medieval Culture.* Cambridge: Cambridge University Press.

Carruthers, Mary,and Jan M. Ziolkowski (eds.) 2002. *The Medieval Craft of Memory: An Anthology of Texts and Pictures.* Philadelphia: University of Pennsylvania Press.

Caspar, Erich. 1926. *Die ältesten Römischen Bischofsliste.* Schriften der Königsberger Gelehrten Gesellschaft, Geisteswissenschaftliche Klasse, 2,vol. 4. Berlin: Deutsche Verlagsgesellschaft für Politik und Geschichte.

Casson, Lionel. 2001. *Libraries in the Ancient World.* New Haven: Yale University Press.

Cavallera, Ferdinand 1922. *Saint Jérôme: sa vie et son oeuvre.* Louvain: "Spicilegium Sacrum Lovaniense."

Cavallo, Guglielmo, Mario Capasso, and Tiziano Dorandi. 1971. "Un secolo di 'paleografia' ercolanese." *Cronache ercolanesi* 1:11–22.

———1983. *Libri, scritture, scribi a Ercolano: introduzione allo studio dei materiali greci.* Naples: G. Macchiaroli.

———1984. "I rotoli di Ercolano come prodotti scritti. Quattro riflessioni." *Scrittura e Civiltà* 8:5–30.

————1989. "Scuola, 'scriptorium,' biblioteca a Cesarea." In Cavallo (ed.) 1989, 65–78.

Cavallo, Guglielmo, Mario Capasso, and Tiziano Dorandi (eds.). 1984. *Libri, editori e pubblico nel mondo antico*, 3rd. ed. Rome: Laterza.

————1989. *Le biblioteche nel mondo antico e medievale*. Bari: Laterza.

————1989–1991. *Lo spazio letterari di Roma antica*. 5 vols. Rome: Salerno.

Cerrato, J. A. 2002. *Hippolytus between East and West: The Commentaries and the Provenance of the Corpus*. Oxford: Oxford University Press.

Chabot, J. B. 1901. "A propos des Hexaples." *Journal Asiatique* ser. 9 17: 349f.

Chartier, Roger. 1988. *Cultural History: Between Practices and Representations*. Cambridge: Polity.

————1994. *The Order of Books: Readers, Authors, and Libraries in Europe between the Fourteenth and Eighteenth Centuries*. Stanford: Stanford University Press.

Chesnut, Glenn. 1986. *The First Christian Historians*, 2nd ed. Macon, Ga · Mercer University Press.

Chroust, A. H. 1962. "The Miraculous Disappearance and Recovery of the *Corpus Aristotelicum*." *Classica et Medievalia* 23:51–67.

Clark, Elizabeth. 1992. "Eusebius on Women in Early Church History." In Attridge and Hata (1992), 256–269.

————1999. *Reading Renunciation: Asceticism and Scripture in Early Christianity*. Princeton: Princeton University Press.

Clarke, Katherine. 1999. *Between Geography and History: Hellenistic Constructions of the Roman World*. Oxford: Clarendon Press.

Clements, Ruth. 1997. "Peri Pascha: Passover and the Displacement of Jewish Interpretation within Origen's Exegesis." Th.D. diss., Harvard Divinity School.

————2000. "Origen's *Hexapla* and Christian-Jewish Encounter in the Second and Third Centuries." In Donaldson (ed.) 2000, 303–329.

Cohen, Marcel (ed.). 1963. *L'écriture et la psychologie des peuples: XXIIe semaine de synthèse.* Paris: Librairie Armand Colin

Collomp, Paul. 1947. "La place de Josèphe dans la technique de l'historiographie hellénistique." *Etudes historiques de la Faculté des Lettres de Strasbourg,* 106:81–92. Paris: Les Belles Lettres.

————1973. "Der Platz des Josephus in der Technik der hellenistischen Geschichtsschreibung." In *Zur Josephus-Forschung,* ed. Abraham Schalit, tr. Günter Mayer, 278–293. Darmstadt: Wissenschaftliche Buchgesellschaft.

Coman, J. 1981. "Utilisation des Stromates de Clément d'Alexandrie par Eusèbe de Césarée dans la Préparation Evangélique." *Texte und Untersuchungen* 125:134.

Copenhaver, Brian. 1978. "The Historiography of Discovery in the Renaissance: The Sources and Composition of Polydore Vergil's *De Inventoribus Rerum libri I-III.*" *Journal of the Warburg and Courtauld Institutes* 41:192–214.

Corcoran, Simon. 1996. *The Empire of the Tetrarchs: Imperial Pronouncements and Government, A.D. 284–324.* Oxford: Clarendon Press.

Coudert, Allison, and Jeffrey Shoulson (eds.). 2004. *Hebraica Veritas? Christian Hebraists and the Study of Judaism in Early Modern Europe.* Philadelphia: University of Pennsylvania Press.

Cox, Patricia. 1983. *Biography in Late Antiquity.* Berkeley: University of California Press.

Cranz, F. Edward. 1952. "Kingdom and Polity in Eusebius of Caesarea." *Harvard Theological Review* 45:47–66.

Cribiore, Raffaella. 1996. *Writing, Teachers, and Students in Graeco-Roman Egypt.* Atlanta: Scholars Press.

————2001. *Gymnastics of the Mind: Greek Education in Hellenistic and Roman Egypt.* Princeton: Princeton University Press.

Croke, Brian. 1982. "The Originality of Eusebius' Chronicle." *American Journal of Philology* 103:195–200.

————1983. "The Origin of the Christian World Chronicle." In Croke and Emmett (eds.) 1983, 116–131.

————1984–1985. "The Era of Porphyry's Anti-Christian Polemic." *Journal of Religious History* 13:1–14.

Croke, Brian, and Alanna Emmett (eds.). 1983. *History and Historians in Late Antiquity*. Sydney: Pergamon.

Crouzel, Henri, S.J. 1962. *Origène et la philosophie*. Théologie 52. Paris: Aubier.

————1977. *Une controverse sur Origène à la Renaissance: Jean Pic de la Mirandole et Pierre Garcia*. Paris: Vrin.

————1979. "Faut-il voir trois personnages en Grégoire le Thaumaturge?" *Gregorianum* 20:287–320.

————1985 [1989]. *Origène*. Paris and Namur: Lethielleux and Culture et vérité. English tr. by A. S. Worrall (1989), San Francisco: Harper and Row.

————1988. "The Literature on Origen, 1970–1988." *Theological Studies* 49: 499–516.

Culham, Phyllis. 1989, "Archives and Alternatives in Republican Rome." *Classical Philology* 84: 100–115.

————1991. "Documents and *Domus* in Republican Rome." *Libraries and Culture* 26:119–134.

Daly, Robert H. (ed.). 1992. *Origeniana Quinta*. Papers of the 5th International Origen Congress, Boston College, 14–18 August 1989. Leuven: Leuven University Press

Daniélou, Jean. 1955. *Origen*. New York: Sheed and Ward.

Darnton, Robert. 1990. *The Kiss of Lamourette: Reflections in Cultural History*. New York: Norton.

Dawson, David. 1992. *Allegorical Readers and Cultural Revision in Ancient Alexandria*. Berkeley: University of California Press.

de Lange, N. R. M. 1976. *Origen and the Jews: Studies in Jewish-Christian Relations in Third-Century Palestine*. Cambridge: Cambridge University Press.

Del Corso, Lucio. 2005. *La lettura nel mondo ellenistico*. Rome and Bari: Laterza.

de Romilly, Jacqueline. 1988. "Plutarch and Thucydides or the Free Use of Quotations." *Phoenix* 42:22–34.

Devreesse, Robert. 1954. *Introduction à l'étude des manuscrits grecs.* Paris: Klincksieck.

Dillon, John. 1977. *The Middle Platonists.* London: Duckworth.

Dillon, John, and A. A. Long (eds.). 1988. *The Question of "Eclecticism": Studies in Later Greek Philosophy.* Berkeley: University of California Press.

Dilke, O. A. W. 1987. "Itineraries and Geographical Maps in the Early and Late Roman Empire." In Harley and Woodward (eds.) 1987–, 1, 234–257.

Dines, Jennifer. 2004. *The Septuagint.* Ed. Michael Knipp. London: Clark.

Ditchfield, Simon. 1995. *Liturgy, Sanctity, and History in Tridentine Italy: Pietro Maria Campi and the Preservation of the Particular.* Cambridge: Cambridge University Press.

Donaldson, Terence (ed.). 2000. *Religious Rivalries and the Struggle for Success in Caesarea Maritima.* Waterloo, Ontario: Wilfrid Laurier University Press.

Dorandi, Tiziano. 1991. "Den Autoren über die Schulter geschaut: Arbeitsweise und Autographie bei den antiken Schriftstellern." *Zeitschrift für Papyrologie und Epigraphik* 87:11–33.

————1993. "Zwischen Autographie und Diktat: Momente der Textualität in der antiken Welt." In Kullmann and Althoff 1993, 71–83.

Dörries, Hermann. 1954. *Das Selbstzeugnis Kaiser Konstantins.* Abh. d. Akad. d. Wiss. in Göttingen, phil.-hist. Kl., 3.34. Göttingen: Vandenhoeck & Ruprecht.

Dortmund, Annette. 2001. *Römisches Buchwesen um die Zeitenwende. War T. Pomponius Atticus (110–32 v. Chr.) Verleger?* Wiesbaden: Harrassowitz.

Douglass, Laurie. 1996. "A New Look at the *Itinerarium Burdigalense.*" *Journal of Early Christian Studies* 4:313–333.

Downey, Glanville. 1965. "The Perspective of the Early Church Historians." *Greek, Roman and Byzantine Studies* 6:57–70.

Drake, H. A. 1965. "Assyria in Classical Universal Histories." *Historia* 14:119–142.

————1975. "The Babylonian Chronicles and Berossus." *Iraq* 37:39–55.

————1976. *In Praise of Constantine: A Historical Study and New Translation of Eusebius' Tricennial Orations.* Berkeley: University of California Press.

————1985. "Eusebius on the True Cross." *Journal of Ecclesiastical History* 36:1–22.

————1988. "What Eusebius Knew: The Genesis of the Vita Constantini." *Classical Philology* 83:20–38.

————2000. *Constantine and the Bishops: The Politics of Intolerance.* Baltimore: Johns Hopkins University Press.

Dufour, Richard. 2002. *Plotinus: A Bibliography, 1950-2000.* Leiden: Brill.

Düring, Ingemar. 1950. "Notes on the History of the Transmission of Aristotle's Writings." *Göteborgs Högskolas Arsskrift* 56:35-70.

————. 1956. "Ariston or Hermippus?" *Classica et Medievalia* 17: 11–21.

————1957. *Aristotle in the Ancient Biographical Tradition.* Göteborg: Elanders.

Ebach, Jürgen. 1979. *Weltentstehung und Kulturentwicklung bei Philo von Byblos: e. Beitr. zur Uberlieferung d. bibl. Urgeschichte im Rahmen d. altoriental. u. antiken Schöpfungsglaubens.* Stuttgart: Kohlhammer.

Edwards, Mark (ed.). 1997. *Optatus: Against the Donatists.* Liverpool: Liverpool Classical Press, 1997.

————2002. *Origen against Plato.* Aldershot and Burlington, Vt: Ashgate.

Ehrhardt, Albert. 1892. "Die griechische Patriarchal-Bibliothek von Jerusalem. Ein Beitrag zur griechischen Paläographie." *Römische Quartalschrift* 5:217–265; 6:339–365.

Ehrman, Bart. 1995. "The Text as Window: New Testament Manuscripts and the Social History of Christianity." In *The Text of the New Testament in Contemporary Research: Essays on the Status* quaestionis, ed. Bart Ehrman and Michael Holmes, 361–379. Grand Rapids, Mich.: Wm. B. Eerdmans.

Elliott, C. J. 1877–1887. "Hebrew Learning among the Fathers." In *A Dictionary of Christian Biography*, 4 vols., ed. William Smith and Henry Wace, II, 851–872. London: J. Murray.

Elliott, T. G. 1991. "Eusebian Frauds in the Vita Constantini." *Phoenix* 45:162–171.

Elsner, Jás. 2000. "The *Itinerarium Burdigalense*: Politics and Salvation in the Geography of Constantine's Empire." *Journal of Roman Studies* 90:18–195.

Fatio, Olivier, and Pierre Fraenkel (eds.). 1978. *Histoire de l'exégèse aux XVIe siècle*. Geneva: Droz.

de Faye, Eugène. 1923–1928. *Origène, sa vie, son oeuvre, sa pensée*. 3 vols. Paris: E. Leroux.

Feldman, Louis H., and Gohei Hata (eds.). 1987. *Josephus, Judaism, and Christianity*. Detroit: Wayne State University Press.

Findlen, Paula (ed.). 2004. *Athanasius Kircher: The Last Man Who Knew Everything*. New York: Routledge.

Fitzgerald, John, Dirk Obbink, and Glenn Holland (eds.). 2004. *Philodemus and the New Testament World*. Leiden: Brill.

Flinterman, Jaap-Jan. 1995. *Power, Paideia, and Pythagoreanism: Greek Identity, Conceptions of the Relationship between Philosophers and Monarchs, and Political Ideas in Philostratus' Life of Apollonius*. Amsterdam: J. C. Gieben.

Fordyce, Edgar John. 1956. *Greece before Homer: Ancient Chronology and Mythology*. London: Max Parrish.

Fowden, Garth. 1986. *The Egyptian Hermes: A Historical Approach to the Late Pagan Mind*. Cambridge: Cambridge University Press.

———1993. *Empire to Commonwealth: Consequences of Monotheism in Late Antiquity*. Princeton: Princeton University Press.

Frazier, Alison. 2005. *Possible Lives: Authors and Saints in Renaissance Italy*. New York: Columbia University Press.

Frenchkowski, Marko. 2003. "Der Text der Apostelgeschichte und die Realien antiker Buchproduktion." In *The Book of Acts as Church History: Text, Textual Traditions, and Ancient Interpretations*.

Apostelgeschichte als Kirchengeschichte. Text, Texttraditionen und antike Auslegungen, ed. Tobias Nicklas and Michael Tilly, 87–107. Berlin and New York.

————Forthcoming. *Studien zur Geschichte der Bibliothek von Cäsarea*. In Tobias Nicklas et al., eds., *The World of New Testament Manuscripts* (forthcoming).

Frye, Richard. 1962. *The Heritage of Persia*. London: Weidenfeld and Nicolson.

Gamble, Harry. 1995. *Books and Readers in the Early Church: A History of Early Christian Texts*. New Haven: Yale University Press.

Ganz, Peter (ed.). 1992. *Das Buch al magisches und als Repräsentationsobjekt*. Wolfenbütteler Mittelalter-Studien, 5. Wiesbaden: In Kommission bei Otto Harrassowitz.

Gardiner, Alan. 1997. *The Royal Canon of Turin*. Oxford: Griffith Institute.

Geerlings, Wilhelm, and Christian Schulze (eds.). 2002. *Der Kommentar in Antike und Mittelalter: Beiträge zu seiner Erforschung*. Leiden: Brill.

Gelzer, Heinrich. 1880–1885. *Sextus Julius Africanus und die byzantinische Chronographie*. 2 vols. Leipzig: Hinrichs.

Gershevitch, Ilya. 1985. *The Cambridge History of Iran*. Vol. II: *The Median and Achaemenian Periods*. Cambridge: Cambridge University Press.

Gerson, Lloyd. 1994. *Plotinus*. London: Routledge.

Gerson, Lloyd P. (ed.). 1996. *The Cambridge Companion to Plotinus*. Cambridge: Cambridge University Press.

Geus, Klaus. 2002. *Eratosthenes von Kyrene. Studien zur hellenistischen Kultur- und Wissenschaftsgeschichte*. Munich: Beck.

Gigante, Marcello. 1979. *Catalogo dei papiri ercolanesi*. Naples: Bibliopolis.

————1983. *Ricerche filodemee*, 2nd ed. rev. and corrected. Naples: G. Macchiaroli.

————1987. *La bibliothèque de Philodème et l'épicurisme romain*. Paris: Les Belles Lettres.

————1990. *Filodemo in Italia*. Florence: Le Monnier

————1995. *Philodemus in Italy: The Books from Herculaneum*. Tr. Dirk Obbink. Ann Arbor: University of Michigan Press.

Gleason, Maud. 1995. *Making Men: Sophists and Self-Presentation in Ancient Rome*. Princeton: Princeton University Press.

Gnoli, Gherardo. 1985. *De Zoroastre à Mani: quatre leçons au Collège de France*. Paris: Klincksieck.

Gödecke, Monika. 1987. *Geschichte als Mythos: Eusebs "Kirchengeschichte."* Frankfurt: Peter Lang.

Godin, André. 1978. "Fonction d'Origène dans la pratique exégètique d'Erasme: les Annotations sur l'Épitre aux Romains." In Fatio and Fraenkel (eds.) 1978, 17–44.

————1982. *Erasme Lecteur d'Origène*. Geneva: Droz.

Goldhill, Simon (ed.). 2001. *Being Greek under Rome: Cultural Identity, the Second Sophistic, and the Development of Empire*. Cambridge: Cambridge University Press.

Gordis, Robert. 1971. *The Biblical Text in the Making: A Study of the Kethib-Qere*, agmented ed. New York: Ktav.

Gottschalk, H. B. 1972. "Notes on the Wills of the Peripatetic Scholarchs." *Hermes* 100:3147–342.

Goulot-Cazé, Marie-Odile (ed.). 2000. *Le commentaire entre tradition et innovation*. Actes du Colloque International de l'Institut des Traditions Textuelles (Paris and Villejuif, 22–25 September 1999). Paris: Vrin.

Grabbe, Lester. 1992. *Judaism from Cyrus to Hadrian*. 2 vols. Minneapolis: Augsburg Fortress.

Grafton, Anthony. 1975. "Joseph Scaliger and Historical Chronology: The Rise and Fall of a Discipline." *History and Theory* 14:156–185.

————1983–1993. *Joseph Scaliger*. 2 vols. Oxford: Clarendon Press.

————1990. *Forgers and Critics*. Princeton: Princeton University Press.

————2004. "Kircher's Chronology." In Findlen (ed.) 2004.

Grafton, Anthony (ed.). 1993. *Rome Reborn: The Vatican Library and Renaissance Culture*. Vatican City: Biblioteca Apostolica Vaticana;

Washington, D.C.: Library of Congress; New Haven: Yale University Press.

Grafton, Anthony, and Noel Swerdlow. 1985. "Technical Chronology and Astrological History in Varro, Censorinus, and Others." *Classical Quarterly* n.s. 35:454–465.

———1986. "Greek Chronography in Roman Epic: The Calendrical Date of the Fall of Troy in the *Aeneid*." *Classical Quarterly* n.s. 36:212–218.

———1988. "Calendar Dates and Ominous Days in Ancient Historiography." *Journal of the Warburg and Courtauld Institutes* 51:14–42.

Grant, Robert M. 1971. "Early Alexandrian Christianity," *Church History* 40:133–144.

———1973. "Porphyry among the Early Christians." In *Romanitas et Christianitas: studia Iano Henrico Waszink a. d. VI Kal. Nov. a. MCMLXXIII XIII lustra complenti oblata*, ed. Willem den Boer et al., 181–187. Amsterdam: North Holland.

———1975. "Eusebius and His Lives of Origen In *Forma Futuri: Studi in onore del Cardinale M. Pellegrino*, 635–649. Turin: Bottega d'Erasmo.

———1980. *Eusebius as Church Historian*. Oxford: Clarendon Press.

Greenberg, Moshe. 1956 [1974]. "The Stabilization of the Text of the Hebrew Bible, Reviewed in the Light of the Biblical Materials from the Judean Desert." *Journal of the American Oriental Society*, 76. Repr. in Leiman (ed.) 1974, 298–326.

Griffin, Miriam, and Jonathan Barnes (eds.) 1989. *Philosophia Togata [I]*. Oxford: Oxford University Press. Corrected paperback ed., 1997.

———1997. *Philosophia Togata II*. Oxford: Clarendon Press.

Groh, Dennis. 1985. "The *Onomasticon* of Eusebius and the Rise of Christian Palestine." *Studia Patristica* 18 (1)23–31.

Gustafsson, B. 1961. "Eusebius' Principles in Handling his Sources, as Found in his Church History, Books I-VII." *Studia Patristica*, 4 433–435.

Habinek, Thomas. 1998. *The Politics of Latin Literature: Writing,*

Identity, and Empire in Ancient Rome. Princeton: Princeton University Press.

Hadot, Pierre. 1995. *Philosophy as a Way of Life*. Ed. Arnold I. Davidson; English tr. by Michael Chase. Malden, Mass.: Blackwell.

———1993. *Plotinus, or, The Simplicity of Vision*. Chicago: University of Chicago Press.

Haines-Eitzen, Kim. 2000. *Guardians of Letters: Literacy, Power, and the Transmitters of Early Christian Literature*. Oxford: Oxford University Press.

Halbertal, Moshe. 1997. *People of the Book: Canon, Meaning, and Authority*. Cambridge: Harvard University Press.

Halévy, J. 1901. "L'origine de la transcription du texte hébreu en caractères grecs dans les Hexaples d'Origène." *Journal Asiatique*, ser. 9 17:335 ff.

Hall, Linda Jones. 2004. *Roman Berytus: Beirut in Late Antiquity*. London: Routledge.

Hall, Stuart. 1993. "Eusebian and Other Sources in Vita Constantini I." In *Logos: Festschrift für Luise Abramowski*, ed. H. Brennecke et al., 239–263. Berlin: DeGruyter.

———1998. "Some Constantinian Documents in the *Vita Constantini*." In *Constantine: History, Historiography, and Legend*, ed. Samuel Lieu and Dominic Montserrat. London: Routledge.

Halporn, James. 1981. "Methods of Reference in Cassiodorus." *Journal of Library History* 16:71–91.

Hamilton, Alistair. 1993. "Eastern Churches and Western Scholarship." In Grafton (ed.) 1993, 225–249.

Hanson, Ann. 1998. "Galen: Author and Critic" In Most (ed.) 1998, 22–53.

Hanson, R. P. C. 1954. *Allegory and Event: A Study of the Sources and Significance of Origen's Interpretation of Scripture*. London: S.P.C.K.

Harl, Kenneth. 1996. *Coinage in the Roman Economy*. Baltimore: The Johns Hopkins University Press.

Harley, J. B., and David Woodward. 1987–. *A History of Cartography*. 4 vols. to date. Chicago: University of Chicago Press.

Harnack, Adolf von. 1893. *Dogmengeschichte,* 2nd rev. ed. Freiburg i.B.: Akademische Verlagsbuchhandlung von J. C. B Mohr (Paul Siebeck).

———1902 [1962]. *The Mission and Expansion of Christianity in the First Three Centuries,* tr. James Moffatt. New York: Harper. Original ed. *Die Mission und Ausbreitung des Christentums in den ersten drei Jahrhunderten;* Leipzig: J. C. Hinrichs.

Harris, William. 1989. *Ancient Literacy.* Cambridge: Harvard University Press.

———1991. "Why Did the Codex Supplant the Book-Roll?" In *Renaissance Society and Culture: Essays in Honor of Eugene F. Rice, Jr.,* 71–85. New York: Italica Press.

Hartmann, Martina. 2001. *Humanismus und Kirchenkritik: Matthias Flacius Illyricus als Erforscher des Mittelalters.* Stuttgart: Thorbecke.

Hasan-Rokem, Galit. 2003. *Tales of the Neighborhood: Jewish Narrative Dialogue in Late Antiquity.* Berkeley: University of California Press.

Haugen, Kristine. 2001. "Richard Bentley: Scholarship and Criticism in Eighteenth-Century England." Ph.D. diss., Princeton University.

Hays, Robert S. 1983. "Lucius Annaeus Cornutus' *Epidrom* (Introduction to the Traditions of Greek Theology): Introduction, Translation, and Notes." Ph.D. diss., University of Texas at Austin.

Helm, Rudolf. 1924. *Eusebius' Chronik und ihre Tabellenform.* Abhandlungen der Preussischen Akademie der Wissenschaften, 1923, Philosophisch-historische Klasse, 4. Berlin: Verlag der Akademie der Wissenschaften, in Kommission bei Walter de Gruyter.

———1929. *Hieronymus' Zusätze in Eusebius's Chronik und ihr Wert für die Literaturgeschichte. Philologus.* Supplement 21, vol. II. Leipzig: Dieterich.

Higbie, Carolyn. 2003. *The Lindian Chronicle and the Greek Creation of Their Past.* Oxford: Oxford University Press.

Hirshman, Marc G. 1995. *A Rivalry of Genius: Jewish and Christian Biblical Interpretation in Late Antiquity.* Tr. Batya Stein. Albany: State University of New York Press.

Hollerich, Michael. 1990. "Religion and Politics in the Writings of Eusebius: Reassessing the First 'Court Theologian.'" *Church History* 59:309–325.

———1999. *Eusebius of Caesarea's* Commentary on Isaiah: *Christian Exegesis in the Age of Constantine.* Oxford: Clarendon Press.

Hopkins, Keith. 1998. "Christian Number and Its Implications," *Journal of Early Christian Studies* 6:185–226.

Horsfall, Nicholas. 1993. "Empty Shelves on the Palatine." *Greece and Rome* 40:58–67.

Hunger, Herbert. 1989. *Schreiben und Lesen in Byzanz: Die byzantinische Buchkultur.* Munich: Beck.

Hunt, E. D. 1982. *Holy Land Pilgrimage in the Later Roman Empire, AD 312-460.* Oxford: Clarendon Press.

Inglebert, Hervé. 1996. *Les romains chrétiens face a l'histoire de Rome: histoire, christianisme et romanités en Occident dans l'Antiquité tardive (IIIe-Ve siècles).* Paris: Etudes augustiniennes.

———2001. *Interpretatio christiana: les mutations des savoirs, cosmographie, géographie, ethnographie, histoire, dans l'antiquité chrétienne, 30-630 après J.-C.* Paris: Institut d'études augustiniennes.

Irigoin, Jean. 1984. "Les éditions de textes." In *La philologie grecque à l'époque hellénistique et romaine,* ed. Franco Montanaru, 39–82. Entretiens sur l'Antiquité Classique, 40. Vandoeuvres-Geneva: Fondation Hardt.

———2001. *Le livre grec des origines à la Renaissance.* Paris: Bibliothèque Nationale de France.

Jakab, Attila. 2001. *Ecclesia alexandrina: évolution sociale et institutionnelle du christianisme alexandrin, IIe et IIIe siècles.* Bern: Peter Lang.

Jardine, Lisa. 1993. *Erasmus, Man of Letters*. Princeton: Princeton University Press

Jay, Pierre. 1985. *L'exégèse de saint Jérôme d'après son "Commentaire sur Isaïe."* Paris: Etudes augustiniennes.

Jellicoe, Sidney. (ed.) 1974. *Studies in the Septuagint: Origins, Recensions, and Interpretations*. New York: Ktav.

Jenkins, R. G.. 1998. "The First Column of the Hexapla: The Evidence of the Milan Codex (Rahlfs 1098) and the Cairo Genizah Fragment (Rahlfs 2005)." In Salvesen (ed.) 1998, 88–102.

Johnson, William. 2000. "Toward a Sociology of Reading in Classical Antiquity." *American Journal of Philology* 121:593–627.

Jones, A. H. M., and T. C. Skeat. 1954. "Notes on the Genuineness of the Constantinian Documents in Eusebius's *Life of Constantine*," *Journal of Ecclesiastical History* 5:196–200.

Junot, Pierre. 1987. "Origène vu par Pamphile dans la lettre-préface de l'*Apologie*." In Lies (ed.) 1987, 128-135.

Kahle, Paul. 1947. *The Cairo Geniza*. London: Published for the British Academy by Geoffrey Cumberlege, Oxford University Press.

———1960, "The Greek Bible Manuscripts Used by Origen," *Journal of Biblical Literature* 79:111–118.

Kalligas, Paul. 2001. "Traces of Longinus' Library in Eusebius' *Praeparatio Evangelica*." *Classical Quarterly* 51:584–598.

Kalmin, Richard. 1989. *The Redaction of the Babylonian Talmud: Amoraic or Saboraic?* Cincinnati: Hebrew Union College Press.

———1994. *Sages, Stories, Authors, and Editors in Rabbinic Babylonia*. Atlanta: Scholars Press.

Kamesar, Adam. 1993. *Jerome, Greek Scholarship, and the Hebrew Bible: A Study of the "Quaestiones Hebraicae in Genesim."* Oxford: Clarendon Press.

Kannengiesser, Charles. 1992. "Eusebius of Caesarea, Origenist" In Attridge and Hata (ed.) 1992, 435–466.

Kannengiesser, Charles, and William Petersen (eds.). 1988. *Origen of Alexandria: His World and His Legacy*. Vol. I: *Christianity and*

Judaism in Antiquity. Notre Dame: University of Notre Dame Press.

Kaplan, Julius. 1933. *The Redaction of the Babylonian Talmud.* New York: Bloch.

Kaster, Robert. 1988. *Guardians of Language: The Grammarian and Society in Late Antiquity.* Berkeley: University of California Press.

Kelly, J. N. D. 1975. *Jerome: His life, Writings, and Controversies.* London: Duckworth.

Knowles, David. 1963. *Great Historical Enterprises: Problems in Monastic History.* London: Nelson.

Kleberg, Tönnes. 1984. "Commercio librario ed editoriale nel mondo antico." In Cavallo (ed.) 1984, 27–80.

Klepper, Deanna. 1999. "Nicholas of Lyra and Franciscan Interest in Hebrew Scholarship." In *Nicholas of Lyra: The Senses of Scripture,* ed. Philip Krey and Lesley Smith. Leiden and Boston: Brill.

———Forthcoming. *The Insight of Unbelievers: Nicholas of Lyra and Christian Reading of Jewish Text in the Later Middle Ages.*

Koch, Hal. 1932. *Pronoia und Paideusis: Studien über Origenes und sein Verhältnis zum Platonismus,* Berlin: de Gruyter.

Koester, Helmut. 1991. "Writing and the Spirit: Authority and Politics in Ancient Christianity." *Harvard Theological Review* 84:353–372.

Kofsky, Aryeh. 2000. *Eusebius of Caesarea against Paganism.* Jewish and Christian Perspectives Series, 3. Leiden: Brill.

Konstan, David. 1996. *Friendship in the Classical World.* Cambridge: Cambridge University Press.

Kraft, Heinz. 1955. *Kaiser Konstantins religiöse Entwicklung.* Beiträge zur Historischen Theologie, 20. Tübingen: Mohr (Siebeck).

Krautheimer, Richard. 1965. 1986. *Early Christian and Byzantine Architecture.* 4th ed., rev. with Slobodan Coric. Baltimore, Penguin Books; New Haven: Yale University Press.

Kuhrt, Amélie. 1986. "Berossus' *Babyloniaka* and Seleucid Rule in Babylonia" In Kuhrt and Sherwin-White (eds.) 1986, 32–56.

Kuhrt, Amélie, and Susan Sherwin-White (eds.). 1986. *Hellenism in the East: Interaction of Greek and Non-Greek Civilizations from Syria to Central Asia after Alexander.* London: Duckworth.

Kullmann, Wolfgang, and Jochen Althoff (eds.). 1993. *Vermittlung und Tradierung von Wissen in der griechischen Kultur.* Script Oralia 61. Tübingen: Gunter Narr.

Lamberton, Robert. 1986. *Homer the Theologian: Neoplatonist Allegorical Reading and the Growth of the Epic Tradition.* Berkeley: University of California Press.

Lamberton, Robert, and John J. Keaney (eds.). 1992. *Homer's Ancient Readers.* Princeton: Princeton University Press.

Lampe, Peter. 2003; tr. from German 2nd ed., 1989. *From Paul to Valentinus: Christians at Rome in the First Two Centuries,* Tr. from the German 2nd ed. (1989) by Marshall Johnson. Minneapolis: Fortress Press.

Laqueur, Richard. 1929. *Eusebios als Historiker seiner Zeit.* Leipzig and Berlin: de Gruyter.

Lauffer, Siegfried. 1971. *Diokletians Preisedikt.* Berlin: de Gruyter.

Lawlor, H. J. 1912. "On the Use by Eusebius of Volumes of Tracts." In *Eusebiana,* 136–178. Oxford: Clarendon Press

Le Boulluec, Alain. 1987. "L'école d'Alexandria. De quelques aventures d'un concept historiographique" In *Alexandrina:. Héllenisme, judaïsme, et christianisme à Alexandrie,* 403–417. Mélanges offerts au P. Claude Mondésert. Paris: Editions du Cerf.

———1999. Aux origines, encores, de l'école' d'Alexandrie *Adamantius* 5:8–36.

———2000. "L'école' d'Alexandrie." In *Le nouveau peuple,* 531–578. Histoire du Christianisme, 1. Paris: Editions du Cerf.

Leiman, Sid (ed.). 1974. *The Canon and Masorah of the Hebrew Bible: An Introductory Reader.* New York: Ktav.

Lendon, J. E. 1997. *Empire of Honour: The Art of Government in the Roman World.* Oxford: Clarendon Press.

Levine, Lee. 1975. *Caesarea under Roman Rule.* Leiden: Brill.

Levine, Lee. (ed.). 1999. *Jerusalem: Its Sanctity and Centrality to Judaism, Christianity, and Islam.* New York: Continuum

Lewis, Naphtali. 1974. *Papyrus in Classical Antiquity.* Oxford: Clarendon Press.

Lieberman, Saul. 1939–1944. "The Martyrs of Caesarea." *Annuaire de l'Institut de philologie et d'histoire orientales et slaves* 7:395–446.

———. 1942. *Greek in Jewish Palestine.* New York: Jewish Theological Seminary of America.

Lies, Lother (ed.). 1987. *Origeniana Quarta.* Innsbruck: Tyrolia-Verlag.

Linder, Amon. 1976. "Ecclesia and Synagoga in the Medieval Myth of Constantine the Great." *Revue Belge de Philologie et d'Histoire* 54:1029–30.

Long, A. A. 1992. "Stoic Readings of Homer." In Lamberton and Keaney (eds.) 1992, 41–66.

Lord, Carnes. 1986. "On the Early History of the Aristotelian Corpus." *American Journal of Philology* 107:147–161.

Louth, A. 1990. "The Date of Eusebius' *Historia Ecclesiastica.*" *Journal of Theological Studies* n.s. 41:111–123.

Lubac, Henri de. 1954–1964. *Exégèse médiévale: les quatre sens de l'Écriture.* 4 vols. Paris: Aubier.

Luraghi, Nino (ed.). 2001. *The Historian's Craft in the Age of Herodotus.* Oxford: Oxford University Press.

Lyon, Gregory. 2003. "Baudouin, Flacius, and the Plan for the Magdeburg Centuries." *Journal of the History of Ideas* 64:253–272.

Maas, Michael. 1992. *John Lydus and the Roman Past: Amtiquarianism and Politics in the Age of Justinian.* London: Routledge.

Mango, Cyril. 1985. *Le Développement urbain de Constantinople (IVe-VIIe siècles).* Paris: Diffusion de Boccard.

Marichal, Robert. 1963. "L'écriture latine et la civilisation occidentale du Ier au XVIe siècle." In Cohen (ed.) 1963, 199–247.

Marincola, John. 1997. *Authority and Tradition in Ancient Historiography.* Cambridge: Cambridge University Press.

Markus, Robert. 1975. "Church History and Early Church Historians." In *The Materials, Sources, and Methods of Ecclesiastical His-*

tory, ed. Derek Baker, 1–17. Studies in Church History, 11. Oxford: Blackwell.

———1990. *The End of Ancient Christianity.* Cambridge: Cambridge University Press.

Marrou, Henri-Irénée. 1949 [1976]. "Le technique de l'édition à l'époque patristique." *Vigiliae Christianae* 1949:208–224. Repr. in *Patristique et humanisme: Mélanges,* 239–252. Patristica Sorbonensia, 9. Paris: Seuil.

———1964. *A History of Education in Antiquity.* Tr. George Lamb. New York: New American Library.

Marsden, Richard. 1995. "Job in His Place: The Ezra Miniature in the Codex Amiatinus." *Scriptorium* 49 3–15.

Martin, Donald. 1984. "The Statilius-subscription and the Editions of Late Antiquity." In *Classical Texts and Their Traditions: Studies in Honor of C. R. Trahman,* ed. David Bright and Edwin Ramage, 147–154. Chico, Cal.: Scholars Press.

McCormick, Michael. 1985. "The Birth of the Codex and the Apostolic Life-Style." *Scriptorium* 39:150–158.

McDonnell, Myles. 1996. "Writing, Copying, and Autograph Manuscripts in Ancient Rome." *Classical Quarterly* 46:460–491.

McGuckin, John. 1992. "Caesarea Maritima as Origen Knew It." In *Origeniana Quinta. Historica—Text and Method—Biblica—Philosophica—Theologica—Origenism and Later Developments,* ed. Robert Daly, 3–25. Papers of the 5th International Origen Congress, Boston College, 14-18 August 1989. Leuven: Leuven University Press.

McKitterick, Rosamond. 2004. *History and Memory in the Carolingian World.* Cambridge: Cambridge University Press.

Méhat, André. 1966. *Etudes sur les "Stromates" de Clément d'Alexandrie.* Paris: Seuil.

Mendels, Doron. 1999. *The Media Revolution of Early Christianity: An Essay on Eusebius's Ecclesiastical History.* Grand Rapids: Eerdmans.

Mercati, Giovanni. 1896. "D'un palimpsesto Ambrosiano contenente i Salmi esapli e di un'antica versione latina del commentario perduto di Teodoro di Mopsuestia al Salterio." *Atti della Reale Academia di Scienze di Torino* 31 655–76

————1901a. "D'alcuni frammenti esaplari sulla Va e VIa edizione greca della Bibbia." *Studi e Testi* 5:28–46.

————1901b. "Sul testo e sul senso di Eusebio H.E. VI 16." *Studi e testi* 5:47–60.

————1941. *Nuove note di letteratura biblica e cristiana antica.* Studi e Testi, 95. Vatican City: Biblioteca Apostolica Vaticana.

————1947. "Il problema della colonna II del Esaplo" *Biblica* 28:181 ff.

————1948. *Osservazioni a proemi del Salterio di Origene, Ippolito, Eusebio, Cirillo Alessandrino e altri, con frammenti inediti.* Vatican City: Biblioteca Apostolica Vaticana.

Mercati, Giovanni (ed.). 1958. *Psalterii Hexapli reliquiae cura et studio Ioh. Card. Mercati editae. Pars prima A: Codex rescriptus bybliothecae Ambrosianae O 39 Sup. phototypice expressus et transcriptus.* Vatican City: Bibliotheca Vaticana.

Merrills, A. H. 2005. *History and Geography in Late Antiquity.* Cambridge: Cambridge University Press.

Metzger, Bruce. 1963. *Chapters in the History of New Testament Textual Criticism.* Grand Rapids: Wm. B. Eerdmans.

————1968. *Historical and Literary Studies: Pagan, Jewish, and Christian.* Grand Rapids: Wm. B. Eerdmans.

————1980. *New Testament Studies: Philological, Versional, and Patristic.* Leiden: Brill.

————1981. *Manuscripts of the Greek Bible.* New York: Oxford University Press.

————1987. *The Canon of the New Testament: Its Origin, Development, and Significance.* Oxford: Clarendon Press.

————1992. *The Text of the New Testament: Its Transmission, Corruption, and Restoration,* 3rd ed. New York: Oxford University Press.

Millar, Fergus. 1977. *The Emperor in the Roman World.* London: Duckworth;Ithaca: Cornell University Press.

Miller, Peter. 2001. "The 'Antiquarianization' of Biblical Scholarship and the London Polyglot Bible (1653–57)." *Journal of the History of Ideas* 62:463–482.

Milne, H. J. M., and T. C. Skeat, with Douglas Cockerell. 1938. *Scribes and Correctors of the Codex Sinaiticus.* London: British Museum.

Mizugaki, Wataru. 1987. "Origen and Josephus" In Feldman and Hata (eds.) 1987, 325–337.

Möller, Astrid. 2001. "The Beginnings of Chronography: Hellanicus' *Hiereiai.*" In Luraghi (ed.) 2001, 241–262.

———2004. *Time and Temporality in the Ancient World.* Ed. Ralph Rosen. Philadelphia: University of Pennsylvania Press.

———Forthcoming a. "Epoch-Making Eratosthenes." Forthcoming in *Greek, Roman, and Byzantine Studies.*

———Forthcoming b. "Felix Jacoby and Ancient Greek Chronography." Forthcoming in *Aspetti dell' opera di Felix Jacoby,* ed. C. Ampolo.

Möller, Astrid, and Nino Luraghi. 1995. "Time in the Writing of History: Perceptions and Structures." *Storia della Storiografia* 28:3–15.

Momigliano, Arnaldo. 1963. "Pagan and Christian Historiography in the fourth century A.D." In Momigliano (ed.) 1963.

———1975. *Alien Wisdom.* Cambridge: Cambridge University Press.

———1977a. "Eastern Elements in Post Exilic Jewish, and Greek, Historiography." In *Essays in Ancient and Modern Historiography,* 25–35. Oxford: Blackwell.

———1977b. "Mabillon's Italian Disciples." In *Essays in Ancient and Modern Historiography,* 00–00. Oxford: Blackwell.

———1991. *The Classical Foundations of Modern Historiography.* Ed. Riccardo Di Donato. Berkeley: University of California Press.

Momigliano, Arnaldo(ed.). 1963. *The Conflict between Paganism and Christianity in the Fourth Century.* Oxford: Oxford University Press.

Montanari, Franco. 1998. "Zenodotus, Aristarchus, and the *Ekdosis* of Homer." In Most (ed.) 1998, 1–21.

Moraux, Paul. 1951. *Les listes anciennes des ouvrages d'Aristote.* Louvain: Editions Universitaires de Louvain.

————1973. *Der Aristotelismus bei den Griechen: von Andronikos bis Alexander von Aphrodisias,* I. Berlin: De Gruyter.

Morgan, Teresa. 1998. *Literate Education in the Hellenistic and Roman Worlds.* Cambridge: Cambridge University Press.

Mortley, Raoul. 1990. "The Hellenistic Foundations of Ecclesiastical Historiography." In *Reading the Past in Late Antiquity,* ed. Graeme Clark, 225–250. Rushcutters Bay: Australian National University Press.

————1996. *The Idea of Universal History from Hellenistic Philosophy to Early Christian Historiography.* Lewiston, N.Y.: Edwin Mellen.

Most, Glenn. 1989. "Cornutus and Stoic Allegoresis: A Preliminary Report." In *Aufstieg und Niedergang der Römischen Welt,* ed. H. Temporini and W. Haase, 2.36.3, 2014–2065. Berlin and New York: De Gruyter, 1972–.

Most, Glenn (ed.). 1998. *Editing Texts—Texte edieren.* Göttingen: Vandenhoeck & Ruprecht.

Mras, Karl (ed.). 1954. *Eusebius Werke VIII: Die Praeparatio Evangelica.* I, liv-lviii. Berlin.

Munson, Rosaria Vignolo. 2005. *Black Doves Speak: Herodotus and the Languages of Barbarians.* Washington, D.C.: Center for Hellenic Studies.

Münzer, Friedrich. 1905. "Atticus als Geschichtschreiber." *Hermes* 40:50–100.

Murphy, Harold. 1959. "The Text of Romans and 1 Corinthians in Minuscule 93 and the Text of Pamphilus." *Harvard Theological Review* 52:119–130

Murray, Oswyn. 1969. Review of Ramsay MacMullen, *Enemies of the Roman Order. Journal of Roman Studies* 59:261–265.

Nautin, Pierre. 1961. *Patristica II: Lettres et écrivains chrétiens des IIe et IIIe siècles.* Paris: Editions du Cerf.

————1977. *Origène: Sa vie et son oeuvre* Paris: Beauchesne.

Neuschäfer, Bernhard. 1987. *Origenes al Philologe.* 2 vols.

Schweizerische Beiträge zur Altertumswissenschaft, 18, 1–2. Basel: Friedrich Reinhardt Verlag.

Norman, A. F. 1960. "The Book Trade in Fourth-Century Antioch" *Journal of Hellenic Studies* 80:122–126.

Obbink, Dirk. 2004. "Craft, Cult, and Canon in the Books from Herculaneum." In Fitzgerald, Obbink, and Holland (eds.) 2004, 73–84.

Obbink, Dirk (ed.). 1995. *Philodemus and Poetry.* New York: Oxford University Press.

O'Donnell, James. 1998. *Avatars of the Word from Papyrus to Cyberspace.* Cambridge: Harvard University Press.

O'Meara, Dominic J. 1993. *Plotinus: An introduction to the Enneads.* Oxford: Clarendon Press.

Olson, Oliver. 2002. *Matthias Flacius and the Survival of Luther's Reform.* Wiesbaden: Harrassowitz in Kommission.

Origen and Frederick Field. 1875. *Origenis Hexaplorum quae supersunt; Veterum interpretum graecorum in totum Vetus Testamentum fragmenta.* Oxford: Clarendon Press.

Osborne, Catherine. 1987. *Rethinking Early Greek Philosophy: Hippolytus of Rome and the Presocratics.* London: Duckworth.

Otranto, Rosa. 2000. *Antiche liste di libri su papiro.* Rome: Storia e letteratura.

Overbeck, Franz. 1892 [1965]). *Über die Anfänge der Kirchengeschichtsschreibung.* Programm zur Rektoratsfeier der Universität Basel, Basel. Repr. Darmstadt: Wissenschaftliche Buchgesellschaft.

Pabel, Hilmar. 2002. "Reading Jerome in the Renaissance: Erasmus's Reception of the *Adversus Jovinianum." Renaissance Quarterly* 55:470–497.

Pagels, Elaine. 1973. *The Johannine Gospel in Gnostic Exegesis: Heracleon's Commentary on John.* Society of Biblical Literature Monographs 17. Nashville, Tenn.: Abingdon Press.

Pasquali, Giorgio. 1910. "Die Composition der *Vita Constantini* des Eusebius." *Hermes* 46:369–386., Repr. in Pasquali 1986 I, 466–483

————1986. *Scritti filologici.* 2 vols. Ed. Fritz Bornmann, Giovanni Pascucci, and Sebastiano Timpanaro, introduction by Antonio La Penna. Florence: Olschki.

Pattie, T. S. 1998. "The Creation of the Great Codices." In Sharpe and Van Kampen 1998, 61–72.

Pecere, Oronzo. 1982. "La 'subscriptio' di Statilio Massimo e la tradizione delle 'Agrarie' di Cicerone." *Italia Medioevale e Umanistica* 25:73–123.

————1984. "Esemplari con *Subscriptiones* e tradizione dei testi latini. L'Apuleio Laur. 68, 2." In *Atti del Convegno internazionale Il Libro e Il Testo Urbino, 20-23 settembre 1982,* ed. Cesare Questa and Renato Raffaelli, 113–137. Urbino: Università degli studi di Urbino.

————1986. "La tradizione dei testi latini tra IV e V secolo attraverso i libri sottoscritti." In *Tradizioni dei classici, trasformazioni della cultura,* ed. Andrea Giardina, 19–81.Rome: Laterza.

Petitmengin, Pierre, and Bernard Flusin. 1984. "Le Livre antique et la dictée: nouvelles recherches" In *Mémorial André-Jean Festugière,* ed. E. Lucchesi and H. D. Saffrey, 247–262.Geneva: Cramer.

Phillips, John. 1989. "Atticus and the Publication of Cicero's Works." *Classical World* 79:227–237.

Pietri, Charles. 1983. "Constantin en 324: propagande et théologie impériales d'après les documents de la *Vita Constantini.*" In *Crise et redressement dans les provinces européennes de l'Empire (milieu du IIIe au IVe siècle ap. J.C.,* Actes du Colloque de Strasbourg (December 1981), 63–90. Strasbourg: Presses de l'Université. Repr. in Pietri 1997, I, 253–280.

———— 1997. *Christiana Respublica: éléments d'une enquête sur le Christianisme antique.* 3 vols. Rome: Ecole Française de Rome.

Places, E. des. 1956. "Eusèbe de Césarée juge de Platon dans la Préparation Evangélique." In *Mélanges de philosophie Grecque offerts à Mgr. Dies,* 72. Paris: Vrin.

————1982. *Eusèbe de Césarée commentateur: Platonisme et écriture sainte.* Paris: Beauchesne.

Pohlkamp, W. "Textfassungen, literarische Formen und Geschichtliche Funktionen der römischen Silvester-Akten." *Francia* 19: 115–196.

Porten, Bezalel. 1968. *Archives from Elephantine: The Life of an Ancient Jewish Military Colony*. Berkeley: University of California Press.

Posner, Ernst. 1972. *Archives in the Ancient World*. Cambridge: Harvard University Press.

Press, Gerald. 1982. *The Development of the Idea of History in Antiquity*. Kingston: McGill-Queen's University Press.

Puglia, E. 1982. "La filologia degli Epicurei." *Cronache ercolanesi* 12:125–173.

Quillen, Carol. 1998. *Rereading the Renaissance: Petrarch, Augustine, and the Language of Humanism*. Ann Arbor: University of Michigan Press.

Raban, Avner, and Kenneth Holum (eds.). 1996. *Caesarea Maritima: A Retrospective after Two Millennia*. Leiden: Brill.

Rebenich, Stefan. 1992. *Hieronymus und sein Kreis: prosopographische und sozialgeschichtliche Untersuchungen*. Stuttgart: F. Steiner.

————1993. "Jerome: the 'Vir Trilinguis' and the 'Hebraica Veritas.'" *Vigiliae Christianae* 47:50–77.

Redepenning, Ernst Rudolf. 1841–1846. *Origenes: eine Darstellung seines Lebens und seiner Lehre*. 2 vols. Bonn: E. Weber.

Reymond, Antoine. 1987. "*Apologie* pour Origène: un état de la question." In Lies (ed.) 1987, 136–145.

Reynolds, Joyce, and Robert Tannenbaum (eds.). 1987. *Jews and Godfearers at Aphrodisias: Greek Inscriptions with Commentary. Texts from the Excavations at Aphrodisias Conducted by Kenan T. Erim*. Cambridge: The Cambridge Philological Society.

Reynolds, L. D. and N. G. Wilson. 1991. *Scribes and Scholars: A Guide to the Transmission of Greek and Latin Literature*, 3rd ed. Oxford: Clarendon Press.

Rice, Eugene. 1985. *Saint Jerome in the Renaissance*. Baltimore: Johns Hopkins University Press.

Rist, John. 1981. "Basil's 'Neoplatonism': Its Background and Nature." In *Basil of Caesarea: Christian, Humanist, Ascetic*, 2 vols., I, 137–220. Toronto: Pontifical Institute of Mediaeval Studies.

Robbins, Gregory. 1989. "'Fifty Copies of the Sacred Writings' (VC 4:36): Entire Bibles or Gospel Books?" *Studia Patristica* 19:91–98.

Robbins, John. 1986. "Peri tôn endiathêkôn graphôn- Eusebius and the Formation of the Christian Bible." Ph.D. diss., Duke University.

Roberts, Bleddyn. 1951. *The Old Testament Text and Versions: The Hebrew Text in Transmission and the History of the Ancient Versions.* Cardiff: University of Wales Press.

Roberts, Colin. 1979. *Manuscript, Society, and Belief in Early Christian Egypt.* The Schweich Lectures of the British Academy, 1977. London: Published for the British Academy by the Oxford University Press.

Roberts, Colin, and T. C. Skeat. 1983. *The Birth of the Codex.* London: Published for the British Academy by the Oxford University Press.

Robinson, J. Armitage. 1895. *Euthaliana: Studies of Euthalius, Codex H of the Pauline Epistles, and the Armenian Version.* Cambridge: Cambridge University Press.

Rosenberg, Daniel. 2004. "The Trouble with Timelines." *Cabinet* 13:85.

Rossi, Paolo. 1984. *The Dark Abyss of Time: The History of the Earth and the History of Nations from Hooke to Vico.* Tr. Lydia Cochrane. Chicago: University of Chicago Press.

Rouse, Mary, and Richard Rouse. 1982[1991]. "*Statim invenire*: Schools, Preachers, and New Attitudes to the Page." In *The Renaissance of the Twelfth Century*, ed. R. L. Benson, G. Constable, and C. Lanham. Cambridge: Harvard University Press. Repr. in Mary Rouse and Richard Rouse 1991, 191–219.

1991. *Authentic Witnesses: Approaches to Medieval Texts and Manuscripts.* Notre Dame: Notre Dame University Press.

Rouse, Richard, and Charles McNelis. 2000 [2001. "North African Literary Activity: A Cyprian Fragment, the Stichometric Lists, and a Donatist Compendium." *Revue d'Histoire des Textes* 30:189–238.

Ruggini, L. Cracco. 1977. "The Ecclesiastical Histories and the Pagan Historiography: Providence and Miracles." *Athenaeum* n.s. 55:107–126.

Runia, David. 1993. *Philo in Early Christian Literature: A Survey.* Compendia Rerum Iudaicarum ad Novum Testamentum, III, 3. Assen: Van Gorcum; Minneapolis: Fortress Press.

———1996. "Caesarea Maritima and the Survival of Hellenistic-Jewish Literature." In Raban and Holu, (eds.) 1996, 476–495.

Rutgers, L. V. , P. W. van der Horst, H. W. Havelaar and L. Teugels (eds.). 1998. *The Use of Sacred Books in the Ancient World.* Contributions to Biblical Exegesis and Theology, 22. Leuven: Peeters.

Saller, Richard. 1982. *Personal Patronage under the Early Empire.* Cambridge: Cambridge University Press.

———1983. "Martial on Patronage and Literature." *Classical Quarterly* 33:246–257.

Salvesen, Alison (ed.). 1998. *Origen's Hexapla and Fragments: Papers Presented at the Rich Seminar on the Hexapla, Oxford Centre for Hebrew and Jewish Studies, 25th July-3rd August 1994.* Tübingen: Mohr Siebeck.

Salzman, Michele. 1990. *On Roman Time: The Codex Calendar of 354 and the Rhythms of Urban Life in Late Antiquity.* Berkeley: University of California Press.

———1999. "The Christianization of Sacred Time and Sacred Space." *The Transformations of Urbs Roma in Late Antiquity* Supp. Ser. 33, ed. William Harris:123–134.

Sanders, Jack T. 2000. *Charisma, Converts, Competitors: Societal and Sociological Factors in the Success of Early Christianity.* London: SCM.

Sandy, Gerald N. 1997. *The Greek World of Apuleius: Apuleius and the Second Sophistic.* Leiden: Brill.

Sautel, Jacques-Hubert. 2000. "Aspects de la mise en page des manuscrits grecs à chaînes exégétiques (Paris, BnF, fonds Coislin)." In Goulot-Cazé (ed.) 2000, 89–98.

Schäfer, Peter. 1997. *Judeophobia: Attitudes toward the Jews in the Ancient World*. Cambridge: Harvard University Press.

Schär, Max. 1979. *Das Nachleben des origines im Zeitalter des Humanismus*. Basel: Helbing & Lichtenhahn.

Schlunk, Robin. 1993. *The Homeric Questions*. New York, Robin Lang.

Schmid, Ulrich. 0000. Review of Kim Haines-Eitzen, *Guardians of Letters*. *TC: A Journal of Biblical Textual Criticism* [http://purl.ord/ TC] 7.

Schöne, Hermann. 1939. "Ein Einbruch der antiken Logik und Textkritik in die altchristliche Theologie." In *Pisciculi: Studien zur Religion und Kultur des Altertums, Franz Joseph Dölger zum sechzigsten Geburtstage dargeboten von Freunden, Verehrern und Schülern*, ed. Theodor Klauser and Adolf Rücker, 252–265. Münster in Westfalen: Aschendorff.

Schroeder, Frederic M. 1987. "Ammonius Saccas." In *Aufstieg und Niedergang der Römischen Welt*, ed. H. Temporini and W. Haase, 2.36.1, 493–526. Berlin and New York: De Gruyter, 1972–.

———1992. *Form and Transformation: A Study in the Philosophy of Plotinus*. Montreal: McGill-Queen's University Press.

Schwartz, Eduard. 1903a [963]. "Zur Geschichte der Hexapla." *Nachrichten von der königlichen Gesellschaft der Wissenschaften zu Göttingen*, phil.-hist. Kl. 1903:693–700. Repr. in Eduard Schwarz, *Gesammelte Schriften, 5: Zum Neuen Testament und zum Frühen Christentum, 183–191*. Berlin: De Gruyter, 1963.

———1903b. "Zu Eusebius Kirchengeschichte I. Das Martyrium Jakobus des Gerechten" *Zeitschrift für Neutestamentliche Wissenschaft* 4:48–61.

———1903c. "Zu Eusebius Kirchengeschichte I. Zur Abgarlegende." *Zeitschrift für Neutestamentliche Wissenschaft* 4:61–66.

———1909. "Eusebios von Caesarea." *RE* 6:1370–1409.

Schwartz, Seth. 2001. *Imperialism and Jewish Society, 200 B.C.E. to 640 C.E.* Princeton: Princeton University Press.

Sedley, David. 1989. "Philosophical Allegiance in the Greco-Roman World." In Griffin and Barnes (ed.) 1989, 97–119.

Seeck, Otto. "Die Urkunden der Vita Constantini" *Zeitschrift für Kirchengeschichte* 18:321-345.

Segal, M. H. 1953 [1974]. "The Promulgation of the Authoritative Text of the Hebrew Bible" *Journal of Biblical Literature* 72:35–47. Repr. in Leiman (ed.) 1974, 285–297.

Shalev, Zur. 2004. "Geographia sacra: Cartography, Religion, and Scholarship in the Sixteenth and Seventeenth Centuries." Ph.D. diss., Princeton University.

Sharpe, John, and Kimberly van Kampen (eds.). 1998. *The Bible as Book: The Manuscript Tradition.* London: The British Library; New Castle: Oak Knoll Press, in association with The Scriptorium: Center for Christian Antiquities.

Shaw, Brent. 1993. "The Passion of Perpetua." *Past and Present* 139:3–45.

Shelford, April. 1997. "Faith and Glory: Pierre-Daniel Huet and the Making of the Demonstratio Evangelica (1679)." Ph.D. diss., Princeton University.

Sirinelli, Jean. 1961. *Les vues historiques d'Eusèbe de Césarée durant le période prénicéenne.* Dakar: Publications de la section de langues et littératures, University of Dakar.

Skeat, T. C. 1956. "The Use of Dictation in Ancient Book-Production." *Proceedings of the British Academy* 42:179–208.

———1982. "The Length of the Standard Papyrus Roll and the Cost-Advantage of the Codex." *Zeitschrift für Papyrologie und Epigraphik* 45:169–175.

———1999. "The Codex Sinaiticus, the Codex Vaticanus, and Constantine." *Journal of Theological Studies* n.s. 50:583–625.

———2004. *The Collected Biblical Writings.* Ed. J.K. Elliott. Supplements to Novum Testamentum, 113. Leiden and Boston: Brill.

Small, Jocelyn Penny. 1997. *Wax Tablets of the Mind: Cognitive Studies of Memory and Literacy in Classical Antiquit.*, London: Routledge.

Smith, M. 1989. "Eusebius of Caesarea: Scholar and Apologist. A Study of his Religious Terminology and Its Application to the Emperor Constantine." Ph.D. diss., University of California, Santa Barbara.

Smith, William (ed.). 1867. *Dictionary of Greek and Roman Biography and Mythology.* Boston: Little, Brown.

Snyder, H. Gregory. 2000. *Teachers and Texts in the Ancient World: Philosophers, Jews, and Christians.* New York: Routledge.

Soisanon-Soininen, Ilmari. 1959. *Der Charakter der asterisierten Zusätze in der Septuaginta.* Annales Academiae Scientiarum Fennicae, series B, 114. Helsinki: Suomalainen Tiedeakatemia.

Sommer, R. 1926. "Pomponius Atticus und die Verbreitung von Ciceros Werken." *Hermes* 61:389–422.

Sorabji, Richard. 1997. *Aristotle and After.* Bulletin of the Institute of Classical Studies, supplement 68. London: Institute of Classical Studies, School of Advanced Study, University of London.

Speigl, J. 1971. "Eine Kritik an Kaiser Konstantin in der Vita Constantini des Euseb." In *Wegzeichen: Festgabe zum 60. Geburtstag von Prof. Dr. Hermenegild H. Biedermann OSA,* 83–94. Würzburg: Augustinus-Verlag.

Staden, Heinrich von. 1995. "Anatomy as Rhetoric: Galen on Dissection and Persuasion." *Journal of the History of Medicine and the Allied Sciences* 50:47–66.

———1997. "Galen and the Second Sophistic." In Sorabji (ed.) 1997, 33–54.

Stark, Rodney. 1996. *The Rise of Christianity: A Sociologist Reconsiders History.* Princeton: Princeton Unversity Press.

Starr, Raymond. 1987. "The Circulation of Literary Texts in the Roman World." *Classical Quarterly* 37:213–223.

Stein, Peter. 1966. *Regulae iuris: From Juristic Rules to Legal Maxims.* Edinburgh: Edinburgh University Press.

Stemberger, Günter. 2000. *Jews and Christians in the Holy Land: Pal-*

estine in the Fourth Century. Tr. Ruth Tuschling. Edinburgh: T. & T. Clark.

Stevenson, James. 1929. *Studies in Eusebius.* Cambridge: CambridgeUniversity Press.

Stock, Brian. 1996. *Augustine the Reader : Meditation, Self-Knowledge, and the Ethics of Interpretation.* Cambridge, : Harvard University Press.

————2001. *After Augustine: The Meditative Reader and the Text.* Philadelphia: University of Pennsylvania Press.

Sterling, Gregory. 1992. *Historiography and Self-Definition: Josephus, Luke-Acts, and Apologetic Historiography.* Supplements to *Novum Testamentum*, 64. Leiden: Brill.

Strocka, Volker Michael. 1981. "Römische Bibliotheken." *Gymnasium* 88:298–329.

Swain, Simon. 1996. *Hellenism and Empire: Language, Classicism, and Power in the Greek World, AD 50-250.* Oxford: Clarendon Press.

Swete, Henry. 1900. *An Introduction to the Old Testament in Greek.* Cambridge: Cambridge University Press.

Tabbernee, W. 1997. "Eusebius' 'Theology of Persecution': As Seen in the Various Editions of his Church History." *Journal of Early Christian Studies* 5:319–334.

Tarán, L. 1981. Review of Paul Moraux, *Der Aristotelismus bei den Griechen. Gnomon* 53 724–731.

Taylor, Charles. 1900. *Hebrew-Greek Cairo Genizah Palimpsests from the Taylor-Schechter Collection: Including a Fragment of the Twenty-Second Psalm According to Origen's Hexapla.* Cambridge: Cambridge University Press.

Taylor, Joan. 1993. *Christians and the Holy Places: The Myth of Jewish-Christian Origins.* Oxford: Clarendon Press.

Teitler, H. C. 1985. *Notarii and Exceptores: An Inquiry into Role and Significance of Shorthand Writers in the Imperial and Ecclesiastical Bureaucracy of the Roman Empire (from the Early Principate to c. 450 A.D.).* Dutch Monographs on Ancient History and Archaeology, 1. Amsterdam: Gieben.

Thee, Francis. 1984. *Julius Africanus and the Early Christian View of Magic*. Tübingen: J. C. B. Mohr (Paul Siebeck).

Thomsen, Peter. 1903. "Palästina nach dem Onomasticon des Eusebius." *Zeitschrift des deutschen Palästina-Vereins* 26:97–141.

Timpanaro, Sebastiano. 1986. *Per la storia della filologia virgiliana antica*. Rome: Salerno.

Timpe, Dieter. 1989. "Was ist Kirchengeschichte? Zum Gattungscharakter der Historia Ecclesiastica des Eusebius." *Xenia*, 22:171–204

———1995. "Che cos'è la storia della chiesa? La Historia Ecclesiastica di Eusebio. Caratteristiche di un genere." In *Lo spazio letterario della Grecia classica*, ed. Guido Cambiano, Luciano Canfora, and Diego Lanza, II, 389–435. Rome: Laterza.

Too, Yun Lee (ed.). 2001. *Education in Greek and Roman Antiquity*. Leidenn: Brill.

Torjesen, Karen Jo. 1986. *Hermeneutical Procedure and TheologicalSstructure in Origen's Exegesis*. Berlin: De Gruyter.

Trigg, Joseph Wilson. 1981a. "A Decade of Origen Studies." *Religious Studies Review* 7:21–26.

———1981b. "The Charismatic Intellectual: Origen's Understanding of Religious Leadership" *Church History* 50:5–19.

———1983. *Origen: The Bible and Philosophy in the Third-Century Church*. Atlanta: John Knox Press.

———1992. "Origen, Man of the Church" In Daly (ed.) 1992, 51–56.

———1998. *Origen*. London: Routledge.

———2001. "God's Marvelous *Oikonomia*: Reflections on Origen's Understanding of Divine and Human Pedagogy in the Address Ascribed to Gregory Thaumaturgus." *Journal of Early Christian Studies* 9:27–52.

Trithemius, Johannes. 1531. *Catalogus scriptorum ecclesiasticorum*. Cologne.

———1559. *Chronicon insigne Monasterij Hirsaugiensis, Ordinis S. Benedicti*. Basel: Oporinus.

―――. 1690. *Annalium Hirsaugiensium Opus numquam hactenus editum, & ab Eruditis semper desideratum, complectens historiam Franciæ et Germaniæ, gesta Imperatorum, Regum, Principum, Episcoporum, Abbatum, et illustrium virorum.* 2 vols. St Gallen: Schlegel.

―――1974. *In Praise of Scribes [De laude scriptorum]* Ed. Klaus Arnold, tr. Roland Behrendt, O.S.B. Lawrence, Kans.: Coronado.

Troiani, Lucio. 1983. "Contributo alla problematica dei rapporti fra storiografia greca e storiografia vicino-orientale." *Athenaeum* 71:427–438.

Trompf, Gary. 1983. "The Logic of Retribution in Eusebius of Caesarea." In Croke and Emmett (ed.) 1983, 132-146.

Tropper, Amram. 2004a. *Wisdom, Politics, and Historiography: Tractate Avot in the Context of the Graeco-Roman Near East.* Oxford: Oxford University Press.

―――2004b. "The Fate of Jewish Historiography after the Bible: A New Interpretation." *History and Theory* 43:179–197.

Trout, Denis. 2003. "Damasus and the Invention of Early Rome." *Journal of Medieval and Renaissance Studies* 33:517–536.

Tufte, Edward. 1983. *The Visual Display of Quantitative Information.* Cheshire, Conn.: Graphics Press.

Turner, Eric. 1974. "Towards a Typology of the Early Codex (3rd-6th Centuries A.D.): Classification by Outward Characteristics." In *La Paléographie hébraïque médiévale*, Colloques internationaux du Centre National de la Recherche Scientifique, 547, Paris, 11–13 September, 1972, 137–152. Paris: Centre Nationale de la Recherche Scientifique: 1974.

―――1977. *The Typology of the Early Codex.* Philadelphia: University of Pennsylvania Press.

Ulrich, Eugene. 1988. "Origen's Old Testament Text: The Transmission History of the Septuagint to the Third Century, C.E." In Kannengiesser and Petersen (eds.) 1988, 3–33.

―――1992. "The Old Testament Text of Eusebius: The Heritage of Origen" In Attridge and Hata (eds.) 1992, 543-562.

Ulrich, Jörg. 1999. *Euseb von Caesarea und die Juden. Studien zur Rolle der Juden in der Theologie des Eusebius von Caesarea.* Berlin: Walter de Gruyter.

Van den Hoek, Annewies. 1992. "Origen and the Intellectual Heritage of Alexandria: Continuity or Disjunction?" In Daly (ed.) 1992, 40–50.

————1996. "Techniques of Quotation in Clement of Alexandria: A View of Ancient Literary Working Methods." *Vigiliae Christianae* 50:223–243.

Vanderkam, James. 2000. *From Revelation to Canon: Studies in the Hebrew Bible and Second Temple Literature.* Leiden: Brill.

Van Elderen, Bastiann. 1998. "Early Christian Libraries," in Sharpe and Van Kampen (1998), 45–59

Vannicelli, Pietro. 2001. "Herodotus' Egypt and the Foundations of Universal History." In Luraghi (ed.) 2001, 211–240.

Veltri, Giuseppe. 2004. "Idiom des Leidens." *Frankfurter Allgemeine Zeitung* 77 (31 March) N 3.

Vessey, Mark. 1993. "Jerome's Origen: The Making of a Christian Literary Persona," *Studia Patristica* 28:135–145.

————1994. "Erasmus' Jerome: The Publishing of a Christian Author." *Erasmus of Rotterdam Yearbook* 14:62–99.

Vianès, Laurence. 2000. "Aspects de la mise en page dans les manuscrits de chaînes sur Ezéchiel." In Goulot-Cazé (ed.) 2000, 79–78.

Von Leyden, W. 1949. "Spatium historicum." *Durham University Journal* 11:89–114.

Vööbus, Arthur. 1975. *The Pentateuch in the Version of the Syro-Hexapla. A fac-simile edition of a Midyat MS. discovered 1964.* Louvain: Corpus Scriptorum Christianorum Orientalium.

Wacholder, Ben Zion. 1968, "Biblical Chronology in the Hellenistic World Chronicles." *Harvard Theological Review* 61:451–481. Repr. in Wacholder 1976.

————1976. *Essays on Jewish Chronology and Chronography.* New York: Ktav.

Walker, P. W. L. 1990. *Holy City, Holy Places? Christian Attitudes to Je-*

rusalem and the Holy Land in the Fourth Century. Oxford: Clarendon Press.

Wallace-Hadrill, D. S. 1974. "Eusebius of Caesarea's Commentary on
Luke: Its Origin and Early History" *Harvard Theological Review*
67:55–63.

Warmington, B. H. 1986. "The Sources of Some Constantinian Documents in Eusebius' Ecclesiastical History and Life of
Constantine." *Studia Patristica* 18 (1): 93–98.

———1993. "Eusebius of Caesarea's Versions of Constantine's Laws
in the Codes." *Studia Patristica* 24:201–207.

Wendel, Carl. 1974. *Kleine Schriften zum antiken Buch- und
Bibliothekswesen.* Cologne: Greven.

Whealey, Alice. 2003. *Josephus on Jesus: The Testimonium Flavianum
Controversy from Late Antiquity to Modern Times.* New York: Peter
Lang.

White, L. Michael. 1990. *Building God's House in the Roman World:
Architectural Adaptation among Pagans, Jews, and Christians.* Baltimore: Johns Hopkins University Press.

White, Peter. 1978. *"Amicitia* and the Profession of Poetry in Early
Imperial Rome." *Journal of Roman Studies* 68:74–92.

———1993.*Promised Verse: Poets in the Society of Augustan Rome.*
Cambridge: Harvard University Press.

Whitmarsh, Tim. 2005. *The Second Sophistic.* Oxford: Oxford University Press, published for the Classical Association.

Wildberg, Christian. 1993. "Simplicius und das Zitat. Zur
Überlieferung des Anführungszeichens." In *Symbolae Berolinenses
für Dieter Harlfinger*, ed. Friederike Berger et al., 187–199. Amsterdam: Hakkert.

Williams, Megan. Forthcoming. *Jerome and the Making of Christian
Scholarship.* Chicago: University of Chicago Press.

Wilson, Nigel. 1983. *Scholars of Byzantium.* Baltimore: Johns Hopkins
University Press.

Winkelmann, Friedhelm. 1962a. *Die Textbezeugung der Vita
Constantini des Eusebius von Caesarea.* Texte und Untersuchungen
84. Berlin: Akademie-Verlag.

————1962b. "Zur Geschichte des Authentizitätsproblems der Vita Constantini," *Klio* 40:187–243. Repr. in Winkelmann 1993, 00–00.

————1977. "Probleme der Zitate in den Werken der oströmischen Kirchenhistoriker." In *Das Korpus der griechischen christlichen Schriftsteller: Historie, Gegenwart, Zukunft*, ed. J. Irmscher and K. Treu, 195–207. Berlin: Akademie-Verlag.

————1993. *Studien zu Konstantin dem Grossen und zur byzantinischen Kirchengeschichte: ausgewählte Aufsätze.* Ed. W. Brander and J. F. Haldon. Birmingham: University of Birmingham, Center for Byzantine, Ottoman, and Modern Greek.

Winkelmann, Friedhelm (ed.). 1975. *Eusebus Werke, I. 1: Über das Leben des Kaisers Konstantin.* GCS. Berlin: Akademie-Verlag.

Wolf, C. U. 1964. "Eusebius of Caesarea and the *Onomasticon.*" *Biblical Archaeologist* 27:66–96.

Wright, John. 1988. "Origen in the Scholar's Den: A Rationale for the Hexapla." In Kannengiesser and Petersen (eds.) 1988, 48–95.

Zecchini, G. 1987. "La conoscenza di Diodoro nel Tardoantico." *Aevum* 61:43–52.

Zerubavel, Eviatar. 2003. *Time Maps: Collective Memory and the Social Shape of the Past.* Chicago: University of Chicago Press.

Zetzel, James. 1973. "*Emendavi ad Tironem:* Some Notes on Scholarship in the Second Century A.D." *Harvard Studies in Classical Philology* 77:225–243.

————1980. "The Subscriptions in the Manuscripts of Livy and the Meaning of *Emendatio.*" *Classical Philology* 75:38–59.

————1981. *Latin Textual Criticism in Antiquity.* New York: Arno Press.

Zetzel, James (ed.). 1939. *Isaias.* Göttingen: Vandenhoeck and Ruprecht.

Zuntz, G. 1953a. *The Text of the Epistles.* The Schweich Lectures of the British Academy, 1946. London: Printed for the British Academy by the Oxford University Press.

————1953b. "Euthalius = Euzoius?" *Vigiliae Christianae* 7:16–22.

Notes

See the Bibliography for full citations of works cited below in abbreviated form.

Introduction

1. On Trithemius see the standard biography of Arnold 1991, which remains the most accurate and comprehensive work, and the studies of Brann 1981 and 1999.

2. E.g. clm 830, a copy of the Mainz MS of the letters of Boniface, finished in August 1497 by the Sponheim novice Fraciscus Hofyrer.

3. Trithemius 1531, liiii vo. The codex is now Herzog August Bibliothek, Wolfenbüttel, MS 34 Aug. fol.

4. Trithemius 1531, xxiii vo, distilling what he had written in another Sponheim manuscript, Herzog August Bibliothek, MS 78 Aug. fol. 196 vo, col. 2.

5. British Library, MS Add. 15, 102, fol. 1 vo.

6. Arnold 1991, 134.

7. Trithemius 1559 and 1690. The former rests on the holograph now in the Vatican Library, Cod. Vat. Pal. lat. 929, fol. 1r-258r. The

latter, a second recension in 2 vol.s, is modeled on MSS now in Munich. On his procedures in drawing up his tables Trithemius writes (1690, I [)(4 ro]): "Omnium dare indiculum, quae memoratu digna in hac prima parte Hirsaugianae continentur historiae, quam non sine magno labore comportavimus, et difficile judicamus et inutile: tum propter variam multitudinem gestorum, tum quod satius esse iudicavimus, si totum legas, quam partem. Verum ne Hirsaugiensibus in hoc videar defuisse, qui Patrum suorum merita et laudes sub una cupiant serie intueri, omissis non solum multis et variis, sed etiam pene infinitis memoratu dignis, quae facili Ordine registrari nequeunt, sequentium tabulam ordinavi." A list of the 11 tables follows.

    8. Trithemus 1974; O'Donnell 1998.

    9. Trithemius 1531, viii ro, xi ro, xiii ro.

    10. See e.g. Marrou 1964, Brown 1992, Kaster 1988, Inglebert 1996 and 2001, Momigliano 1963, Barnes 1981.

    11. See Quillen 1998 and, for Stock's work on specifically late antique materials, Stock 1996 and 2001.

    12. Roberts and Skeat 1983. See also Hunger 1989, 23–27; Harris 1991; Blanck 1992, 75–101.

    13. See Cavallo 1983 and 1984, Cavallo (ed.) 1984 and 1988, Casson 2001, Gamble 1995.

    14. Metzger 1968 and 1981, Haines-Eitzen 2000 (to be used with some caution; see Schmid 2002.

    15. Chartier 1988 and 1994, Darnton 1990, Carruthers 1990, Chia 2002. For an interesting recent application of book history to the study of the New Testament see Frenchkowski 2003.

    16. Martial, *Epigrammata* 14. See Blanck 1992, 97–99; Irigoin 2001, 64–65; And see more generally Dortmund 2001.

    17. The notion of "social capital" used here derives from the work of Pierre Bourdieu, e.g. Bourdieu 1977.

    18. On literary patronage in the Roman Empire, see (with contradictory conclusions) White 1978 and 1993 vs, Saller 1983; on the larger context of patronage in the empire, see Saller 1982 and Lendon 1997.

For literary patronage in a Christian context, see Williams forthcoming.

19. For Origen's biography, our principal primary source is Eusebius, *HE (Church History)* 6. Our sense of Origen's thought depends, of course, on his own surviving works, but also on the *Farewell Oration* of Gregory Thaumaturgus, his student. General discussions of Origen's life and works can be found in Crouzel 1985 and Nautin 1977 (the latter to be used with caution).

20. For the chronology of Origen's works, which is based on internal evidence and on the evidence of Eusebius, we follow Crouzel 1985 in preference to Nautin 1977.

21. Apollonius, *Epistles* 11.

22. See in general the still useful synthesis in Levine 1975, and two massive recent collections of articles on everything from archaeology to ethnography: Raban and Holum (eds.) 1996 and Donaldson (ed.) 2001.

23. See Adler 1989, and for the works of Berossos and Manetho see the recent translation and commentary in Verburgghe and Wickersham 1996 (repr. 2001).

24. Julius Africanus, *Kestoi* 5.1.50–54, in Africanus 1971.

25. For Pamphilus, see Chapter 4 below.

1. Origen at Caesarea

1. Adamantius: see *HE* 6.14.10. The title can be compared to the nickname Chalcenterus, or "Brazen-boweled," applied to the first-century BCE grammarian Didymus, in recognition of his immense productivity, as Jerome does in his comparison between the two men in *Epistolae* 33.

2. For example, Jerome called Origen the "first teacher of the church after the Apostles." Modern biographies of Origen include Daniélou 1948, English tr. by Walter Mitchell, 1955; Crouzel 1985, English tr. by A. S. Worrall 1989; Nautin 1977, by far the most author-

itative study presently available, though it has a number of serious flaws (see Crouzel 1988, 505–506, for a brief but balanced criticism of the work's strengths and defects); and Trigg 1998, who provides a useful, if brief biographical introduction (1–66) to his volume of selections from Origen's works, drawing upon his earlier work in Trigg 1983.

3. Trigg 1981, 22, gives a helpful overview of the nineteenth-century scholars and their influence on the mid-twentieth-century situation. Harnack 1893, following F. C. Baur earlier in the century, saw Origen as misinterpreting the original Christian revelation by casting it entirely in terms of Greek philosophy. De Faye 1923–1928 followed on this philosophical interpretation of Origen, but in a more sympathetic light, while Koch 1932 reinterpreted Origen's Platonism as intrinsic to, and fully integrated with, his "fanatical" Christian commitment. But Redepenning 1841–1846 had established a more influential tradition, taken up especially by French Catholic scholars after World War II (e.g. de Lubac 1954–1964, I), which emphasized instead Origen's orthodoxy, and minimized the importance of philosophy in his thought. Crouzel 1962 reviews the scholarship up to his time, which he then saw as tending to favor the idea of Origen as a Christian philosopher, but rejects it, 11: "Cependant [Origen] n'est philosophe ni par son but ni par sa méthode." Crouzel remained the most influential spokesperson for this perspective for several decades: e.g. Crouzel 1988, 499, surveys the debate, again coming down on the side of the thesis that Origen the theologian was not a Greek philosopher. Even Trigg 1998, who had been an advocate for rejecting the tradition founded by Redepenning, saw strong links to philosophy but concluded, "Origen became the archetypal Christian scholar." Edwards 2002, 1, sums up the tradition as a whole, with enthusiasm for its results: "The assiduous researches of such scholars as Simonetti and Crouzel have made it clearer to the modern world that Origen was before all else a Churchman, who availed himself of philosophy in the service of exegesis and the defense of ecclesiastic tradition. In the work of Joseph Trigg indeed he becomes almost a Protestant, beholden to no authority but the Bi-

ble; in such interpretations as those of Alviar and Laporte he is, on the contrary, a catholic, devoted to the sacraments and contemplative prayer."

4. The author of the *Farewell Oration* has traditionally been identified as Gregory Thaumaturgus, the wonder-working bishop of Pontus in northern Asia Minor and subject of a biography by Gregory of Nyssa, written in the mid-fourth century. Nautin 1977 183–184, challenged this identification, but his claims have largely been rejected by subsequent scholars: see Crouzel 1979. On the interpretation of the *Farewell Oration,* see now Trigg 2001. The quotation is Gregory Thaumaturgus 1969, 128 (*PG* 1072B; 8.84.75–76).

5. Eusebius, *HE* 6.19.1–10. See Schroeder 1987 on Ammonius, with a full discussion (494–508) of his relation both to an Origen, mentioned in Porphyry's *Life of Plotinus* (Porphyry 1966, for which see below), who was a fellow pupil of Plotinus's, and to our Origen, the Christian, concluding that Origen the Christian was merely a member of the outer circle of Ammonius's students. Beatrice 1992 mounts a spirited and interesting, if ultimately unconvincing, attack on the idea of the two Origens, one Christian and one pagan, in the course of which he presents a helpful historical interpretation of the passage of Porphyry's *Against the Christians* quoted by Eusebius.

6. Eusebius, *HE* 6.3.9. In support of the interpretation that Origen, despite his Christianity and his rejection of "pagan" learning unpurged of non-Christian associations, in his way of life followed the model of contemporary Greek philosophers, see Trigg 1998, 13: "But specific doctrines are not the point; Origen became a philosopher. He made his own the precise use of language and the inquiring, critical approach to reality inculcated by a rigorous philosophical training. As a teacher himself, Origen would seek to replicate his formation by evoking from his students 'the part of the soul that exercises judgment.' [Plato, *Theatet.* 176b] As Pierre Hadot has pointed out, for Origen, as for all ancient lovers-of-wisdom, philosophy was a way of life." This statement summarizes, and places in a broader context, the lengthier discussion of Trigg 1983, esp. 52–75. For the larger cultural

context, see Hadot 1995, with a discussion of Gregory Thaumaturgus's praise of Origen at 163–164.

7. Origen 1969, 1–2 (*PG* 11, 88A:10, B:19–26), 187, 188 in *Sources chrétiennes* 148 (Crouzel [ed.] 1969).

8. Porphyry, *Adversus Christianos, apud* Eusebius, *HE* 6.19.5–10.

9. On Origen's powers as a biblical exegete, which include all fields of inquiry under one (hyperbolical) umbrella, see Gregory Thaumaturgus, 1969, 170 (*PG* 10, 1096A; 15.182.41–47): "For that reason nothing was unspeakable [*arrēton,* the language of the mysteries] for us, nothing was hidden and inaccessible; rather, it was possible for us to learn every field of knowledge [*logos*], both barbarian and Greek, whether connected with religious secrets or with public affairs, both divine and human."

10. The ground-breaking work on the Second Sophistic was Bowersock 1969, with the papers collected in Bowersock 1974; see also Bowersock 2002 specifically on philosophy; since then, the field has exploded, producing an impressive bibliography in the last fifteen years, from Anderson 1993, Gleason 1995, and Swain 1996 through the essays collected in Goldhill (ed.) 2001, and the recent work of Borg 2004 and Whitmarsh 2005. On specific authors, see e.g. Anderson 1976 on Lucian and Sandy 1997 on Apuleius.

11. See, for a particularly striking example, von Staden 1997, giving the general context in relation to medicine and, specifically, Galen's practice of public dissection; von Staden 1995 makes specific connections between learning and performance, as alluded to in the text above. For the influence of this element of late Roman culture on a subject as far afield from rhetoric as astrology, see Barton 1994a, 139–141, and, at greater length, Barton 1994b, on astrology, physiognomy, and medicine as shaped by sophistic culture.

12. See e.g. Seneca, *Letters* 108.38: in criticizing philosophers who make their calling into a trade, Seneca summarizes his attack as follows, "All the words these men say, which they cast before a listening crowd, are those of others: Plato said that, Zeno something else, Chrysippus, and Posidonius and an immense mass of our own [Stoic]

school as many more excellent things. I shall show you how men can prove that their words are their own: they do what they have said."

13. The increasing eclecticism of philosophy over the course of the second century CE is a major thesis of the classic study by Dillon 1977; see more recently on this theme the articles collected in Dillon and Long (eds.) 1988. Sedley 1989 draws a detailed portrait of philosophical culture that exhibits many of the traits described in the text. For general bibliography, see the volume in which this essay appears, and its successor, in particular their extensive and judicious bibliographies: Griffin and Barnes (eds.) 1989 and Griffin and Barnes (eds.) 1997.

14. The *Kestoi* have been fully studied, with a translation of the fragments, in Africanus 1971; see also Thee 1984..

15. Eusebius 1923, 296; 1984, 214.

16. George Syncellus, *Chronographia* 439.15–20 Mosshammer. For this interpretation of Africanus's career, as for much else, we are indebted to William Adler, whose forthcoming study and collaborative edition of Africanus will shed a vast amount of light on this obscure but centrally important figure.

17. For an authoritative synthesis of Roman religion under the empire, see Beard, North, and Price 1998, especially 313–363 on the period and issues in question here.

18. Historia Augusta *Severus Alexander* 29.2.

19. On Philostratus and the *Life of Apollonius*, see Flinterman 1995 and Anderson 1986.

20. Philostratus dedicated his biography of Apollonius of Tyana to Julia Domna: *Life of Apollonius*, 1.3.

21. Snyder 2000. See also Del Corso 2005, 31–61.

22. Porphyry in Eusebius, *HE* 6.19.1–9; on Ammonius, see n. 5 above. On Plotinus, there are a number of useful recent surveys and introductions, e.g. O'Meara 1993, on which see the review in *Bryn Mawr Classical Review*, 6 April 2004, by John Peter Kenney, with helpful discussion of the bibliographic context. See also Gerson 1996 and 1993, Schroeder 1992; for an interpretation by one of the greatest living historians of Greek philosophy, see Hadot 1993. There is a reli-

able translation of the *Enneads* in the Loeb Classical Library series (Plotinus and A. H. Armstrong 1966–1988) and a full bibliography through 2000 in Dufour 2002.

23. Classically, *Phaedrus* 274c ff, and *Republic* 3.386b–397 and 10.595a–608b; note however that in the *Timaeus*, written records are an index of the superiority of Egyptian historical traditions to mere Greek memories: 21b–26a. The question, therefore, is not of the appropriateness of writing for cultural activity of any kind, but of its usefulness for transmitting philosophical truth, and of the philosophical utility of literature.

24. Porphyry 1966, 3.24–36: "Erennius, Origen, and Plotinus had made an agreement not to disclose any of the doctrines of Ammonius which he had revealed to them in his lectures. Plotinus observed the agreement, and though he associated with those who came to him, he guarded the secrecy of Ammonius's doctrines. Erennius was the first to break the agreement, and Origen followed Erennius, who had anticipated him; but he wrote nothing except the treatise *On the Daimones* and, in the reign of Gallienus, *That the King Is the Only Maker.*" Plotinus, however, kept the secret and wrote nothing. (Note that the translations from Porphyry are our own, but draw upon those of Armstrong wherever we found that we could not improve upon his wording.)

25. For a translation of the surviving fragments of Porphyry's *Homeric Questions,* see Schlunk 1993; a recent edition is that of A. R. Sodano, 2 vols. (Naples: Giannini, 1970–1973. An essay of Porphyry's, giving an allegorical interpretation of *Odyssey* 13.102–112, appeared in a revised text with English translation in Porphyry 1969; the work has also been translated with a full introduction in Porphyry and Lamberton 1983.

26. Porphyry 1966, 20.58–72.

27. Porphyry 1966, 3.33–36, continuing the passage quoted in n. 24.

28. Porphyry 1966, 4.10–17.

29. Porphyry 1966, 20.6–10.

30. Porphyry 1966, 8.1–7.

31. Porphyry 1966, 14.1–3.

32. Porphyry 1966, 18.6–8.

33. Porphyry 1966, 14.18–20.

34. See e.g. the story of Porphyry's poem "The Sacred Marriage," read out during the celebration of Plato's birthday, which was "expressed in the mystic and veiled language of *enthusiasmos*," and which Plotinus heartily approved, calling his student "at once poet, philosopher, and hierophant" (Porphyry 1966, 15.1–6).

35. Porphyry 1969, 14.10–14. On this passage see Snyder 2000, 116–117.

36. Porphyry 1966, 18.10–24.

37. This aspect of the Platonic circle portrayed in the *Life of Plotinus* has strong parallels in other traditions, particularly those of the Aristotelians. See esp. Chroust 1962, Moraux 1973 with Tarán 1981, and Lord 1986.

38. Porphyry 1966, 16.

39. For other pseudepigrapha exposed by Porphyry, see his dissection of the biblical Book of Daniel in the fragments of his *Against the Christians* (collected in Hoffmann [ed.] 1994), and his exposure of Hermes Trismegistus as a contemporary author rather than a sage of remotest antiquity, both discussed in Grafton 1990, 75–79.

40. Longinus *apud* Porphyry 1966, 19.15–19.

41. Porphyry 1966, 19.13–15.

42. Longinus *apud* Porphyry 1966, 19.8–13.

43. Porphyry 1966, 24.7–16.

44. On the editing of Aristotle's works in antiquity see esp. Moraux 1951 and 1973, with the review of the latter by Tarán 1981; Lord 1986.

45. Snyder 2000, 94–99.

46. Porphyry 1966, 26.28–41.

47. Porphyry 1966, 23.18–21.

48. Long 1992, 48.

49. Snyder 2000, 14–44.

50. Snyder 2000, 34; Sedley 1989, 119, portrays Seneca as an exception, while Snyder sees him as more typical of Stoics, who are less reverential toward the founders than some other schools.

51. See e.g. Letter 108.23–25, on the interpretation of the Virgilian phrase *fugit inreparabile tempus*. Seneca sums up the entire discussion in advance by saying scornfully, "Itaque quae philosophia fuit, facta philologia est." On this passages see Snyder 2000, 33, citing Seneca, *Letters* 108.30, in particular the claim there that "cum Ciceronis librum de Re Publica prendit hinc philologus aliquis, hinc grammaticus, hinc philosophiae deditus, alius alio curam suam mittit." As the discussion that follows in letter 108 shows, Seneca found the concerns of the *philologi* and the *grammatici* rather trivial, though better than pointless.

52. *De tranquillitate animi* 9.4–5: "Studiorum quoque quae liberalissima impensa est tamdiu rationem habet, quam diu modum. Quo innumerabiles libros et bybliothecas, quarum dominus uix tota uita indices perlegit? Onerat discentem turba, non instruit, multoque satius est paucis te auctoribus tradere, quam errare per multis. Quadraginta milia librorum Alexandriae arserunt; pulcherrimum regiae opulentiae monimentum alius laudaverit, sicut T. Livius, qui elegantiae regum curaeque egregium id opus ait fuisse. Non fuit elegantia illud aut cura, sed studiosa luxuria, immo ne studiosa quidem, quoniam non in studium sed in spectaculum comparauerant, sicut plerisque ignaris etiam puerilium litterarum libri non studiorum instrumenta sed cenationum ornamenta sunt." Tr. Basore, LCL, with our own slight adaptations.

53. Snyder 2000, 35–37.

54. For a brilliant summary of Seneca's place in this tradition, see Stock 1996, 14 with n. 203.

55. Hays 1983, 30, based on Cornutus's full name, L. Annaeus Cornutus.

56. On Cornutus, see Long 1992, Most 1989, Hays 1983, with a very thorough discussion of the philosophical background and the

life of Cornutus, and a translation of the *Introduction;* the text is Cornutus, *Theologiae Graecae Compendium,* Lang (ed.) 1881.

57. Suetonius, *De poetis et grammaticis, Vita Auli Persi Flacci* 15–17, 40–46, 49–58 (Suetonius, Rostagni [ed]. 1979, 169–176). On their relationship, see Hays 1983, 31–32, Most 1989, 2050–2053, and Snyder 2000, 39–40.

58. Some of the papyri from Herculaneum, to be discussed below, preserve works of Chrysippus, e.g. *P. Herc.* 307 *(Logical Inquiries);* 1038 and 1421 *(On Providence).*

59. Snyder 2000, 46–61, provides a competent and readable overview of Philodemus's Epicureanism, from a point of view very close to our own. There is no general study of Philodemus, beyond that of Gigante 1995 in its various versions, which is impressionistic rather than exhaustive. For bibliography on Philodemus, see Griffin and Barnes (eds.) 1989, 267–268, dated but judicious; more recent bibliography is reflected in the articles collected in Fitzgerald et al. (eds.) 2004. Editions of Philodemus's writings remain in progress, though many of his major philosophical works have been edited since the 1990s, including *On Poems* (by Richard Janko), *On Frank Criticism* (by David Konstan), *On Piety* (by Dirk Obbink), and his epigrams (re-edited by David Sider). The essays collected by Obbink 1995 and David Armstrong 2004 deal with the relation between Philodemus's thought and poetry, either in theory or in the work of contemporary Latin authors thought to have come directly or indirectly under his influence. Continuing investigations of on the rolls from Herculaneum themselves, together with many studies of various aspects of Philodemus's life and work, have appeared in *Cronache ercolanesi* since 1971; an index of papyri published in that journal through 1995 appeared as Amarante et al. 1995. Further specific studies are cited in the notes below.

60. Gigante 1995 is an authoritative summary of the evidence from the papyri and the archaeological excavations, by a scholar who dedicated his career to the study of the library and its contents; the book is

an English translation of Gigante 1990, and repeats much of what Gigante had previously argued in French in Gigante 1987. Gigante's impassioned enthusiasm for Philodemus, and for maximal exploitation of the evidence to reconstruct his life in as much detail as possible, demands a degree of caution. Specifically, some of the more speculative scholarly reconstructions of the physical layout and social role of the library, presumed to have been formed and used in the mid-first century BCE on the site where it was entombed over a century later, invite skepticism. The library at Herculaneum has not been, and may never be, fully catalogued. Not only are many of the carbonized papyrus rolls recovered from the site unreadable, but there is no knowing how many of the books the library originally contained have been destroyed or will never be successfully excavated. Though many scholars connect the site with two known figures from the first century BCE, the Epicurean philosopher Philodemus—author of many of the books found at Herculaneum—and his patron Calpurnius Piso, it is unlikely that this conjecture will ever be confirmed by direct evidence.

61. *P. Herc.* 817, Rabirius *Carmen de bello Actiaco sive Alexandrino.*

62. Gigante 1987, 37.

63. The index of Gigante 1979, the most recent catalogue of the Herculaneum papyri, lists 38 separate works of Philodemus and 23 Greek works by other authors, including several of uncertain authorship and/or title. But this list is now somewhat outdated, and in any case the identification of some of the works (especially for writings previously unknown or not elsewhere preserved) is controversial.

64. On the composition of the library, see Snyder 2000, 46–47, summarizing information from Gigante 1979 and more recent publications.

65. Sedley 1989, 100: "Under the Roman empire the large centralized schools gave way to individual teachers with their small groups of adherents, but the role of loyalty to scriptures remained integral to the philosophical enterprise. To meet the demand, the forgery industry gathered pace, and innumerable epistles of Socrates, Diogenes the

Cynic, Aristotle, and others came into circulation. For the vast majority of thinkers in this period, however, the revered text was either that of Plato, commonly regarded as divine, or of course the Old and/or New Testament, which were taken to represent, most prominently, the authority of Moses and St. Paul respectively. Even a double allegiance, such as to Plato *and* the Bible, was not uncommon." (Emphasis in the original.)

66. Sedley 1989, 101: "So far I must have given the impression of trying to reduce ancient philosophy, as practised from the fourth century BC down to the sixth century AD, to a rather mindless enterprise, in which the *ex cathedra* pronouncements of long-dead saints counted for more than open-minded inquiry and debate. This is by no means the correct consequence to draw. The role of scriptural authority was to provide a philosophical movement with a *raison d'être* and a framework within which it could preserve its cohesion *while* continuing to inquire and debate." (Emphasis in the original.) But cf. Obbink 2004, who rejects the idea of Epicureanism as a "Hellenistic cult or religion," and the suggestion that Philodemus treated the texts of Epicurus as Scripture, specifically targeting Sedley's analysis. Sedley reads, to us, as if he were at times exaggerating for effect; Obbink's criticisms are well taken, but need not obviate the point crucial to the present discussion, that Philodemus's brand of Epicureanism involved a great deal of work with texts, especially those of earlier Epicureans.

67. The phases of Philodemus's career are discussed by Gigante 1995, 20–46.

68. Sedley 1989, 105, citing Diogenes Laertius, 10.3, 10.24. Discussed also in Gigante 1995, 21, who suggests that Diogenes also depended on Philodemus in his *Life of Epicurus.*

69. *P. Herc.* 307, Chrysippus, *Logical Questions; P. Herc.* 1038, 1421, Chrysippus, *On Providence; P. Herc.* 1020, an unknown work by Chrysippus.

70. *P. Herc.* 1041, *Life of Epicurus,* by an unknown author; *P. Herc.* 1044, *Life of Philonides,* by an unknown author.

71. Gigante 1979, 53; a number of the identifications are conjectural, and since Gigante's work more rolls containing parts of *On Nature* have been identified, so that a precise number cannot be given.

72. Cavallo et al. 1983.

73. See Gigante 1995, 18–20, on Demetrius of Laconia as a philologist and textual critic of Epicurus; Snyder 2000, 50–53, citing especially Puglia 1982. Puglia sees the absence of philological argument in the preserved works of Philodemus as proving that he took no interest in such studies, but this argument from silence is not entirely convincing.

74. E.g. *P. Herc.* 1021 + 1064, *History of the Academy;* see Gigante 1987 34; on copies of *On the Stoics,* of which P.Herc. 339 is a draft and *P. Herc.* 155 a finished copy, see Gigante 1987, 39; Cavallo et al. 1983.

75. Cavallo produces this argument, in typically allusive fashion, in Cavallo et al. 1983 and in Cavallo 1984, esp. 12, where he explains that the ancient "editions" "si presentano omogenee sotto l'aspetto tecnico-grafico, vale a dire a blocchi testuali dovuti ciascuno alla medesima mano o a mani fortemente affini, indicando perciò un programma 'editoriale' più o meno organico nella trascrizione delle diverse opere," and goes on to point out that there is too much uniformity for the production to have been done in outside "botteghe librarie" or by scholars themselves. Characteristically, he is rather more reserved in his conclusions than Gigante.

76. Cavallo et al. 1983.

77. On the scope of this undertaking, and of *On Rhetoric* and *On Poetry,* see e.g. Gigante 1995, 20–29, discussing the findings of Cavallo et al. 1983.

78. On Roman libraries in the first century BCE, see Casson 2001, 51–84.

79. On literary education in the Hellenistic and Roman worlds, Marrou 1949 [1976] is still a standard reference; more recent studies, supporting the same notion of a narrow emphasis on certain canonical authors, include Morgan 1998; Cribiore 1996 on the Greek school pa-

pyri from Egypt; Cribiore 2001, placing the papyrological evidence in a broader context; and the articles assembled in Too (ed.) 2001.

80. Sedley 1989, 104, and Obbink 2004, 79, agree on this point.

81. The story as recounted in the text is a composite of the testimonies of Strabo, *Geography* 13.609, and Plutarch, *Life of Sulla* 26. Only Plutarch transmits the story of Andronicus's editing and promulgation of the Aristotelian corpus. See Düring 1950, 1956, and 1957; Moraux 1951 and 1973, the latter with Tarán 1981; Chroust 1962; Gottschalk 1972; Lord 1986.

82. Millar 1977.

83. For a survey of the issue, see Konstan 1996.

84. See Lendon 1997 for a nuanced presentation of this insight.

85. Marrou 1964, 206–217, 305–308.

86. For the chronology, see Nautin 1977, 363–409.

87. For a discussion of typical codex formats in the third century, see Chapter 2 below.

88. *HE* 6.16.1–3: "[Origen] personally acquired the original Scriptures current among the Jews, in Hebrew characters, and tracked down the editions of those others who, after the Seventy, had translated the Holy Scriptures. And beside the beaten track of translations, those of Aquila and Symmachus and Theodotion, he discovered certain other translations, long unknown, which he brought to light from I know not what hidden store-chambers. With regard to these, since they were so obscure (for he did not know whose they were), he indicated only that he had found one in Nicopolis near Actium, and another in some such other place. At any rate in the Hexapla of the Psalms, after the well-known four editions, he inserted not only a fifth, but even a sixth and a seventh translation, and indicated that one of these had been found in Jericho in a jar in the time of Antoninus the son of Severus."

89. Clements 1997, 85 with n. 134.

90. For this date, see Nautin 1977, 418.

91. Clements 1997, 98–100, provides a particularly detailed explo-

ration of the situation that Origen encountered at Rome, with full bibliography in her notes.

92. Hippolytus 1986, 32.

93. Osborne 1987. Recent work on Hippolytus has questioned whether he was a Roman or, indeed, a single individual, e.g. Cerrato 2002; cf. Brent 1995. While it remains to be seen what scholarship will make of these challenges to the integrity and authorship of the Hippolytan corpus, its individual components remain as testimony to the effort devoted by Christians of the late second century to textual, heresiological, and chronographic researches.

94. On the possible influence of the Roman scene of that time on Origen's scholarship, see Clements 1997, 98–100, perhaps the most full-blown statement of the possibilities.

95. Runia 1993, 157–183; Clements 1997, 71–82.

96. Origen refers to Aristobulus in *Contra Celsum* 4.51, discussed in Clements 1997, 76, and Runia 1993, 161–162.

97. Jakab 2001, 71.

98. Date of Origen's commentary on John: Nautin 1977 427–438; Herakleon and his commentary: Pagels 1973.

99. On this and other sources that Origen may have used, see Hanson 1954.

100. Hopkins 1998, 199, discusses the relatively large number of letters that a rough estimate would predict circulated among the Christian communities in the period 50–150 (10,000), in comparison to the few (50) that survive from that century.

101. See Carriker 2003, 6–8, for these authors in Origen's library.

102. See Mizugaki 1987 with list of citations.

103. DeLange 1976, 15–17.

104. Carriker 2003, 8. For Origen's use of Philo of Byblos, see e.g. *Contra Celsum* 1.15, which may in fact cite another work of Philo's, his *De iudaeis;* on this problem, see the commentary of Baumgarten 1981, 249; the work is also an authoritative source for other questions regarding Philo.

105. The fragments have been collected and translated into Ger-

man in Ebach 1979, and edited, translated into English, and annotated in Attridge and Oden 1981.

106. Gregory Thaumaturgus 1969 158 (*PG* 10, 1088A; 13.150.7–11).

107. Gregory Thaumaturgus 1969 142 (*PG* 10, 1077C; 8.11–13.7–22).

108. Further in this vein, in a discussion of philosophical sectarianism, Gregory writes (Gregory Thaumaturgus 1969, 162 [*PG* 10, 1089C; 14.162.24–28]): "Such have been the philosophical habits of our noble, most eloquent and most critical Greeks; for each one, driven by some impulse of which he remains unaware, declares whatever he happened to run into first to be the sole truth, and all other philosophies to be deception and nonsense." Characterizing Origen's teaching (Gregory Thaumaturgus 1969, 166 [*PG* 1092C-1093A; 14.170.73–76)], he writes: "Therefore, in order that we might not suffer the same fate as most do, he did not introduce us to some one kind of philosophical opinion, nor did he see fit for us to go away following any one of them, but he introduced us to them all, not wishing that we should leave untested any Greek doctrine."

109. Porphyry, *Against the Christians* book 3, *apud* Eusebius, *HE* 6.19.9–10.

110. The *Oxford Classical Dictionary*, s.v., gives his dates as ca. 213–273. When Porphyry studied with him, he was teaching at Athens, but he later relocated to Syria, specifically to Tyre in Lebanon.

111. Beatrice 1992, 352.

112. Beatrice 1992, 356, gives the dates of Porphyry's studies at Athens as 253–263.

113. See Porphyry 1966, 19.5, 36, for Longinus's location.

114. Porphyry 1966, 20.36–37.

115. Beatrice 1992, 354–355, explicitly discusses this passage as evidence for Origen's library.

116. Dillon 1977, 361–379; Origen repeatedly refers to Numenius (362) and mentions his allegorical interpretations of the Hebrew Bible in his *Contra Celsum* 4.51 = Numenius, frag. 1C (365); Numenius laid "great emphasis . . . on the teachings of the Brahmans, Jews, Magi, and

Egyptians" (363); "he was certainly acquainted with the results of allegorical exegesis of the Pentateuch" (378, on frag. 1).

117. Dillon 1977, 344–351.

118. Dillon 1977, 362, 379

119. Smith 1870, I, 246, s.v. Apollophanes (1), citing Athenaeus, *Deipnosophistae* 7.281, Diogenes Laertius, *Lives of the Philosophers* 7.140.

120. Dillon 1977, 352–360.

121. Dillon 1977, 382.

122. For the fragments of Chaeremon, see the collection, with text, English translation, and commentary, of Van der Horst 1983. Chaeremon was active in the lifetime of Nero. The titles of three of his works survive: the *Egyptian History, On Hieroglyphics,* and *Peri Kometon.* He is identified as both a Stoic and a *hierogrammateus,* a sacred scribe trained in an Egyptian temple.

123. On Origen's allegorical interpretation—discussed of course in all general treatments of the man and his work—see esp. Hanson 1954, Torjesen 1986, and Clements 1997. One fragment of Chaeremon's history of Egypt is transmitted by Eusebius, *PE* 6.10.

124. *HE* 6.3.8–9.

125. E.g. Nautin 1977, 417, describes this moment as "une authentique conversion"; he is followed by Jakab 2001, 157 ff. But cf. Crouzel 1985 [1989], 8: "This gesture of selling his library marks a complete renunciation of secular studies. But he was not slow to realize that secular knowledge was of great value in explaining the Scriptures and for his missionary work, and he would soon return to what he had intended to abandon."

126. For a similar interpretation, see Trigg 1998, 14; in detail, Neuschäfer 1987 passim, but especially 122–138, 202–239, 287–292.

127. Jerome, *Epistolae 33*; see Nautin 1977, 214, on this list and its deficiencies.

128. This division of Origen's exegesis into subgenres comes from Jerome, *Epistolae 33.*

129. For substantiation of this, see Nautin 1977, 428 with n. 60, on

the exemplars of his works that Origen took with him when he left Alexandria for Athens in 232; for this, Nautin cites a letter of Origen's to friends at Alexandria, which he reconstructs on the basis of a fragment transmitted by Jerome and Rufinus, discussed at Nautin 1977, 161–168.

130. *HE* 6.23.1–2.

131. Scholarship on the "school of Alexandria" has such a long history that it has begun to generate a historiography of its own: see Le Boulluec 1987, 1999, 2000. Specific items of bibliography relevant to our problem are cited in the notes that follow.

132. See on this topic Jakab 2001, who although he accepts the idea that Demetrius of Alexandria initially played a role in conferring an official imprimatur on Origen's teaching when he began to operate as a "catechist" early in his career (150), nevertheless judges, with Joseph Trigg 1981, whose work Jakab appears to ignore entirely, that by the early 230s, "Demetrios pouvait désormais le [i.e., Origen] percevoir commme un rival, auquel une partie des chrétiens devait se sentir attachée . . . Dès lors, nous pouvons aisément concevoir qu'Origène . . . par-dessus de tout à cause de l'autonomie que lui assurait Ambroise, ait pu être perçu comme une menace" (169).

133. *HE* 2.16.1; Jakab 2001, 45–49, rejects entirely the idea that Mark brought the Gospel to Alexandria, considering this story a late third-century, if not a Eusebian, invention.

134. For this, see Jakab 2001, 216–222; Jakab's bibliography provides full references to the previous literature, particularly in French; Trigg 1981b, 5–7 and n. 13, citing Harnack 1902, 1965, I, :463, Bauer 1934, 1971, 53–54, and Roberts 1979, 71.

135. *HE* 6.3.8.

136. *HE* 6.15.11–16.1.

137. *HE* 6.6.1.Jakab 2001, 117, having reviewed all the evidence for the career of Pantaenus, embarks on his study of Clement by saying of Eusebius's description of the succession of catechetical teachers at Alexandria that it "n'a guère de chances d'être vrai."

138. For a nice appreciation of the inconsistencies, see Daniélou 1955.

139. Bauer 1934; tr. 1971, 44–60; cited by Trigg 1981b, 7.

140. Stark 1996 3–27, far better founded than much of the rest of the book; Hopkins 1998.

141. Lampe 2003, 397–408.

142. Jakab 2001.

143. Hopkins 1998, 187–192.

144. For this model for the growth of modern new religious movements, see Stark 1996, 3–27; Sanders 2000, 82–97, with discussion of a variety of sociological models, including Stark's. The figures are cited from Hopkins 1998, fig. 1 and 192–193, who follows Stark 1996 at this point in his argument.

145. Lampe 2003, 359–408, analyzes the evidence gathered in the first 350 pages of the book, concluding that the monarchical episcopate emerged at Rome at the earliest "after the middle of the second century," probably after the 180s (406–407); but see Lampe 2003, 410, for caveats regarding extending the Roman model to the much smaller cities of the rest of the empire, though as he acknowledges, both Alexandria and Antioch were large enough to face similar problems. Hopkins 1998, 198–203, comes to the same conclusion on the basis of demographic hypothesis, rather than close examination of the evidence for a single city.

146. The foundational analysis of this phenomenon remains that of Krautheimer 1965, 1986, 23–37, cited and discussed by White 1990, 19–21. White's study, however, addresses the early period here under discussion in considerably greater detail than does Krautheimer's treatment, which is the first chapter of a book that continues through the end of the Byzantine Empire. White's work therefore will be the basis for our discussion.

147. White 1990, 108–109, figs. 17, 18, show the *domus ecclesiae* at Dura; for the term, see White 1990, 111; discussion of the Dura structure, 120–122; on the Dura synagogue and a Mithraeum in comparison with the church building (all located on the same street), see White 1990, 8.

148. White 1990, 4–5.

149. Eusebius, *HE* 8.1.5, cited and discussed by White 1990, 127; see also *HE* 7.30.18–19, White 1990, 129–130, on the church constructed by Paul of Samosata at Antioch, whose ownership, disputed between the followers of Paul and his opponents, the emperor Aurelius assigned to the "orthodox" party, Paul's opponents. Lactantius, *De mortibus persecutorum* 12.4–5, cited and discussed by White 1990, 130, describes the Christian church in the imperial city of Nicomedia in 303, at the onset of Diocletian's persecution, as a prominent structure, visible from the palace.

150. White 1990, 103–110.

151. Hopkins 1998, 204, 209.

152. As evidenced by the collection for the church at Jerusalem mentioned by Paul, 1 Cor. 8–9.

153. For the use of rented halls and rooms by new religious groups, see White 1990, 32.

154. Lampe 2003, 366–368, lists and describes the third-century church buildings excavated at Rome underneath the present churches of SS. Giovanni e Paolo (the earliest monumental Christian building, perhaps mid-third century); S. Martino ai Monti (perhaps a "house church," a term Lampe uses in the same sense that White employs *domus ecclesiae*, i.e., a house architecturally adapted for full-time use by a Christian assembly); and San Clemente (perhaps adapted into a Christian hall of assembly by the mid-third century).

155. The same data from San Clemente and SS. Giovanni e Paolo, and those from another Roman site, San Crisogono (not rebuilt as a church until around 310), are discussed at somewhat greater length by White 1990, 114, 131–134, in the course of a synthetic argument that entirely concurs with that of Lampe, in concluding that Christians at Rome did not even begin to adapt large structures as regular meeting places until at least the mid-third century. Lampe 2003 notes White's dissertation, the basis of his 1990 book, in his bibliography, but the two authors were in fact working at the same time, since Lampe's original German edition was published in 1987, and the revised second edition that formed the basis for the English translation in 1989.

156. See Hopkins 1998, 201, for a similar conclusion.

157. Jakab 2001, 30–35, esp. 34, n. 165, with the following citation from Roberts 1979, 58: "From the two hundred and twenty years between 117 and 337 only forty-four documents with allusions to Jews are known, a figure that contrasts with nearly three hundred for the first one hundred and fifty years of Roman rule. It is precisely when the evidence for Judaism grows scarce that that for Christianity begins to appear." On the revolt, see the standard works of Grabbe 1992, II, 596–599, suggesting that the Alexandrian community, though severely damaged by the revolt, may have had more survivors than did Jewish communities elsewhere in Egypt, and Barclay 1996, 78–81, who concluded that "the most glorious centre of Jewish life in the diaspora, which had produced the finest literary and intellectual products of Hellenized Judaism, and which had once wielded such military, economic and political influence, was all but snuffed out in a frenzy of intercommunal violence" (81).

158. See e.g. the letters of Ignatius of Antioch, usually dated to the years immediately after 110, which constantly assert the centrality of a single bishop in each city's Christian community, though they acknowledge at the same time considerable resistance to this concept.

159. Lampe 2003, 399–408.

160. See Nautin 1977, 35–42, 47–48, on Eusebius, *HE*, as a source for Origen's teaching at Alexandria; see 415–417 on the first phase of Origen's career as a Christian teacher at Alexandria, begun during a persecution that Demetrius and the rest of the Alexandrian clergy escaped by fleeing the city, and approved by Demetrius after the fact, when the persecution had relented; see 419–420 on Origen's teaching after his return from Rome at the end of 216; and 429–430 on the final conflict between Demetrius and Origen, occasioned by Origen's ordination by the bishops of Caesarea and Jerusalem, and ended only by Demetrius's death.

161. Trigg 1981b, 5–7.

162. Nautin 1961, 117–118, 140; 1977, 420. On Clement's relation to Origen, see Trigg 1998, 9–10; however, Trigg's argument that Clement

and Origen formed part of "a distinct school of thought, a learned Christianity distinguished from Gnosticism by its loyalty to the church's rule of faith, which was already flourishing in Alexandria," seems to come perilously close to inventing a social milieu on the basis of literary and intellectual similarities alone. Perhaps, as Trigg argues, "it is hardly conceivable that Origen, with his insatiable intellectual curiosity, would have neglected a figure as deeply learned as Clement, as long as the two were, as they seem to have been, in the same city at the same time." But we have no evidence for such a relationship; nor did Eusebius, as far as we can tell. For the evidence, in the form of textual parallels between the works of Clement and Origen, see van den Hoek 1992; she concludes that "the evidence seems persuasive that Origen was indeed acquainted with at least parts of Clement's works. Some striking similarities were found, and on a few occasions he seems to refer explicitly to his predecessor . . . [Origen] supposedly used similar reference works and frequented the same libraries that Clement did . . . But beyond such generalities, it is very hard to specify the nature of the kinship between Clement and Origen. In fact, many more dissimilarities than similarities can be pointed out" (44–45).

163. Nautin 1977, 419.

164. Nautin 1961 250–253 (text 250–251, translation 251). Nautin notes that Eusebius probably quoted this passage in book 6 of the *Apology for Origen*, as part of an effort to show that some of his writings could have gone into circulation without his permission. Jerome offers a slightly scrambled account of the same letter in *Epistolae* 43, 1: "Ambrosius, quo chartas, sumptus, notarios ministrante tam innumerabiles libros vere Adamantius et noster Χαλκέντερος explicavit, in quadam epistula quam ad eundem de Athenis scripserat refert nunquam se cibos Origene praesente sine lectione sumpsisse, nunquam venisse somnum nisi e fratribus aliquis sacris littteris personaret; hoc diebus egisse vel noctibus, ut et lectio orationem susciperet et oratio lectionem." See the discussion in Nautin 1961, 260–261.

165. Note though that the patron, for all his passion for all Bible, all the time, did not feel the need to rival his friend's personal asceti-

cism in other respects: Origen goes on to tell Africanus that Ambrose's "faithful wife Marcella, and the children, greet you" (*Ad Africanum* 24).

166. Eusebius, *HE* 6.21.3: "Origen's fame was now [i.e., at the beginning of the reign of Alexander Severus] universal, so as to reach the ears of the emperor's mother, Mamaea by name, a religious woman if ever there was one. She set great store on securing a sight of the man, and on testing that understanding of divine things which was the wonder of all. She was then staying at Antioch, and summoned him to her presence with a military escort. And when he had stayed with her for some time, and shown her very many things that were for the glory of the Lord and the excellence of the divine teaching, he hastened back to his accustomed duties."

167. Chaeremon, the Egyptian priest turned Stoic philosopher, may provide a partial parallel, but the phenomenon remained very rare in Greek philosophical circles.

168. Lieberman 1942 is the classic statement of this view.

169. The continuing importance of translation from the Hebrew, in the form of the *targum,* for Jewish congregations for whom Aramaic was the primary language of scholarship and liturgy, does not mitigate the force of the separatist impulse that drove rabbinic Jews to create a non-Greek learned culture in a region where Greek had been for centuries the only legitimate language of learning.

170. *HE* 6.16.1; see Chapter 2 for a discussion of this passage and the controversies over its interpretation.

171. See on this issue Fowden 1986, and for earlier Greek ways of dealing with "barbarian" languages see the fascinating work of Munson 2005.

172. The references are collected, with citations to the secondary literature, by Clements 1997, 102–114.

173. See de Lange 1976, Clements 1997, Clements 2000, and the works of Kimelman and Halperin cited and discussed in Clements 1997, 114–117; also Hirshman 1995.

174. For the milieu, see e.g. Levine 1975 and Hirshman 1995.

175. See the work of Leonard Rutgers on the Jewish community at

Rome; a general survey of the earlier period is Barclay 1996. Jakab 2001 assembles much of the bibliography for the Jewish community at Alexandria; Clements 1997 similarly for Caesarea. On Hellenistic Judaism in Palestine, see also Schwartz 2001.

176. For a comprehensive discussion of the data that underlie this view, together with an analysis that supports—although it does not precisely conform to—our view, see Schwartz 2001. For a specific example, see the large Jewish inscription, in Greek, from Aphrodisias in Caria (Asia Minor), published in Reynolds and Tannenbaum (eds.) 1987. The stone was inscribed over the course of the second and third centuries. It lists the members of the community, its patrons (not all Jewish), and a number of proselytes and "God-fearers" *(theosebeis)*, presumably Gentile sympathizers who did not undergo full conversion.

177. See Levine 1976, 70–71 and nn.; for the texts, see e.g. J Sota VII, 1, 21bm, cited at Levine 1976, 197, n. 119: "R Levi bar Hita came to Caesarea and heard voices reciting the Shema in Greek. He wanted to stop them. R. Jose heard about it and became angry (with R. Levi). He said: 'This I say: If they cannot say it in Hebrew, should they then not say it at all? Rather they are permitted to say it in any language.'" Note also Abbahu's giving permission to read the scroll of Esther in Greek (J. Megilla II, 1, 73a) and to have Torah scrolls in Greek (B. Megilla 9b). All of these passages should be read as reflecting not rabbinic *control* over the practices of other Jews, but rabbinic *awareness* of those practices, with which the rabbis had to come to terms.

178. On the Jewish translations after the Septuagint, the fundamental work is Barthélemy 1963.

179. On the expression of Egyptian religious ideas in Greek form, see Fowden 1986 with extensive discussion of the Egyptian elements in "Greco-Roman" magic.

2. Origen's Hexapla

1. And Aramaic, in Daniel and Job.
2. The early tradition culminated in the great edition of Freder-

ick Field (Origen and Frederick Field 1875); see also Shelford 1997. Contemporary scholarship is best represented by De Lange 1976; see also the articles in Salvesen (ed.) 1998 and in Kannengiesser and Petersen (eds.) 1988.

3. The debate will be rehearsed in detail in the notes below.

4. Origen, *Ad Africanum*, 5; *Commentarius in Mattheam*, 15.14.

5. Though the consensus may be shifting: cf. Neuschäfer 1987, 96–97, arguing that the critical signs did appear in the fifth column, with Dines 2004, 101–102, agreeing with our view that their presence there would have been illogical; both authors provide citations to the large bibliography on this problem.

6. On Theodotion, see Barthélemy 1963, 1971, 1978; more recently, Clements 1997, 83–85; Dines 2004, 81–91, a very thorough and judicious discussion.

7. *HE* 6.16: Τοσαύτη δὲ εἰσήγετο τῷ Ὠριγένει τῶν θείων λόγων ἀπηκριβωμένη ἐξέτασις, ὡς καὶ τὴν Ἑβραΐδα γλῶτταν ἐκμαθεῖν τάς τε παρὰ τοῖς Ἰουδαίοις φερομένας πρωτοτύπους αὐτοῖς Ἑβραίων στοιχείοις γραφὰς κτῆμα ἤδιον ποιήσασθαι ἀνιχνεῦσαί τε τὰς τῶν ἑτέρων παρὰ τοὺς ἑβδομήκοντα τὰς ἱερὰς γραφὰς ἑρμηνευκότων ἐκδόσεις καί τινας ἑτέρας παρὰ τὰς κατημαξευμένας ἑρμηνείας ἐναλλαττούσας, τὴν Ἀκύλου καὶ Συμμάχου καὶ Θεοδοτίωνος, ἐφευρεῖν, ἃς οὐκ οἶδ᾽ ὅθεν ἔκ τινων μυχῶν τὸν πάλαι λανθανούσας χρόνον ἀνιχνεύσας προήγαγεν εἰς φῶς ἐφ᾽ ὧν διὰ τὴν ἀδηλότητα, τίνος ἄρ᾽ εἶεν οὐκ εἰδώς, αὐτὸ τοῦτο μόνον ἐπεσημήνατο ὡς ἄρα τὴν μὲν εὕροι ἐν τῇ πρὸς Ἀκτίοις Νικοπόλει, τὴν δὲ ἐν ἑτέρῳ τοιῷδε τόπῳ· ἔν γε μὴν τοῖς Ἑξαπλοῖς τῶν ψαλμῶν μετὰ τὰς ἐπισήμους τέσσαρας ἐκδόσεις οὐ μόνον πέμπτην, ἀλλὰ καὶ ἕκτην καὶ ἑβδόμην παραθεὶς ἑρμηνείαν, ἐπὶ μιᾶς αὖθις σεσημείωται ὡς ἐν Ἱεριχοῖ εὑρημένης ἐν πίθῳ κατὰ τοὺς χρόνους Ἀντωνίνου τοῦ υἱοῦ Σευήρου. ταύτας δὲ ἁπάσας ἐπὶ ταὐτὸν συναγαγὼν διελών τε πρὸς κῶλον καὶ ἀντιπαραθεὶς ἀλλήλαις μετὰ καὶ αὐτῆς τῆς Ἑβραίων σημειώσεως, τὰ τῶν λεγομένων Ἑξαπλῶν ἡμῖν ἀντίγραφα καταλέ-

λοιπεν, ἰδίως τὴν Ἀκύλου καὶ Συμμάχου καὶ Θεοδοτίωνος ἔκδοσιν ἅμα τῇ τῶν ἑβδομήκοντα ἐν τοῖς Τετρασσοῖς ἐπισκευάσας." Words given in brackets in the translation do not appear in the Greek, but are added to clarify the sense of Eusebius's description, whose tone is almost hysterical in its enthusiasm. The translation also omits (with ellipses) the details given in the Greek text regarding the additional versions found by Eusebius, since this material will be discussed in detail in Chapter 4.

8. Eusebius clearly refers to the presence of a column in Hebrew written in Hebrew letters, and describes the order in which the columns were arranged just as it is preserved in the fragments. Pierre Nautin reinterpreted the passage of Eusebius to imply that no column in Hebrew letters was present in the original synopsis (Nautin, 1977, 314–316); this view has been widely rejected: see the refutation in the appendix to Jay 1985, 411–417, the comments on this phrase of Barthélemy 1978, and the article of Rebenich 1993.

9. Ulrich 1988 criticizes such overInterpretations.

10. *Commentarii in Epistolam ad Titum*, 3.9 (*PL* 26 734D-735A): "in quibus et ipsa Hebraea propriis sunt characteribus uerba descripta: et Graecis litteris tramite expressa uicino. Aquila etiam et Symmachus, Septuaginta quoque et Theodotio suum ordinem tenent. Nonnulli uero libri et maxime hi qui apud Hebraeos uersu compositi sunt, tres alias editiones additas habent: quam quintam, et sextam, et septimam translationem uocant: auctoritatem sine nominibus interpretum consecutas." Jerome also describes the Hexapla in his *De viris illustribus:* there, however, he is clearly dependent on Eusebius' description in *HE* 6.16, discussed above. The description in the Commentary on Titus is shorter, yet gives more detail regarding the arrangement of the work. Nautin 1977, 303–361, in addition to challenging the interpretation of *HE* 6.16.1, 4, also argued that the Hexapla was never copied, and that Jerome never saw it. For refutations of Nautin's views on Jerome, see the appendix of Jay 1985, cited above, Kamesar 1993, 4–28, and Rebenich 1993, 57–62.

11. For further details, see Williams 2001.

12. Epiphanius, *Panarion* 64.3.5 (*GCS* 31): τοῦ μὲν Ἀμβροσίου τὰ πρὸς τροφὰς αὐτῷ τε καὶ τοῖς ὀξυγράφοις [καὶ] τοῖς ὑπηρετοῦσιν αὐτῷ ἐπαρκοῦντος, χάρτην τε καὶ τὰ ἄλλα τῶν ἀναλωμάτων, καὶ τοῦ Ὠριγένους ἔν τε ἀγρυπνίαις καὶ ἐν σχολῇ μεγίστῃ τὸν κάματον τὸν περὶ τῆς γραφῆς διανύοντος. ὅθεν τὸ πρῶτον αὐτοῦ ἐπιμελῶς φιλοτιμησαμένον συναγαγεῖν τῶν ἐξ ἑρμηνειῶν, Ἀκύλα Συμμάχον τῶν τε ἑβδομήκοντα δύο καὶ Θεοδοτίωνος, πέμπτης τε καὶ ἕκτης ἐκδόσεως ⟨τὰς βίβλους ἐξέδωκεν⟩, μετὰ παραθέσεως ἑκάστης λέξεως Ἑβραϊκῶς καὶ αὐτῶν ὁμοῦ τῶν ⟨Ἑβραϊκ ν⟩ στοιχείων· ἐκ παραλλήλου δὲ ἄντικρυς, δευτέρᾳ σελίδι χρώμενος κατὰ σύνθεσιν Ἑβραϊκῶς μὲν τῆς λέξεως, δι' Ἑλληνικῶν δὲ τῶν γραμμάτων ἑτέραν πάλιν πεποίηκε σύνθεσιν· ὡς εἶναι μὲν ταῦτα καὶ καλεῖσθαι Ἑξαπλᾶ, ἐπὶ ⟨δὲ⟩ τὰς Ἑλληνικὰς ἑρμηνείας ⟨γενέσθαι⟩ δύο ὁμοῦ παραθέσεις, Ἑβραϊκῶς φύσει δι' ⟨Ἑβραϊκ ν⟩ στοιχείων καὶ Ἑβραϊκῶς δι' Ἑλληνικῶν στοιχείων, ὥστε εἶναι τὴν πᾶσαν παλαιὰν διαθήκην δι' Ἑξαπλῶν καλουμένων καὶ διὰ τῶν δύο τῶν Ἑβραϊκ υ ῥημάτων."

13. Epiphanius, *De mensuris et ponderibus* 510–535: "And Origen himself, who was also called Adamantius, having suffered many things no sooner attained the end of martyrdom. But he went to Caesarea, Strato's city, and spent a little time in Jerusalem, then went to Tyre for twenty-eight years, as the story has it, where he became a citizen, and translated the Scriptures. At that time he put together both the Hexapla and the two columns in Hebrew opposite in parallel, one translation beside the other, naming the books Hexapla, so that he could examine them both vertically and across the breadth. But finding the fifth and sixth translations of the books in the manner that we said, and not knowing who their translators were, according to the sequence in which they were found, after the four he had alread composed together in juxtaposition, he named the one fifth, writing the fifth letter for the number five and thus making clear the name, and then writing the distinguishing mark on the accompanying one, he made clear the

name of the sixth translation. But he worked this out this cleverly, inasmuch as it had escaped the notice of some of the philologists. For some, encountering the Hexapla or the Octapla—for the Tetrapla are the Greek, in which the translations of Aquila and Symmachus and the Seventy-two and Theodotion are arranged together; but these four columns having been added to the two Hebrew ones is called the Hexapla; but if also the fifth and the sixth translations are adjoined following these it is called Octapla; I refer indeed to the six translations and the other two, the one in Hebrew letters and words, the other in Greek letters but in Hebrew words. Now some, one might think, encountering these books and finding the two Hebrew columns lying in the first place, and after these arranged Aquila, after that Symmachus, then the Seventy-two, and after these arranged together Theodotion and next the fifth and the sixth, might think that Aquila translated first, then, Symmachus, then the Seventy-two according to the order in which they were placed, which is not the case. But Origen, perceiving that the translation of the Seventy-two was accurate, put this one in the middle, so that he might refute utterly those on either side. This Origen alone did usefully." Καὶ αὐτὸς δὲ Ὠριγένης ὁ καὶ Ἀδαμάντιος κληθεὶς πολλὰ πεπονθὼς εἰς τέλος τοῦ μαρτυρίου οὐκ ἔφθασεν. Ἐλθὼν δὲ εἰς Καισάρειαν τὴν Στράτωνος καὶ διατρίψας εἰς Ἱεροσόλυμα χρόνον ὀλίγον, εἶτα ἐλθὼν εἰς Τύρον ἐπὶ ἔτη κη΄, ὡς ὁ λόγος ἔχει, τὴν μὲν πολιτείαν ἐνῃσκεῖτο, τὰς δὲ γραφὰς ἡρμήνευσεν, ὅτε καὶ τὰ ἐξαπλᾶ καὶ τὰς δύο τῶν ἑβραϊκ ν σελίδας ἄντικρυ ἐκ παραλλήλου μιᾶς ἑρμηνείας πρὸς τὴν ἑτέραν συνέθηκεν ἐξαπλᾶ τὰς βίβλους ὀνομάσας, καθ᾽ ἅπερ ἄνω διὰ πλάτους εἴρηται. Εὑρὼν δὲ τῆς πέμπτης καὶ ἕκτης ἐκδόσεως τὰς βίβλους καθ᾽ ὃν εἴπομεν τρόπον, καὶ μὴ γνοὺς τίνες εἶεν οἱ ἑρμηνεύσαντες αὐτάς, καθ᾽ οὓς εὑρέθησαν χρόνους ταῖς πρὸ αὐτῶν τέσσαρσιν ἀκολούθως τῇ παραθέσει συνυφήνας, τὴν μίαν πέμπτην ὠνόμασεν, ἐπιγράψας διὰ τοῦ πέμπτου στοιχείου τῆς πέμπτης τὸν ἀριθμὸν καὶ δηλώσας τὸ ὄνομα ὡσαύτως δὲ καὶ τῇ μετ᾽ αὐτὴν τὸ ἐπίσημον ἐπιγράψας τὸ τῆς ἕκτης ἑρμηνείας ὄνομα ἐδήλωσεν. Ἀλλὰ καὶ τεχνικῶς τοῦτο εἰργάσατο, ὅπερ τῶν φιλολόγων τινὰς λανθάνει. Ἐντυγχάνοντες γάρ τινες τοῖς ἑξαπλοῖς ἢ ὀκταπλοῖς—τετραπλᾶ γάρ εἰσι τὰ ἑλληνικά, ὅταν αἱ τοῦ Ἀκύλα καὶ Συμμάχου καὶ τῶν ἑβδομήκοντα δύο καὶ Θεοδοτίωνος ἑρμηνεῖαι συντεταγμέναι ὦσι·τῶν τεσσάρων δὲ τούτων σελίδων ταῖς δυσὶ ταῖς ἑβραϊκαῆς συναφθεισῶν ἑξαπλᾶ καλεῖται·ἐὰν δὲ καὶ ἡ πέμπτη καὶ ἡ ἕκτη ἑρμηνεία συναφθῶσιν ἀκολούθως τούτοις ὀκταπλᾶ καλεῖται·φημὶ δὴ ταῖς ἐξ ἑρμηνείαις καὶ ταῖς ἄλλαις δυσὶ τῇ μὲν ἑβραϊκοῆς στοιχείοις καὶ ῥήμασιν αὐτοῖς γεγραμμένη, τῇ δὲ ἑλληνικοῖς μὲν στοιχείοις ῥήμασι δὲ ἑβραϊκοῆς. Τινὲς τοίνυν, ὡς ἔφην, ταύταις ταῖς βίβλοις ἐντυγχάνοντες καὶ εὑρίσκοντες τὰς δύο ἑβραϊκ ς πρώτας κειμένας, μετὰ ταύτας δὲ πρώτην τὴν τοῦ Ἀκύλα τεταγμένην, μεθ' ἢν καὶ τὴν τοῦ Συμμάχου, ἔπειτα τὴν τῶν ἑβδομήκοντα δύο, μεθ' ἃς ἡ τοῦ Θεοδοτίωνος συντέτακται καὶ ἑξῆς ἡ πέμπτη τε καὶ ἕκτη, δοκοῦσι πρώτους ἑρμηνεῦσαι τὸν Ἀκύλαν καὶ τὸν Σύμμαχον τῶν ἑβδομήκοντα δύο κατὰ τὴν τάξιν τῆς θέσεως, ὅπερ οὐκ ἔστιν. Ἀλλ' Ὠριγένης πυθόμενος τὴν τῶν ἑβδομήκοντα δύο ἔκδοσιν ἀκριβῆ εἶναι, μέσην ταύτην συνέθηκεν, ὅπως τὰς ἐντεῦθεν καὶ ἐντεῦθεν ἑρμηνείας διελέγχῃ. Τοῦτο δὲ μόνον Ὠριγένης χρησίμως ἐποίησεν.

14. Jerome, *Apology* 3.30.2.

15. Rufinus, *HE* 6.16.4 (GCS 9, p. 555, 8 f.): "Unde et illos famosissimos codices primus ipse composuit, in quibus per singulas columellas separatim opus interpretis uniuscuiusque descripsit, ita ut primo omnium ipsa Hebraea uerba Hebraeicis litteris poneret, secundo in loco per ordinem Graecis litteris e regione Hebraea uerba describeret, tertiam Aquilae editionem subiungeret, quartam Symmachi, quintam septuaginta interpretun, quae nostra est, sextam Theodotionis conlocaret, et propter huiuscemodi compositionem exemplaria ipsa nominauit *Exapla,* id est sextiplici ordine scripta."

16. In particular, the discussion of Nautin 1977, 303–309, does not give adequate attention to the differences between the two primary fragments, and thus deduces (308) that the Genizah fragment likely derived from a codex of similar layout to the material published by

Giovanni Mercati, in which the Hexaplaric columns alternate with the Septuagint text and passages from the *catenae*. This seems implausible given the far greater dimensions of the codex represented by the Genizah fragment, in which the six columns of the Hexapla were spread out over two facing pages and written in a majuscule hand. Indeed, Nautin's description of the Mercati fragments bears little relation to the actual appearance of the facsimiles. Nautin refers to the Hexaplaric text of the Psalms as presented in the manuscript as if it gave only brief extracts from each psalm, followed by the corresponding section of the *catena:* "Ordinairement une chaîne se présente ainsi: le caténiste cite un court passage de la Septante (lemme) et met à la suite un ou plusieurs extraits des Pères commentant ce passage. Dans le palimpseste de l'Ambrosienne on a *pour chaque passage:* 1° la partie de la synopse concernant ce passage ; 2° le lemme ordinaire de la Septante; 3° les extraits des Pères" (Nautin 1977, 305; emphasis added). In fact, the Mercati fragments give first the Hexaplaric columns for an *entire psalm,* not merely a passage, then the LXX version of the entire psalm, and finally the *catena*.

17. Taylor 1900, 13–15.

18. Taylor 1900, 25. Note that this figure is entirely independent of the evidence of the material discovered by Mercati, which was published fully only in 1958.

19. Jenkins 1998, 90–100.

20. The ms. is Ambrosianus O 39 sup. The discovery was announced in Mercati 1896; the full publication with facsimiles appeared as Mercati 1958.

21. Mercati 1958, xv–xvi.

22. For the full data on words per line, see Williams 2001.

23. Mercati 1958, xv.

24. Mercati 1958, xvi.

25. On the impact of the transition, see Wilson 1983, 65–68.

26. Jenkins 1998, 89–90.

27. Based on the data presented in Turner 1977, 82 percent of surviving Greek literary manuscripts of the third century are rolls, while only 18 percent are codices.

28. The width of the column that the human eye can comfortably scan is quite invariant: over time, therefore, most written media evolve to present text in columns of a standardized width that conforms to this physiological limitation. Long before the third century CE, roll books had largely adapted to this constraint, so that the width of the columns was more or less fixed. See Lewis 1974.

29. Lewis 1974.

30. The tables in the final section of Turner 1977—which remains the most comprehensive study of the subject—list 186 third-century surviving codices and codex fragments written on papyrus to 29 on parchment, a ratio of roughly one to seven.

31. Sixty-five percent of the third-century papyrus examples listed in the tables of Turner 1977 were written in one column, while 69 percent of his parchment codices and fragments from the same period show a similar format.

32. Ten percent of the papyrus codices listed in Turner 1977 were written in more than one column, while 26 percent of the total are too fragmentary for any determination to be made. Among his parchment codices, 21 percent were written in more than one column, while 10 percent do not allow for a determination. The differences between the data for papyrus and parchment codices are probably best explained not by a difference in their normal arrangement, but by the better preservation of our small sample of parchment codices in comparison to the more numerous, but less well preserved, papyrus codices.

33. On Christians as early adopters of the codex, see Roberts and Skeat 1983.

34. Roberts and Skeat 1983, 37, 38–44.

35. Swete 1902, 74–75, gives an estimate of the size of the Hexapla based on the size of Vaticanus (Codex B) and Sinaiticus (Codex ℵ): "Like the great Vatican MS., it would have exhibited at each opening at least six columns, and in certain books, like the Sinaitic MS., eight. Its bulk, even when allowance has been made for the absence in it of the uncanonical books, would have been nearly five times as great as that of the Vatican or the Sinaitic Old Testament. The Vatican MS.

contains 759 leaves, of which 617 belong to the Old Testament; when complete, the O.T. must have occupied 650 leaves, more or less. From these data it may be roughly calculated that the *Hexapla*, if written in the form of a codex, would have filled 3250 leaves or 6500 pages; and these figures are exclusive of the *Quinta* and *Sexta*, which may have swelled the total considerably." In fact, Swete's figures both under- and overestimate the size of the Hexapla, since he did not take into account the one-Hebrew-word per line format. The number of pages in a Hexapla written with one Hebrew word per line, and 40 lines per page, can be readily calculated, on the basis of the Masoretic lists printed in modern rabbinic Bibles, which give the total number of words in the Hebrew Bible as 304,901. If the Hexapla were laid out three or four columns per page, a copy would fill 15,245 pages. At 400 leaves per codex, that makes 38 codices. However, the codices could have been fairly small, since the columns were considerably narrower than those used in Vaticanus or Sinaiticus. Massive books such as the fourth-century pandect Bibles need not be envisioned.

36. First of all, the Price Edict postdates Origen's literary activity by at least half a century. Second, it was intended to regulate prices at a period of high inflation, and may therefore be out of step with normal prices; in any case it was a rather hopeful piece of legislation, expressive at best of the emperor's intentions, not of economic reality. Third, no surviving version of the Price Edict gives a price for papyrus, though we do have a price for parchment. Finally, the Price Edict's data is probably irrelevant to the cost of the writing of the Hebrew text in the first column.

37. For these figures see Marichal 1963, 214–216 and 14, n. 5; the data are as follows, from the edition of Lauffer 1971, 120:

38 membranario in [qua]t<erni>one pedali pergamen[i uel] croca[ti] D XL

39 scriptori in sc<ri>ptura optima versus n. centum D XXV

40 sequ[enti]s scripturae bersuum no. centum D XX

41 tabellanioni in scriptura libelli bel tabularum [in ver]sibus no. centum[D] X

38. At 304,901 lines (based on one Hebrew word per line), and 20 denarii to copy 100 lines in first-quality writing.

39. At 7,623 pages (based on 40 lines per page), three or four columns per page (so that the six, or more, columns of the Hexapla would have covered a single opening, i.e., two pages), and 40 denarii per quaternio (8 pages) of parchment. Note that, as we will soon see, a copy of the Hexapla would have cost the same as a year's subsistence for 38 laborers, which makes each codex of the Hexapla equal in value to one laborer's annual subsistence.

40. For the grammarian's fee, see Lauffer (ed.) 1971, 7.70–71.

41. Grammarians' earnings are discussed in Kaster 1988 118–123, who also addresses what little evidence we have for the size of classes, which comes mostly from Libanius. Clearly, there was wide variation, but a good-sized class might usually have had about 30 students.

42. For purposes of comparison, the Price Edict sets the price of wheat at 100 denarii per modius, an extremely inflated price (for the context and results of the Price Edict, and the depressed wages set in it, see Harl 1996, 281–283). Subsistence for an adult male laborer is reckoned at the equivalent of about 30–50 modii of wheat per year (what the poor actually ate included not only wheat but other, more costly items, especially oil and wine, here converted into wheat-equivalents; see Harl 1996, 271, 273, for further details). A grammarian, in these terms, could earn enough money from 30 students to support 18 people at subsistence level. In Origen's day, wages were higher in relation to prices, and Egypt (though perhaps not Alexandria) was always a place of low prices, so the figure should perhaps be doubled (see Harl 1996, 278–280, summarizing the changes in wages and prices over the second and early third centuries, and comparing data from Egypt with that for other regions). The distinction used here, between elite and sub-elite, owes much to the work of Morgan 1998, although we do not adopt her analysis in its entirety. The same distinction is articulated concisely by Hopkins 1998, 208, in the context of a useful description of the probable distribution of wealth among the Roman population at large.

43. This is the annual cost, in Price Edict values, of feeding the 1,500 "widows and persons in distress" supported by Cornelius (Eusebius, *HE* 6.43.11), if they received the standard ration of about 40 modii of wheat-equivalent per year—a risky assumption, which probably inflates the final figure. But even if these nonworking individuals survived on half as much food as required by an adult male laborer, the comparison to the estimated cost of the Hexapla does not change much. In the terms of the Price Edict, Cornelius's distributions cost the same as 40 copies of the Hexapla, or about 800 codices written on parchment—a very large library.

44. According to Hopkins 1998, n. 46 to 208, the annual income of the senator Pliny the Younger in the early second century has been estimated at 1.1 million sesterces, at that time enough to support 8,000 people at subsistence level. This figure, therefore, gives a rough sense of the immense gap between elite and sub-elite, a gap that probably remained constant over the century or so in question. Cornelius's charitable distributions, too, would have been fairly small in comparison to the annual income of a senator or other member of the highest imperial elite.

45. Clements 1997; Clements 2000; the second chapter of the 1997 dissertation contains much relevant material not reproduced in the 2000 article.

46. This strongly implies that the one-Hebrew-word-per-line arrangement of the two fragments represents that of the original Hexapla. It is very unlikely that two separate scribes, each knowing Hebrew, each reworked the *Hexapla* on the Psalms into such an arrangement, producing two separate forerunners to our two fragments.

47. Dines 2004, 101, briefly raises this issue.

48. Vööbus 1971, 7, traces the idea back to Halevy 1901, who relied on J. Sota 7, 1, where R. Levi says that if one can't read square-character Hebrew letters one can carry out the duty to say the Shema in any language one knows (*baqol lashon shehu yodea*). Obviously, Vööbus notes, this refers not to transliterations but to versions of the Shema in other languages. He cites Chabot 1901 and Mercati 1947, and notes, 8,

that "it has become customary since then [citing Jellicoe 1974, 110] to think of the transliterated texts as of Jewish liturgical origin and that they were current in the synagogues in Palestine" and counsels restraint in the interpretation of the relevant sources. See also Kahle 1947, 1960; Nautin 1977.

49. Clements 1997, 95–98, esp. n. 163 to 96.

50. For the idea of a preexisting synopsis, see Nautin 1977, 333–339.

51. This is the argument of Nautin 1977, 334–336. Clements 1997, 96 and ff, proposes an alternative explanation for the order of the columns, which is probably more plausible; her larger argument regarding the place of the Tetrapla and the *Hexapla* in Origen's philological project, with which we generally, will be taken up below.

52. Nautin 1977.

53. Clements 1997, 85, esp. n. 134, which in its use of the Thesaurus Linguae Graecae as a research tool supersedes earlier work on this problem.

54. Roberts 1979 discusses the evidence for Jewish presence before 117, and for the disappearance of Jews from the papyri after that period; for late antique papyri with references to Jews, see Tcherikover and Fuks 1957–1964, III.

55. De Lange 1976.

56. Clements 1997, 2000.

57. One of the best treatments of Origen's (and Jerome's) knowledge of Hebrew, notable for its balance as well as its thorough command of the evidence, remains Elliott 1877–1887; on the limitations of Origen's Hebrew knowledge, see 856–859.

58. There is ample evidence for Jewish/Christian discussion and debate in Caesarea about particular textual details. Jewish scholars seem, for example, to have corrected the text of Philo there. See Barthélemy 1967, 45–78, and Runia 1996, 493–494.

59. *HE* 6.16.4.

60. This interpretation turns entirely on the placement of the reference to the "Tetrassa" after the discussion of the Hexapla, and on

Eusebius's use of the verb *episkeuasas,* "preparing in addition"—weak evidence on which to erect such an important argument.

61. Clements 1997, 97–100, superseding Nautin 1977, 314–316, 333–343, which she cites and discusses in detail.

62. Clements 1997, 96–97, 100.

63. Swete 1902, 241–242.

64. See below on *Ad Africanum,* 3.

65. Swete 1902, 68, argues in a similar vein. Because he believed that Origen's overall purpose was to adjust the LXX to conform to the Hebrew, Swete assumes that the LXX was transposed to fit the Hebrew order. We do not share Swete's understanding of Origen's larger project, but it still seems likelier that one column would be reorganized to fit five, or even three (in the case of an original Tetrapla), than the other way around.

66. Numerous references to asterisks and obeli appear in Jerome's commentaries. See also the prefaces to the Vulgate versions of Job, Chronicles, and the Pentateuch.

67. Kahle 1947, 1960; Dines 2004.

68. Clements 1997.

69. Swete 1900 68–69.

70. Nautin 1977, 351–353.

71. Brock 1970.

72. Kamesar 1993.

73. Clements 1997, 86–100.

74. Clements 1997, 91–94.

75. *Ad Africanum* 4. Translation adapted from NPNF.

76. A similar interpretation is presented by Clements 1997, 94.

77. *Ad Africanum* 9.

78. Clements 1997, 93, 114–117, discussing the work of Kimelman 1977 and Halperin 1988; on the possible interactions between Origen's exegesis and that of Rabbi Yochanan, see also Hirshman 1995.

79. Clements 1997, 120–135.

80. Levine 1975, 46–47, cited by Clements 1997, 121, n. 229.

81. For example, Clements summarizes her findings on Origen's

purposes as a textual scholar as follows: "It was in this cultural setting of struggle with Jews to establish Christian *hegemony* [emphasis added] in the matter of biblical interpretation, and struggle with Christians to establish the authority of his own method of teaching and its results, that Origen composed *Peri Paschā*"—the polemical treatise, written late in Origen's Caesarean period, that is the ultimate object of Clements's investigation (Clements 1997, 135). We would suggest that perhaps mere Christian legitimacy, rather than "hegemony," was still the real stake in debates with Jews in the mid-third century, whatever Origen's rhetoric might imply, and that Origen himself occupied a similarly insecure—rather than firmly, or even potentially, authoritative—position within the Christian communities at both Alexandria and Caesarea.

82. See Clements 1997, 131–132, on the prevalence of Jewish practices and participation in synagogue worship among Caesarean Christians, including the audiences of Origen's homilies.

83. Clements 1997, 91–92, 94.

84. Clements 1997, 94: "it may be more accurate to read *CMt* XV.14 as a disjunctive rather than conjunctive statement. That is, perhaps we should understand the 'healing' of the manuscript tradition as one discrete task, necessitated by the many textual problems within the tradition; and the marking of the differences between the LXX and the Hebrew as a second discrete task, carried out to create a resource for exegesis and disputation. It is clear from both passages [i.e., this passage and the passage from the *Letter* to Africanus discussed above], however, that Origen's main concern is with the LXX itself; *CMt* construes the versions the Hebrew 'as tools for healing the LXX, and the *Letter* makes clear the theological primacy of that translation."

85. Wright 1988, 61; see also the discussion and synthesis of Wright's and Kamesar's work in Clements 1997, 86–88, upon which this paragraph largely depends.

86. Kamesar 1993, 25; Clements 1997, 87–88.

87. Clements 1997, 38–46.

88. Ulrich 1988.

89. See for example the prefaces to his translations of Job and Chronicles *iuxta Hebraeos.*

90. Barthélemy 1963.

3. Eusebius's *Chronicle*

1. On the chronology of Eusebius's work see most recently Burgess 1997, dating the *Chronicle* to 311.

2. Cf. Caspar 1926, 15; and cf. the important general remark of Murray 1969, 263: "There is a relation here between the systematization of astrology and magic, and the forces which led to similar more rigid systematization in government, rhetorical theory, law, philosophy, geography, medicine, and religion, whether Jewish, Christian or pagan." It is not certain whether the maps with which the Byzantine scholar George Planudes (ca. 1260–1310) adorned the text of Ptolemy's *Geography,* and from which the maps in later copies descend, were copied from an original that went back to the work of the Alexandrian engineer Agathodaimon or were reconstructed by Planudes. See in general Stückelberger 1994, 60–61; Berggren and Jones 2000. But the much earlier geographical work of Artemidorus of Ephesus (ca. 100 BCE) was certainly set out as a synthetic prose work with maps, as shown by Gallazzi and Kramer 1998, and Ptolemy's book was certainly intended to be equipped with maps—and thus to represent an even more challenging task for scribes than the *Chronicle* of Eusebius. For the codification of the *Corpus Iuris* see e.g. *Brill's New Pauly,* s.v. *Digesta,* by Wolf Eckart Voss.

3. See Billanovich 1954.

4. Grafton 1983–1993, II, reviews the older scholarship. More recent work is discussed in Mosshammer 1979 and Burgess and Witakowski 1999.

5. Eusebius 1928, 7–9; Eusebius 1984, 9–11. Eusebius writes that Moses "is found to be earlier, than all those, whom the Greeks consider most ancient, that is, Homer, and Hesiod, and the Trojan War, and much earlier Hercules, Musaeus, Linus, Chiron, Orpheus, Castor,

Pollux, Aesculapius, Liber, Mercury, Apollo, and the other gods and holy ones of the Gentiles, or their bards, and also than the deeds of Jove, whom Greece treated as divine. We have shown, I say, that all of those whom we have enumerated were also after Cecrops, the first king of Attica. But the present history will show that Cecrops was a contemporary of Moses and came 350 years before the Trojan War." He then argues, computing backward from the birth of Jesus in the year 15 of Tiberius to the Fall of the Temple and from that to the Fall of Troy, and from that, finally, to the age of Moses, that Cecrops and Moses were contemporaries. For a full discussion of the varied Christian arguments for the priority of Moses see Sirinelli 1961.

6. See Adler 1989 and 1992. In keeping the dynasty lists and narratives that he assembled in book 1 separate from the actual chronological tables in book 2, Eusebius made a clear formal distinction between his documentation and his formal text—a choice in which only a handful of ancient writers on mythology seem to have preceded him. See Cameron 2004.

7. Hunt 1982, 102. Eusebius regularly emphasized the vital role of Abraham in sacred history. See *HE* 1.4.5–14, where he treats Abraham as a model Christian, and *DE* 1.2.14–15. To judge from Constantine's letter to the bishops of Palestine on the shrine at Mamre, preserved by Eusebius at *VC* 3.53.3, he agreed, as Hunt 1982 elegantly demonstrates.

8. See the excellent commentary by Copenhaver in Vergil 2002, and for the Hellenistic and later tradition of recording inventions in their chronological place see Copenhaver 1978 and Geus 2002.

9. Eusebius 1923, 14; 1984, 18–19: "Et, ne forte longus ordo numerorum aliquid turbationis adferret, omnem annorum congeriem in decadas cecidimus, quas ex singulorum gentium historiis congregantes sibi in vicem fecimus esse contrarias ut facilis praebeatur inventio cuius Graeci aetate vel barbari prophetae et reges et sacerdotes fuerint Hebraeorum, item qui diversorum gentium falso crediti dii, qui heroes, quae quando urbs condita, qui de inlustribus viris philosophi poetae principes scriptoresque variorum operum extiterint, et si qua

alia digna memoria putavit antiquitas. Quae universa in suis locis cum summa brevitate ponemus."

10. Eusebius 1911, 3.

11. Eusebius 1923, 269; 1984, 187: "Oportuit enim in isdem diebus paschae eos interfici, in quibus Salvatorem cruci fixerant."

12. The comprehensive character of Eusebius's vision of the past, and its optimistic outcome, are well evoked by Chesnut 1986, 74–76, and set into context by Burgess 1997. See also Sirinelli 1961, 112–115, emphasizing that the notion that the Roman Empire was universal had deep roots in Roman tradition.

13. Tufte 1983. On the history of universal time lines see Rosenberg 2004 and Archibald and Rosenberg 2004.

14. On Eusebius's accomplishment see esp. the classic work of Barnes 1981 and Burgess and Witakowski 1999.

15. Cassiodorus, *Institutiones* 1.17.2 Mynors, quoted in Croke 1982, 198: "Chronica vero, quae sunt imagines historiarum brevissimaeque commemorationies temporum, scripsit graece Eusebius "

16. Barnes 1981, 120; cf. Kannengieser 1992.

17. Fordyce 1956; Asheri 1991–92; Möller 2001 and 2004.

18. Censorinus, *De die natali* 21.6–8: "unless I am mistaken, the present year [238 CE], which has the consulate of Pius and Pontianus as its formal designation, is the year 1014 from the first Olympiad [776 BCE], that is, from the summer solstice, when the Olympic games took place; but it is the year 991 from the foundation of Rome, and more precisely from the Parilia [21 April], from which the city's years are computed; and in Julian years it is 283, from the 1st of January, where Julius Caesar set the beginning of the year that he established." Further references to this work are given in the text.

19. Because the Egyptian year was exactly 365 days long, its first day, 1 Thoth, moved one day earlier in the Julian calendar every four years. Censorinus's conversions are correct.

20. Grafton and Swerdlow 1985.

21. See Mortley 1996.

22. For the larger context see Burstein's comments in Berossus 1978 and Kuhrt 1986.

23. See Von Leyden 1949, Bickerman 1952, and Alonso-Nuñez.

24. Gardiner 1997.

25. Verbrugghe and Wickersham 1996, 98. See also Murray 1972 and Kuhrt 1986.

26. Drews 1965; 130; see also Drews 1975, Burstein's comments in Berossos 1978, and Adler 1989, 27, n. 57, who points out that Berossos was not himself consistently critical or accurate.

27. Drews 1965, 131; Clarke 1999, 322–325.

28. Josephus, *Contra Apionem* 1.73–105, 227–287, 294; 2.1, 16. See the discussion in Schäfer 1997.

29. For fragments and testimonia see *FrGrHist* 685.

30. Plato, *Timaeus* 23E, tr. Bury, cited by Adler and Tuffin, 23, n. 5.

31. Origen, *Contra Celsum* 1.19–20. In the case of chronology Christian scholars did not see Plato as an Attic Moses (cf. also Justin, *Oratio ad Graecos* 12).

32. The only collection of the fragments of Africanus in print remains that of Routh 1814–1818. The fullest study is still Gelzer 1880–1885. Both are seriously in need of replacement.

33. Africanus, frag. XX Routh, in Eusebius, *PE* 10.10.6.

34. Africanus frag. 22 Routh, from book 3, in Eusebius, *PE* 10.10.1–2.

35. Justin, *Oratio ad Graecos* 9–12. Tatian, *Oratio ad Graecos* 31; Whittaker (ed.) 1982, 57: "we shall find that our history is not only earlier than Greek culture, but even than the invention of writing." .For detailed discussion of Jewish and Christian efforts to use chronology to prove the priority of their traditions to those of the Greeks and other pagans, see Sirinelli 1961, 52–59, 497–515.

36. Africanus, frag. 10 Routh, quoted by Syncellus, 18 Mosshammer = Adler and Tuffin 23.

37. Ibid.

38. Ibid., Adler and Tuffin 24.

39. Note Africanus's surviving comment, which makes clear that though he found "many marvellous things" in Daniel, "at present, however, I shall speak only of those things in it that bear on chronology and matters connected with it" (quoted by Eusebius, *DE* 8.389).

40. Eusebius, *DE* 8.389

41. Eusebius 1911, 1–2.

42. Sirinelli 1961, 44–46.

43. For this perspective on Africanus we are indepted to Adler 2003. See also Inglebert 2001. Naturally, Jerome added many notices to the Roman segments of the *Chronicle* when he translated it. On this point, and for the most detailed account of Eusebius's work on the chronology of very recent times, see Burgess and Witakowski 1999.

44. See in general Croke 1983.

45. For further discussion of the tradition of Christian chronography and Eusebius's relation to it, see esp. Mosshammer 1979, Adler 1989 and 1992, Burgess 1997, Burgess and Witakowski 1999, and Inglebert 2001, part 2.

46. Eusebius 1911, 2. In practice, of course, Eusebius normally followed the Septuagint chronology and worked with it as if it were generally valid.

47. Africanus, frag. 6 Routh, quoted by George Syncellus, 91–92 Mosshammer = 116 Adler and Tuffin.

48. See Wacholder 1968, 1976. It is of course also possible that the underlying Hebrew text already gave the longer chronology, but the changes seem more likely to represent a response to rival world histories that circulated in Greek, and thus to be the work of the makers of the Septuagint.

49. Syncellus, 95 Mosshammer; 116 Adler and Tuffin = Eusebius 1911, 39–40.

50. Syncellus, 95 Mosshammer; 119–120 Adler and Tuffin = Eusebius 1911, 40.

51. Syncellus, 20–21 Mosshammer = 27–28 Adler and Tuffin.

52. Eusebius 1911, 38.

53. Cf. Syncellus, 20 Mosshammer =27 Adler and Tuffin: "But it

is agreed by all that Methusaleh was the longest-lived of all men." Syncellus's own proposal, which involved changing the birth-year of Methusaleh, was not more successful; see Adler and Tuffin, 27–28, n. 5.

54. On this strategy and its relation to those of other Jewish and Christian writers who confronted these problems see esp. Adler 1989, 32–40.

55. Syncellus, 96 Mosshammer = 120 Adler and Tuffin = Eusebius 1911, 41.

56. Eusebius 1923, 7; 1984, 8–9: "Neque me fugit in Hebraeis codicibus dissonantes aetatum annos inveniri, plusque vel minus prout interpraetibus visum est lectitari, sequendumque illud potius quod exemplariorum multitudo in fidem traxit."

57. For the importance and distinctiveness of Eusebius's decision see above all Adler, 70–71 and n. 105.

58. Censorinus, *De die natali* 21.1–3. Joseph Scaliger took this periodization as the creation of Varro; Felix Jacoby, influentially, as that of Eratosthenes. Geus 2002 denies the connection to Eratosthenes at 316, n. 29. We have not yet seen Möller forthcoming a and b.

59. Eusebius 1911, 2, quoting Plato, *Timaeus* 22C–23B; cf. Adler 1989, 22.

60. Eusebius 1911, 2.

61. Eusebius 1911, 3.

62. Eusebius 1911, 6.

63. Eusebius 1911, 7 = Syncellus 29 Mosshammer = 38–39 Adler and Tuffin = Verburgghe and Wickersham 1996, 44, as translated by Adler and Tuffin. Cf. Adler 1989, 29 and n. 66.

64. For a much fuller analysis of the ways in which Africanus and Eusebius dealt with antediluvian history, see the standard work, Adler 1989.

65. Eusebius 1911, 9 = Verbrugghe and Wickersham 1996, 46.

66. Cicero, *De divinatione* 1.19, 2.46.

67. Censorinus, *De die natali* 19.4: "et in Aegypto quidem antiquissimum ferunt annum unimestrem fuisse." The same suggestion

occurs in Diodorus, 1.26.3; Plutarch *Numa* 18.4; and Varro, as cited in Lactantius, *Divinae institutiones* 2.12.

68. Proclus 1903, I, 103 = Eudoxus frag. 302 Lasserre: "Εἰ δὲ καὶ ὃ φησιν Εὔδοξος ἀληθές, ὅτι Αἰγύπτιοι τὸν μῆνα ἐνιαυτὸν ἐκάλουν, οὐκ ἂν ἡ τῶν τούτων ἐνιαυτῶν ἀπαρίθμησις ἔχοι τι θαυμαστόν." See Adler 1989, 75–76

69. Africanus, frag. 10 Routh, in Syncellus, 17–18 Mosshammer = Adler and Tuffin 23.

70. Fowden 1993, 34; see also Gnoli 1985, 37–38.

71. *Seder Olam* 1998, 255.

72. Eusebius 1911, 9.

73. Eusebius 1911, 63 = Waddell 1940, 5.

74. Eusebius 1911, 64.

75. Eusebius 1911, 64–65 = Waddell 1940, 9.

76. Grafton 1975; Rossi 1984.

77. Syncellus, 35 Mosshammer = 46 Adler and Tuffin.

78. Syncellus, 36 Mosshammer = 47–48 Adler and Tuffin. See also Adler 1989, 97–99.

79. Orosius, *Historiae adversos paganos* 1.11; see Adler 1989, 19.

80. Eusebius 1911, 2.

81. Grafton 1983–93, II, part 4.

82. Inglebert 2001, 506–507.

83. Inglebert 2001, 505.

84. Inglebert 2001, 504, rightly compares Eusebius's way of dealing with the earliest times to that of Hellenistic chronologers like Eratosthenes.

85. Note that Africanus took what look like varied views at different times on the authority of Scripture. In his letter to Origen, he rejected the LXX story of Susanna and the Elders as a forgery, on philological grounds. But in his letter to Aristides, he insisted on the literal truth of all of the Gospels. The latter attitude seems to have underpinned his chronological studies.

86. See Vööbus 1975, 42–43. The colophon of Exodus in the Pentateuch of the Syro-Hexaplar reads: "However, this (copy of) Exodus

was also collated with an accurate exemplar which has this colophon: 'The tradition of the Seventy was transcribed from (a manuscript of) the Hexapla . . . And (this copy) was corrected by the hand of Eusebius Pamphili, as the epigraph made it clear'"; the colophon to Numbers reads: "The (Book of) Numbers was taken from an exemplar of the Hexapla which is in the library of Caesarea of Eusebius Pamphili." The interest of the fact that the Syro-Hexaplar derived from the work of Pamphilus and Eusebius was noted as early as the 1570s by Andreas Masius, the first Western scholar to use the text and bring it to the attention of his colleagues. See Baars 1968, 2–3, n. 6.

87. Vööbus 1975, 42 (colophon to Exodus): "And (this copy) was corrected by the hand of Eusebius Pamphili, as the epigraph made it clear: from which (copy) the things taken from the Samaritan text have been previously added—alone to an evidence that great pains were taken with the copy"; 43 (colophon to Numbers): "there was also a mark which shows that the Hebrew (text) of this book was collated according to the Hebrew (text) of the Samaritans from which (are) also the traditions to the value of this book in the Hexapla."

88. For a very different presentation, see Inglebert 2001.

89. For Herodotus's efforts to use synchronisms to establish a chronological framework see e.g. Vannicelli 2001. On the calendrical synchronisms in Herodotus's (and later) accounts of important events see Grafton and Swerdlow 1988.

90. Möller 2001, 254–255. On the origins of synchronistic tables— a very controversial question, made no easier by the fact that we have no idea what any of them might have looked like in detail—see Asheri 1991–92 and Möller 2004.

91. FrGrHist 323 (cf. 608).

92. Thucydides 5.20.2–3; cf. 1.97.2

93. FrGrHist 239. More generally, on the material for early chronography cf. the wise words of Möller 2004, 173: "All arguments are built on poor evidence."

94. Polybius 5.35.5.

95. See the discussion in Syncellus, 243–249 Mosshammer = 299– 306 Adler and Tuffin.

96. Polybius 12.11.1.

97. Asheri 1991–92, 54.

98. See Eviatar Zerubavel's pioneering treatment of metaphorical plotlines for time (Zerubavel 2003).

99. Helm 1924; Mosshammer 1979. For earlier Greek chronography see, in addition to the works already cited, Fordyce 1956, Geus 2002, and Möller 2001.

100. For the very different ways—antiquarian and nostalgic—in which the past is tabulated in yet another form of Greek chronography, the Chronicle of Lindos (99 BCE), see Higbie 2003.

101. Cicero's military metaphor, which Denis Feeney called to our attention: "explicatis ordinibus temporum."

102. See Münzer 1905 and Habinek 1998, 94–96.

103. Helm 1924; Burgess and Witakowski 1999. On the survival of Latin erudition in the Greek world see esp. Maas 1992.

104. See esp. Mosshammer 1979 and Burgess and Witakowski 1999.

105. See Burgess and Witakowski 1999, 28–45.

106. McKitterick 2004, 226–227.

107. See Mosshammer 1979 and Barnes 1981, 111–113.

108. Mosshammer 1979; Croke 1982; Adler 1992.

109. Eusebius 1923, 3; 1984, 5: "hoc nobis proprium accedat, quod historia multiplex est habens barbara nomina, res incognitas Latinis, numeros inextricabiles, virgulas rebus pariter ac numeris intertextas, ut paene difficilius est legendi ordinem discere quam ad lectionis notitiam pervenire."

110. On Atticus as publisher see Sommer 1926, Phillips 1986, and Butler 2002.

4. Eusebius at Caesarea

1. Levine 1975, 70–71, 82–83.

2. In fact, though many modern scholars have assumed that the diocesan library of Eusebius rested on foundations laid by Pamphilus, the sources do not state this explicitly. They do, however, make clear

that Eusebius learned many of the practices that he applied to books from Pamphilus.

3. On the date of Pamphilus's death, see Barnes 1981, 153–154, citing Eusebius, *Martyrs of Palestine;* for Constantine's consolidation of power in the East, see Barnes 1981, 77.

4. Well-documented expositions of this thesis include Cavallo 1988, Gamble 1995, 155–160, and above all Carriker 2003, 1–36. A different view is cogently argued by Frenchkowski forthcoming. On the larger context see esp. Cavallo (ed.) 1988, Casson 2001, and Battles 2003.

5. Pamphilus and Eusebius 2002, II, 76, n. 8.

6. For example, in the ingenious, even visionary articles collected in Wendel 1973.

7. See Eusebius, *HE* 6.32.3; 8.13.6.

8. Eusebius, *Martyrs of Palestine* 11.1e-f; Jerome, *De viris illustribus* 75. For Pamphilus's vision of Origen as the ideal theologian see Junod 1987.

9. Jerome, *Contra Rufinum* 1.9; 1982, 8; 1983, 26–28: "'Quis studiosorum amicus non fuit Pamphilus? Si quos videbat ad victum necessariis indigere, praebebat large quae poterat. Scripturas quoque sanctas non ad legendum tantum, sed et ad habendum tribuebat promptissime, non solum viris, sed et feminis quas vidisset lectioni deditas. Vnde et multos codices praeparabat, ut, cum necessitas poposcisset, volentibus largiretur. Et ipse quidem proprii operis nihil omnino scripsit, exceptis epistulis quas ad amicos forte mittebat, in tantum se humilitate deiecerat. Veterum autem scriptorum tractatus legebat studiosissime et in eorum meditatione iugiter versabatur.'"

10. See e.g. Otranto 2000, xxiii, and Bagnall 1992, on Aurelia Ptolemais, a female landowner whose father probably left her the history of Sikyon, Homeric papyri, and a copy of the *Kestoi* of Julius Africanus that formed part of her family's archive; and Otranto 2000, 128–129, on P. Oxy. 4365, fourth century, the writer of which, perhaps Aurelia Soteira, who signed the document on the recto, asks her sister: "lend me Esdras, since I lent you the little *Genesis* [probably *Jubilees,*

though Otranto does not say so]." Pamphilus was by no means the only well-born and well-educated man in Christian circles who took pride in scribal activities: cf. the case of the Roman scribe and lapicide Furius Dionysius Filocalus (ca. 350–380 CE). This brilliant calligrapher actually signed what is now his most famous work, the Calendar of 354, on its title page: "Furius Dionysius Filocalus titulavit." See Salzman 1990, 26, 44, 202–204; Cameron 1992. True, there is no evidence to suggest that Pamphilus felt the sort of aesthetic pride in his work that inspired Filocalus.

11. Eusebius, *HE* 6.33.4.

12. Jerome, *De viris illustribus* 75: "Scripsit, antequam Eusebius Caesariensis scriberet, Apologeticum pro Origene."

13. For an astute defense of Eusebius's and Jerome's denials that Pamphilus wrote any work of his own see Reymond 1987. Reymond, however, misses the point that for Eusebius—and for Pamphilus—compilation was a form of writing, with special qualities and purposes. This theme is developed later in the chapter. These bibliographical puzzles have occupied scholars for a long time: see e.g. Pico della Mirandola's *Apologia* for Origen in Crouzel 1977, 100–113.

14. Eusebius, *HE* 6.32.3.

15. Jerome, *Epistulae* 34.2: " hic cum multa repperiret et inventorum nobis indicem derelinqueret." Jerome echoes Eusebius, *HE* 6.32.3 here.

16. Jerome, *De viris illustribus* 75: "Pamphilus presbyter, Eusebii Caeasriensis episcopi necessarius, tanto Bibliothecae divinae amore flagravit, ut maximam partem Origenis volumina sua manu descripserit, quae usque hodie in Caesariensi bibliotheca habentur."

17. Eusebius, *HE* .36.3. For this interpretation of the phrase ἐν ἰδίαις τόμων περιγραφαῖς see Lawlor and Oulton in Eusebius 1924, II, 225.

18. Jerome, *De viris illustribus* 75: "Sed et in duodecim Prophetas viginti quinque *Exegeseon* Origenis volumina, manu eius exarata reperi, quae tanto amplector et servo gaudio, ut Craesi opes habere me credam."

19. Devreesse 1954, 122 and n 4, from Funk (ed.) 1905, II, 144–148, at 144: "Τοῦ ἁγίου ἱερομάρτυρος Παμφίλου ἐκ τῆς ἐν Ἀντιοχείᾳ τῶν Ἀποστόλων συνόδου, τουτέστιν ἐκ τῶν συνοδικῶν αὐτῶν κανόνων μέρος τῶν εὑρεθέντων εἰς τὴν Ὠριγένους βιβλιοθήκην." The text is spurious, though the evidence that it did not come from Origen's library is purely negative—i.e., that he never cited it (Funk, xxxv–xxxvii). There seems to be no way to know whether Pamphilus collected pagan texts; cf. the ingenious arguments of Kalligas 2001.

20. These subscriptions have long interested students of the text of the Septuagint. Basic studies include Swete 1900; Schwartz 1905; Mercati 1941, the fullest presentation of the evidence; and Devreesse 1954. Skeat 1956 and Petitmengin and Flusin 1984 offer essential help in interpreting the texts.

21. Nautin 1977, 322: "'Ἀντεβλήθη πρὸς παλαιώτατον λίαν ἀντίγραφον δεδιορθωμένον χειρὶ τοῦ ἁγίου μάρτυρος Παμφίλου, ὅπερ ἀντίγραφον πρὸς δὲ τῷ τέλει ὑποσημείωσίς τις ἰδιόχειρος τοῦ αὐτοῦ μάρτυρος ὑπέκειτο ἔχουσα οὕτως· Μετελήμφθη καὶ διωρθώθη πρὸς τὰ Ἑξαπλᾶ Ὠριγένους, Ἀντωνῖνος ἀντέβαλεν, Πάμφιλος διώρθωσα.'"

22. Nautin 1977, 323; cf. Skeat 1956, 194: "'Ἀντεβλήθη πρὸς παλαιώτατον λίαν ἀντίγραφον δεδιορθωμένον χειρὶ τοῦ ἁγίου μάρτυρος Παμφίλου. Πρὸς δὲ τῷ τέλει τοῦ αὐτοῦ παλαιωτάτου βιβλίου . . . τοιαύτη τις ἐν πλάτει ἰδιόχειρος ὑποσημείωσις τοῦ αὐτοῦ μάρτυρος ὑπέκειτο ἔχουσα οὕτως· Μετελήμφθη καὶ διωρθώθη πρὸς τὰ Ἑξαπλᾶ Ὠριγένους ὑπ' αὐτοῦ διορθώμενα. Ἀντωνῖνος ὁμολογητὴς ἀντέβαλεν, Πάμφιλος διώρθωσα τὸ τεῦχος ἐν τῇ φυλακῇ . . . καὶ εἴγε μὴ βαρὺ εἰπεῖν τούτῳ τῷ ἀντιγράφῳ παραπλήσιον εὑρεῖν ἀντίγραφον οὐ ῥάδιον.'"

23. In what follows, "Syh" designates texts translated from the subscriptions in the Syro-Hexaplar. The evidence is handily collected by Devreesse 1954, 123–124, and Nautin 1977, 322–324:

III Reg. (Syh = Mercati 38–39): "Sumptus est hic liber . . . ex Hexaplo, h.e. sex columnis, bibliothecae Caesareae Palestinensis; et collatus est cum exemplari in quo subsignatum erat sic: Εὐσέβιος διώρθωσα ὡς ἀκριβῶς ἐδυνάμην."

IV Reg. (Syh = Mercati 39–43): "Sumpta est haec quoque . . . ex libro Heptaplorum, h.e. septem columnarum bibliothecae Caesareae Palaestinae . . . Et collatus est accurate cum exemplari septem columnarum, cui subscripta erant haec: Quartus Regnorum secundum Septuaginta, isque accurate emendatus. Eusebius emendavi, Pamphilo collationem instituente."

"This book was also drawn . . . from the book of the Heptapla (that is, of the 7 columns) from the library of Caesarea in Palestine . . . And it was carefully collated with an exemplar in 7 columns with the following subscription: Fourth Book of Kings according to the Seventy, corrrected with great care. I, Eusebius, corrected, Pamphilus having done the collation."

Proverbs (Syh = Mercati 43–44): "Μετελήμφθησαν καὶ ἀντεβλήθησαν ἁι Παροιμίαι ἀπὸ ἀκριβοῦς ἀντιγράψου, ἐν ᾧ παρετέθησαν καὶ ἐγράφησαν ἐν τοῖς μετωπίοις σχόλια χειρὶ Παμφίλου καὶ Εὐσεβίου, ἐν ᾧ καθυπετέτακτο ταῦτα· Μετελήμφθησαν ἀφ' ὧν εὕρομεν Ἑξαπλῶν Ὠριγένους. Καὶ πάλιν· αὐτοχειρὶ Παμφίλου καὶ Εὐσεβίου διωρθώσαντο."

"The Proverbs were copied and collated from an accurate copy, in which scholia were placed and written in the front by the hand of Pamphilus and Eusebius, and in which were these words: 'Copied from the Hexapla of Origen that we found.' And, again, 'corrected in their own hand by Pamphilus and Eusebius.'"

Ecclesiastes (Syh = Mercati 44–45, at 45): "Adnotatum erat in libro graeco . . . Ἐκκλησιαστὴς ὁμοίως μετελήμφθη ἀπὸ τοῦ αὐτοῦ ἀντιγράφου, ἐν ᾧ καὶ οἱ λοιποὶ [τὰ λοιπὰ] ἐφεξῆς παρετέθησαν. καὶ πάλιν χειρὶ τοῦ ἁγίου Παμφίλου ταῦτα· Πάμφιλος καὶ Εὐσέβιος διωρθώσαμεν."

Cantica (Syh = Mercati 45–46): "Desumptus est ex Hexaplis, qualia ea reperimus, Origenis secundum versionem reliquorum et iterum manu nostra nosmet Pamphilus et Eusebius correximus"

"'Taken from the Hexapla or Origen, as we found them, according to the translation of the others,' and again, in their own hand, 'We, Pamphilus and Eusebius, corrected.'"

Minor Prophets (Syh = Mercati, 46): "Μετελήμφθησαν οἱ δώδεκα προφῆται ἐκ τῶν κατὰ τὰς ἐκδόσεις τετραπλῶν. Πάμφιλος καὶ Εὐσέβιος ἀκριβῶς διώρθωσαν." "Copied from the Tetrapla according to the editions. Pamphilus and Eusebius corrected accurately."

Isaiah (Marchalianus = Mercati, 8): "Μετελήμφθη ὁ ἠσαΐας ἐκ τῶν κατὰ τὰς ἐκδόσεις ἐξαπλῶν ἀντεβλήθη δὲ καὶ πρὸς ἕτερον ἐξαπλοῦν." (Syh = Mercati, 10, 29): "Μετελήμφθη καὶ παρετέθη ἀπὸ ἀντιγράφου Εὐσεβίου καὶ Παμφίλου, ὃ καὶ αὐτοὶ διωρθώσαντο ἐκ τῆς βιβλιοθήκης Ὠριγένους."

Ezechiel (Marchalianus = Nautin 1977, 323: "Μετελήμφθη ἀπὸ τῶν κατὰ τὰς ἐκδόσεις Ἑξαπλῶν καὶ διωρθώθη ἀπὸ τῶν Ὠριγένους αὐτοῦ Τετραπλῶν, ἅτινα καὶ αὐτοῦ χειρὶ διώρθωτο καὶ ἐσχολιογράφητο, ὅθεν Εὐσέβιος ἐγὼ τὰ σχόλια παρέθηκα. Πάμφιλος καὶ Εὐσέβιος διωρθώσαντο."

"Copied from the Hexapla according to the editions and corrected from Origen's own Tetrapla, which was corrected and annotated in his hand. I Eusebius added the scholia from this source. Pamphilus and Eusebius corrected."

24. Mercati 1941, 19–20, denies that Pamphilus would have boasted of the quality of his work, and notes that a later scribe might more plausibly have marveled at the wonderful manuscript prepared by the martyr Pamphilus. Skeat 1956, 194, takes the sentence as by Pamphilus. Mercati's reasoning seems more plausible—especially in the light of the fact that Pamphilus's other colophons all end with the sentence that identifies him and his associates as the ones who did the actual work. On the other hand, the special circumstances involved in working in prison could have provoked Pamphilus to vary his usual practice.

25. Eusebius, *HE* 5.20.3. See the erudite and precise survey by Pecere 1986, 24–26. Irenaeus's subscription reappears in Latin in

Jerome, *De viris illustribus* 35, with a slight alteration, and elsewhere. See also Gamble 1995, 114–116, 123–125. Further important studies, the results of which differ sharply, include Zetzel 1973, 1980, and 1981, Timpanaro 1986, and Cameron forthcoming.

26. Eusebius, *HE* 5.20.3.

27. See e.g. Soisalon-Soininen 1959.

28. Since we take it that the Septuagint text in the Hexapla was not itself the result of a new recension of the text, but part of the material Origen used for that recension.

29. As textual critics in modern times have regularly complained, their voices rising slightly as they explain the difficulties of working out how much of the Hexapla has entered the "Hexaplaric" form of the text that descends from Caesarea. For a manuscript with the Hexaplaric signs, see e.g. Leiden University Library Vossianus gr. Q 8; Metzger 1981, 38, 70. On the nature of the additions marked with asterisks see Soisalon-Soininen 1959.

30. Jerome, *Praefatio in Paralipomena* (*PL* 28, 1324B): "Alexandria et Aegyptus in Septuaginta suis Hesychium laudant auctorem; Constantinopolis usque ad Antiochiam Luciani martyris exemplaria probat; mediae inter hae provinciae Palaestinos codices legunt, quos ab Origene elaboratos Eusebius et Pamphilus vulgaverunt, totusque orbis hac inter se trifaria varietate conpugnat."

31. Dines 2004, 95–96.

32. Dines 2004, 102.

33. See generally Small 1997 and Van den Hoek 1996, and for this particular case the superb studies of Skeat 1956 and Petitmengin and Flusin 1984. Cf. also Teitler 1985.

34. Petitmengin and Flusin 1984, 250 and n. 35: "Eusebius emendavi Pamphilo collationem instituente"; cf. Mercati 1941, 39.

35. Eusebius, *HE* 5.28.16.

36. Eusebius, *HE* 5.28.18.

37. See Schöne 1939; Metzger 1980, 196–197; Metzger 1992, 150–151;

38. Jerome, *De viris inlustribus* 3.2; 1999, 10: "Porro ipsum hebrai-

cum habetur usque hodie in Caesariensi bibliotheca, quam Pamphilus martyr studiosissime confecit."

39. Metzger 1987, 201–207.

40. On these notoriously slippery texts see Robinson 1895, Zuntz 1953b, Murphy 1959, and Metzger 1992, 26.

41. On this notion see Metzger 1963, 42–72, and Barnes 1981, 124–125.

42. Cf. Pamphilus and Eusebius 2002, II, 79–81, on what "imprisonment" meant in this context.

43. Jerome, *De viris illustribus* 75: "Si enim laetitia est, unam epistolam habere martyris, quanto magis tot millia versuum, quae mihi videtur sui sanguinis signasse vestigiis!"

44. Eusebius, *Martyrs of Palestine* 9.4. Cf. Schwartz 1909.

45. Eusebius, *Martyrs of Palestine* 4.6 (long form of text). Apphianus was martyred on 2 April 306.

46. Eusebius, *Martyrs of Palestine* 5.2 (long form of text).

47. Schwartz 1909; Grant 1980, 123–124, 165.

48. Eusebius, *Martyrs of Palestine* 11.15–19 (long form of text).

49. For the Greek text see E. Nestle and K. Aland, *Novum Testamentum Graece,* 25th ed. (London, 1969), 32*–37*; we quote the translation of Barnes 1981, 121–122.

50. For a particularly splendid case in point see Hamilton 1993.

51. Rondeau 1982–85, 2, 21–135; Trigg 1998, 6, 14, 46, 58, 73, 148, 202, 204, 211, 256 n. 24.

52. Mercati 1948. Rondeau describes this work as "une trace supplémentaire du travail scientifique d'Eusèbe sur le Psautier" (1982–85, 1, 72). For a case in which Eusebius's discussion of the authorship of a psalm was falsely attributed to Pamphilus, see Mercati 1941, 91, and for Eusebius's formal application of "prosopographical" exegesis to the Psalms see Rondeau 1982–1985, 2, 169–195.

53. See http://ccat.sas.upenn.edu/jod/jod.html.

54. Jerome's preface to the *Chronicle* appears in Eusebius 1984, 5: "I should note in advance that the different colors should be preserved, as they have been used in writing. This will prevent anyone

from thinking that this effort was made simply to please the eye and creating a labyrinth of error as he shirks the effort required to copy it. For this was devised so that the red ink would distinguish the series of the different kingdoms, which had become mixed up together because they were too close together, and so that the next part of the text would preserve the position of the color with which the previous parchment had marked a kingdom." A further passage, added to the introduction by the creator of what became the source of a family of manuscripts of the *Chronicle*, describes a still more complex system of colored inks. Relegated to the apparatus in Helm's critical edition (1984, 5), this passage and the manuscripts it describes represent interpolation to the modern textual critic—but can also be seen as reflecting a second, later homage to Eusebius.

55. On the novelty of Eusebius's method see esp. the classic study, Momigliano 1963, 89–91, on which cf. the works by R. Mortley cited above.

56. The treaties quoted word for word by Thucydides are an exception to the rule, accordingly, though a striking one.

57. Hollerich 1999, 2, n. 2: : "Apologetic works like the *Prophetic Selections* and *The Proof of the Gospel* expand on the old proof text tradition, with often lengthy expositions of texts arranged either topically or by biblical book. The *Preparation for the Gospel* uses the same technique of commenting on excerpts from pagan philosophers, many of which would otherwise be lost. In the *Church History* Eusebius pioneered a tradition of ecclesiastical history which placed a special emphasis on documentary quotation. The *Church History* elaborates the theme of the succession of ecclesiastical writers with rich quotations from their writings, about half of which are otherwise unknown (so the estimate of H. J. Lawlor, cited in Young, *From Nicaea to Chalcedon,* 291). Schwartz saw the emphasis on quotation as a Christian analogue to the pagan scholarly tradition of literary and philosophical history (*RE* vi.1395f.). The *Chronology* used extracts from various Hellenistic historians. Although the *Life of Constantine* resembles an encomium as well as a biography, it too relied on the documentary

approach. In its present form imperial letters and orders constitute about a fourth of the whole. Works of controversial theology like the *Against Marcellus* and *On the Ecclesiastical Theology* also used the method of quotation and refutation."

58. Eusebius 1911, 1. For the Greek text and a translation see Burgess 1997, 503–504.

59. *HE* 1.1.3.

60. Cf. Gamble 1995, 172–174, and Pattie 1998.

61. Hollerich 1999, 2.

62. Eusebius and Pamphilus 2002, I, 32–34: "1. Nihil mirum, fratres, videmini mihi esse perpessi, quod ita vos Origenis subterfugit intellectus, ut vos quoque ea aestimetis de illo quae et alii non nulli, qui sive per imperitiam sui, qua non valent sensus eius altitudinem contueri, sive pravitate mentis, qua studium gerunt non solum dicta illius incusare, verum etiam adversum eos qui haec legunt hostiles inimicitias sumere—tam pertinaciter id agentes ut nulla prorsus venia eos dignos haberi putent, ne ea quidem quae impertiri solet, verbi gratia, his qui vel Graecorum saecularium libros vel non numquam etiam haereticorum percunctandi atque agnoscendi studio decurrunt—sibi solis scilicet concedi debere peritiam probandi sermonis putant, ut si quid bene ab aliquo dictum est retinere sciant, ab omni autem specie mala abstinere se noverint, ab his vero qui Origenis libros legunt istud penitus exclusum putant esse mandatum quo iubentur probabiles effici trapezitae, scientes quod bonum est retinere, ab omni autem specie mala se abstinere; sed tantum modo si <quis> legere libros illius visus fuerit, statim ab his haereticorum perfundetur infamia."

63. Eusebius and Pamphilus, *Apology for Origen* 1, 3.

64. Eusebius and Pamphilus, *Apology for Origen* 12–13.

65. Eusebius and Pamphilus, *Apology for Origen* 19: "Quod ita nobis prosequi rectius visum est ut non nostris verbis aut adsertionibus defensionem paremus, sed ex suis propriis vocibus, quibus ipse aliena haec esse quae isti obiciunt proprio sermone testatur, id est omne quicquid praeter fidem catholicam praedicatur, quia si nostris verbis haec adserere velimus suspiciosum forte videri possit, eo quod nos

amore eius si quid ipse pravi senserit celaverimus. Vbi autem eius ipsius qui accusatur vocibus utimur et ad omnes obiectiones accusatorum suis verbis eum, non nostra adsertione defendimus, quae ultra relinqui potest criminationis occasio, saltem his ipsis qui non veri studio, sed velut libidine quadam culpandi semper agitantur? Et quoniam de eo nunc sermo est qui utique apud homines iudices pro defuncto firmius ac fortius valere debet quam litterae et scripta defuncti?"

66. Eusebius, *HE* 6.33.4.

67. Eusebius and Pamphilus 2002, I, 324–335, offers a list of the passages Pamphilus quoted.

68. Photius, *Bibliotheca* codex 118; see Eusebius and Pamphilus 2002, II, 78–79.

69. Méhat 1966, 181.

70. Eusebius, *HE* 6.16.2–3, tr. Oulton, as emended by Kahle 1947, 162.

71. Published by Mercati 1901a, and reprinted by Schwartz 1903; translated by Kahle 1947, 161–162.

72. Schwartz 1903, 187–188, esp. 188: "Eine Tradition, die über die Notizen der Hexapla hinausging, stand Euseb nicht zur Verfügung, so sehr er sich für Origenes Biographie und die Hexapla interessierte: auch hier tritt scharf heraus wie das Wissen der KG aus der Bibliothek von Cäsaerea stammt." This interpretation is accepted by Neuschäfer 1987, II, 375–376n. 46. For a very different point of view, see Grant 1980, 83.

73. Jerome, *Epistulae* 34.1.

74. Cf. esp. Obbink 2004.

75. Carriker 2003. See also the ingenious earlier study by Lawlor 1912.

76. For discussion of the diocesan library see, in addition to Carriker 2003, the older accounts by Wendel 1974, 35–45, characteristically stimulating and characteristically speculative; Cavallo 1989; and Gamble 1995.

77. Africanus mentioned the same library, which, he claimed, pos-

sessed a copy of the interpolated version of the *Iliad* that he quoted in his *Kestoi*.

78. Eusebius, *HE* 6.20.2–3.

79. Eusebius, *HE* 4.15.46–48.

80. Eusebius, *HE* 4.15.47.

81. Lawlor 1912, 167–178; Grant 1980, 116–117; Carriker 2003, 250–255.

82. Eusebius, *HE* 2.18. See Philo 1896–1930, I, iii–iv, xxxv–xxxvii; Runia 1993; Runia 1996; Carriker 2003, 164–177. Eusebius may well have found in the existing collection the work of Diodorus Siculus, from which he drew chronological information and Euhemerist interpretations of Greek myths: and that of Julius Africanus, who came from the same region, and whose work Origen himself had used. See Zecchini 1987.

83. See Kalligas 2001 and Carriker 2003.

84. Gamble 1995, 175–176; Catabiano 1996, 83–84.

85. Gifford in Eusebius 1903, IV, 104, on III, 82d7.

86. Mras 1954, lviii; cf. Grant 1980, 28.

87. Burgess and Witakowski 1999, 71.

88. *HE* 2.23.3.

89. *HE* 4.8.1–2; 4.11.7–11. Eusebius also manipulated the texts he cited from Hegesippus. See Lawlor 1912, 1–107; Grant 1980, 67–70; Mendels 1999. Naturally, he did not always work in this manner: see the recent analysis by Cerrato 2002, 26–44, who argues that Eusebius carefully noted that his materials on Hippolytus came from Christian communities at Jerusalem, Alexandria, and Caearea, and did not mention, much less contribute to the invention of, a Roman Hippolytus.

90. Winkelmann 1977. Cf. also Schwartz 1909; Laqueur 1929, stimulating but, as is well known, to be treated with reserve; Gustafson 1961.

91. Barnes 1981, 124.

92. On the innovative, even "hybrid" character of Eusebius's life of Constantine, see Barnes 1989 and Cameron 1991, chap. 2.

93. See the elegant analysis in Grant 1980, 28–29.

94. Curiously, though Mendels 1999 emphasizes Eusebius's successful effort to create a "media history," and offers stimulating comments on Eusebius's efforts to create a biblical canon (184–193), he pays little attention to the material form of the books Eusebius himself created.

95. Jerome, *De viris illustribus* 113.

96. On the colophon of Euzoios that appears in Vienna theol. gr. 29, 146 verso, "Εὔζοιος ἐπίσκοπος ἐν σωματίοις ἀνενεώσατο" (Cohn, in Philo 1896–1930, I, iii), see now Runia 1993 and Runia 1996, 476–495, 478–482. In *Epistolae* 34.1, written before he arrived in Palestine, Jerome described this renewal of the library, ascribing it to Euzoios and another bishop of Caesarea, Acacius, perhaps his predecessor.

97. Eusebius, *VC* 4.36.1, 4.36.2, tr. Cameron and Hall.

98. Eusebius, *VC* 4.36.3, tr. Cameron and Hall.

99. For the institutional context see the wonderful discussion in Skeat 1999, 604–607.

100. Eusebius, *VC* 4.36.3, tr. Cameron and Hall.

101. Eusebius, *VC* 4.37.1, tr. Cameron and Hall.

102. See e.g. Robbins 1986 and 1989; Gamble 1995, 159.

103. See e.g. Wendel 1974, 37–39; Gamble 1995, 159.

104. Skeat 1999.

105. Skeat 1999, 607–609.

106. Skeat 2004, 279–280.

107. For this dating, *contra* the influential, much earlier date given by Barnes, see Louth 1990, 118–120; Carriker 2003, 39 and n. 15; and Freeman-Greville in Eusebius 2003, 3–4.

108. Eusebius 1904, 2 = Eusebius 2003, 11.

109. For efforts to reconstruct Eusebius's personal exploration of Palestine, and Jerusalem in particular, see Hunt 1982, 101–102, Taylor 1993, and Freeman-Greville in Eusebius 2003, 2–3. By contrast, Groh 1985 dates the work relatively early, argues that some of the formulas that seem to indicate autopsy "should be seen to conform to literary/historical commonplaces rather than pilgrim's interests" (27), and

reduces the role of direct exploration in the *Onomasticon* to what Eusebius learned "from his brief researcher's rambles between the libraries of Jerusalem and Caesarea or from his literary sources" (28). He is followed by Walker 1990, 24, 42–43.

110. Eusebius 1904, 2; 2003, 11. Cf. Douglass 1996, 317–318.

111. See Eusebius's entries on Ailam (1904, 6–8; 2003, 14); Arnon (1904, 10; 2003, 15); Bala (1904, 96); 2003, 57); Thaiman (1904, 96; 2003, 57); Mephaath (1904, 128; 2003, 72; and Rooboth II (1904, 142; 2003, 179). Peter Thomsen remarked that "Eusebius is splendidly informed about the deployment of the Roman troops" (Thomsen 1903, 140, quoted by Klostermann in Eusebius 1904, xvi).

112. Dilke 1987.

113. Thomsen 1903, 140, quoted by Klostermann in Eusebius 1904, xvi. Cf. Hunt 1982, 98.

114. This point is made in passing by Groh 1985, 29. Fascinating and provocative recent studies of late antique visions of Palestine include Douglass 1996, Bowman 1999, and esp. Elsner 2000. On the importance of geography see Merrills 2005.

115. See now Shalev 2004.

116. Barnes 1981, 265–271.

117. See Warmington 1985, 1993.

118. Eusebius *VC* 3.59.4–5, 4.27.3.

119. Eusebius *VC* 3.24, ed. Winkelmenn 1975, 94; tr. Cameron and Hall 1999, 131.

120. Cf. Burgess and Witakowski 1999, 73: "But although he was tendentious, tended to distort reality, and covered up and omitted material Eusebius knew how to research and write history as well as any Christian. His willingness to use and cite documentary evidence was in advance of any pagan historian."

121. For the documents Eusebius merely cited see Barnes 1981, 269. On the larger question of Eusebius's accuracy, Cameron and Hall (eds.) 1999, 16–20, offer a lucid and learned introduction.

122. See also Winkelmann 1962b and Pietri 1983, both of whom

trace the history of the controversy; Seeck 1898; Pasquali 1910; Dörries 1954; Winkelmann (ed.) 1975, esp. li-lii; Warmington 1985; Hall 1998.

123. Cameron and Hall (ed.) 1999, 27, 31.

124. Gigante 1995, 20.

125. Gigante 1995, 18–23, and see further the contrasting treatments of Cavallo 1984, esp. 5–12; Sedley 1989; and Obbink 2004. Obbink points out, unexpectedly, that the Herculaneum papyri show little sign of sustained study of *On Nature*.

126. Porphyry, *Life of Plotinus* 8. Cf. Edwards 2000, 17.

127. Porphyry, *Life of Plotinus* 26. Cf. Edwards 2000, 53. At *VLife of Plotinus* 7 Porphyry states that Plotinus asked him to correct his writings.

128. Cf. Edwards 2000, 53, nn. 316–318.

129. Simplicius *In Categorias* 64.20–25, quoted by Wildberg 1993, 194.

130. Wildberg 1993

131. *BT Kethuboth* 106a: "Rabbah b. Bar Hana said in the name of R. Johanan: Book readers in Jerusalem received their fees from the Temple funds." See Gordis 1971, xl–xlii; Segal 1952, 1974, 288–291; Greenberg 1956, 1974; and more generally Halbertal 1997, 16–19.

132. See Kalmin 1989, 3–4.

133. See Brüll 1876, Kaplan 1932, Kalmin 1989 and 1994, Halbertal 1997, 72–81, and Hasan-Rokem 2003.

134. Rouse and McNelis 2000 [2001], esp. 201–206; quotation at 205, original text at 205, n. 80: "Quoniam indiculum versuum in urbe Roma non ad liquidum sed et alibi avariciae causa non habent integrum, per singulos libros computatis syllabis posui numero XVI versum Virgilianum omnibus libris numerum adscribsi."

135. *Scholia Sinaitica*, in Riccobono et al. 1908, II, 533–546, xvi (II, 544–545); xvii (II, 545); xviii (II, 545).

136. On the law school see Hall 2004, 195–220; she does not discuss this material, or indeed say much about teaching practices. For the suggested connection with Beirut see Stein 1966.

137. For another interesting parallel cf. the mythographers studied by Cameron 2004, 321–323, Parthenius and Antoninus Liberalis, who segregated their source references systematically from their texts and evidently used the services of professional amanuenses capable of following this complex and relatively unusual system.

Coda

1. Eusebius 1923, 3–4; 1984, 5: "Unde praemonendum puto ut, prout quaeque scripta sunt, etiam colorum diversitate serventur, ne quis inrationabili aestimet voluptate oculis tantum rem esse quaesitam et, dum scribendi taedium fugit, labyrinthum erroris intexat. Id enim elucubratum est, ut regnorum tramites, qui per vicinitatem nimiam paene mixti erant, distinctione minii separarentur et eundem coloris locum, quem prior membrana signaverat, etiam posterior scriptura servaret."

2. See Carruthers 1990 and Carruthers and Ziolkowski (ed.) 2002.

3. See Rouse and Rouse 1982 (repr. 1991).

4. See Klepper 2000 and Klepper forthcoming.

5. Allen (ed.) 1906–1958, IX, 311. For Erasmus's interest in Origen see esp. Godin 1978 and 1982.

6. For Erasmus and Jerome see Jardine 1993, Vessey 1994, and Pabel 2002.

7. Miller 2001, 473.

8. Botfield (ed.) 1861. Cf. Bentley 1983 on the New Testament in the Complutensian Polyglot.

9. Miller 2001.

10. See in general Burnett 1996, Coudert and Shoulson (ed.) 2004.

11. Grafton 2004.

12. McKitterick 2004, 226.

13. Bede, *Ecclesiastical History* 5.16–17, 5.22.

14. See most recently Hartmann 2001, Olson 2002, and Lyon 2003.

15. Ditchfield 1995.

16. Momigliano 1977, 278. See further Barret-Kriegel 1988.

17. On the Bollandists and their relation to the Maurists see Knowles 1963; for Bentley see Haugen 2001.

18. Quillen 1998.

19. Rice 1985, Jardine 1993, Vessey 1994, and Frazier 2005.

Acknowledgments

OUR thanks go, first of all, to the wonderful colleagues who have helped us finish what must often seemed to many of them a folie à deux. Alan Cameron, Denis Feeney, Marco French-kowski, Pat Geary, Stephen Menn, Glenn Most, Jim Porter, Brent Shaw, Noel Swerdlow, and other aficionadi of the book and of ancient scholarship—including a number of audience members at lectures and seminars whom we cannot now iden-tify—have offered helpful criticism and vital references. We are especially grateful to Alan Cameron, Denis Feeney, and Marco Frenchkowski for allowing Tony Grafton to read unpublished work. William Adler, Robert Kraft, and another, anonymous referee read the book for Harvard University Press, and we thank all of them heartily for their valuable corrections and sug-gestions.

We are also deeply grateful to the institutions that made our work possible. The libraries of Oberlin College, Princeton

Theological Seminary, Princeton University, the University of California, Los Angeles, the University of Michigan, the University of Montana, and the University of Pennsylvania sustained our research. Microsoft—a firm that neither of us regards with unmixed admiration, but that nonetheless deserves its due praise—created the infrastructure that did for us what zealous, well-trained scribes did for Origen, Pamphilus, and Eusebius. A grant from Princeton University enabled Tony Grafton to spend a month at the Warburg Institute, where Christopher Ligota and his colleagues have built up extraordinary collections on both Origen and Eusebius, and at the Institute for Classical Studies. Further support from Princeton enabled us to pay for illustrations and permissions.

Megan Williams spent much of the time she was engaged in research on this project as a Fellow of the Michigan Society of Fellows and assistant professor in the Department of Near Eastern Studies at the University of Michigan, and thanks both units and the university as a whole for their extraordinary support. The Center for Advanced Judaic Studies in Philadelphia, where Megan Williams was a Fellow during 2001–01, provided not only a congenial environment for research and discussion, but a superb library and the enthusiastic assistance of its interlibrary loan librarian, Judith Leifer. The Center and the Division of Social Sciences and Humanities at Caltech both provided vital hospitality at exactly the right times: heartfelt thanks to David Ruderman of the former and Moti Feingold and Jed Buchwald of the latter institution. Over the course of 2005, Megan tried the Interlibrary Loan Department of the University of Montana's Mansfield Library to its utmost; she is extremely grateful for thelibrarians' willingness to go above and beyond the call of duty in assisting her to gather the resources—often arcane—she needed to complete this manuscript. Lindsay Waters of Harvard University Press enthusiastically agreed to consider, and then to publish, a book on what even he agrees is a recondite subject. Nancy Clemente and Phoebe Kosman turned our heap of files and pictures into a book with care and kindness.

For both of us, Peter Brown has been an incomparable friend and teacher. From the beginning of this project, he urged us forward, advised us, and corrected us. No thanks we could offer would come close to repaying our debt. The best we can do—bronze for gold—is to dedicate this book to him.